Oriole Magic
The O's of '83

Thom Loverro

TRIUMPH
BOOKS
CHICAGO

Library of Congress Cataloging-in-Publication Data

Loverro, Thom.
    Oriole magic : the O's of '83 / Thom Loverro.
      p. cm.
    Includes index.
    ISBN 1-57243-564-X
    1. Baltimore Orioles (Baseball team)—History.   I. Title.

GV875.B2L68 2004
796.357'64'097526—dc22

2003061399

This book is available in quantity at special discounts for your group or organization. For further information, contact:
    Triumph Books
    601 South LaSalle Street
    Suite 500
    Chicago, Illinois 60605
    (312) 939-3330
    Fax (312) 663-3557

Printed in U.S.A.
ISBN 1-57243-564-X
Design by Patricia Frey

Contents

Foreword

had a lot of good fortune throughout my baseball career. I had the good
fortune of growing up in a baseball family; of having a father, Cal Ripken
Sr., who had a love and respect for the game that he was able to pass on
to his sons; and of having a mother who created an atmosphere where I
was able to feel secure and to grow as a baseball player and a young man.

I was also very fortunate to be a part of one of the greatest organiza-
tions of its time in baseball, an organization I was very familiar with: the
Baltimore Orioles. It was particularly special not only because it was my
hometown team, but also because it was the team that my dad was with
for nearly four decades as a minor and major league coach and
manager. In his opening speech to the guys in the minor leagues, Dad
used to say, "Welcome to the greatest organization in baseball. If you can
make it through our organization, you will play in the big leagues." The
Orioles organization took great pride in developing talent and getting
players into the big leagues.

The real proof of the greatness of the Orioles' system became
evident when an injury occurred, as it did with Mike Flanagan in 1983.
The ability to find another young talent in the minor leagues to step in,
as Mike Boddicker did, is one of the Orioles' greatest strengths. Of
course it was depressing when Flanny went down, but when Boddicker
stepped in and started showing what he could do, it was very uplifting.
And in the end, having a hot pitcher—another weapon down the stretch
to carry us into the playoffs and the World Series—was important.

The one team that may personify everything that the Orioles stand for
is the 1983 world championship club. It was the Orioles philosophy at its

best: a team with players who came up through the farm system—such as Eddie Murray, Rich Dauer, Al Bumbry, and pitchers like Scott McGregor and Storm Davis—filled in by players we had traded for who fit into the Orioles style of play, such as John Lowenstein and Ken Singleton.

That 1983 roster was the team concept at its best. We knew we were good. We liked each other and we felt that there was talent and good chemistry on the team. It seemed as if there was a different hero every single night. But after witnessing 20 years of baseball, I know that that is the sign of a good team: contributions from all 25 players. That club was made up of players who filled specific roles, such as Gary Roenicke and Lowenstein in left field. They were a super platoon—we got more production out of two guys than we would have out of one. We certainly weren't the kind of team that has nine men who play every single day. Sure, there were those of us who played every game—Eddie and myself in particular—but the makeup of the club was such that it lent itself to regular contributions from everyone.

I always look back on 1983 with much fondness and satisfaction. I have been on both ends of the spectrum in my career. I was a part of a team that won the whole thing, and I know that very special feeling. I was also part of a team that had an 0–21 start; I was on a team that lost 100 games; and I have gone through a total rebuilding process, where there is a lot of frustration. Those experiences help me to look back on that 1983 team and truly appreciate the unity and the excellence that we were able to achieve. If baseball is a game beyond numbers—a game of determination, a game of dedication, a game of diligence—then the 1983 Baltimore Orioles World Series championship team personified all of that. It is a team I will always be proud to have been a part of.

—Cal Ripken Jr.

Introduction

The term "old school" is thrown around in sports descriptions way too much these days. But sometimes the tag is warranted. In the case of the Baltimore Orioles franchise, for 17 years over a three-decade span, the team was most definitely "old school," with its players taught the game of baseball in the legendary method of the "Oriole Way." It is simply the way of playing the game right and carrying yourself in a professional manner—simple goals that seem to be harder than ever to find in today's world of sports.

But from 1966 through 1983, it was on display at Memorial Stadium and other American League parks throughout the country whenever and wherever the Baltimore Orioles took the field, as the team amassed three World Series championships, six AL pennants, and seven second-place finishes. They deeply respected the game and played it right. You think of Frank Robinson, the 1966 Triple Crown winner whose career was supposedly finished after he was traded by the Cincinnati Reds but who led Baltimore to its first World Series championship. You think of Brooks Robinson and his remarkable play at third base, robbing batters of hits. You think of Jim Palmer, the three-time Cy Young Award winner. You think of Eddie Murray and his clutch RBI hitting. You think of Cal Ripken and his consecutive game streak.

But you also think of Mark Belanger, the slick-fielding shortstop. You think of Paul Blair, the graceful center fielder. You think of Benny Ayala and his pinch-hitting feats. You think of Tippy Martinez and his reliable bullpen work. You think of Rick Dempsey, the fiery catcher who emerged as the hero of the 1983 World Series.

You think of the great players, but you also think of the other players on the rosters through the years, because the Baltimore Orioles were always about team play. You hear that term used often, and it seems ridiculously simple. But when you examine the great run this franchise had from 1966 to 1983, you see the true meaning of team play in action, and the 1983 club epitomized team play. Everyone contributed at one time or another during the season, resulting in the World Series title. You realize that while Cal Ripken was important to that team, so was Jim Dwyer. While Scott McGregor was a key to the success of the pitching staff, so was Bill Swaggerty.

"We weren't the most talented club, but we played together, and that was what made that team special, 25 guys playing together," Eddie Murray said.

What the Baltimore Orioles did during those championship years from 1966 to 1983 should rank them among the greatest sports franchises of all time. This was a small town, without the resources of a New York or Los Angeles franchise. And even those teams with good player-development programs rarely can sustain a 17-year run of success. But the Orioles did. They were the model franchise, relying on player development to win at the major league level. This was not just good for the Orioles; it was good for baseball as well. If you could make it through the Orioles farm system, it was likely that you would become a major league player, whether in Baltimore or someplace else.

You will never again see another franchise in baseball like the Orioles. Today, large-market teams stock up on high-priced free agents, and small-market teams, if they are fortunate, get a few good years out of their young players before having to let them go on to the richer teams—and then rebuild all over again. It's doubtful you will ever see a small-market team—and the Orioles, before the construction of Camden Yards, were considered a small-market team—again have a 17-year player development run.

"The great thing about the Orioles back then was that there was continuity," Jim Palmer said. "You had different generations passing their knowledge on to the next generation."

Now all there is to pass on is memories, but they are great memories. When it comes to "old school," the 1983 world champion Orioles were at the head of the class.

1 | History and Legacy

Eddie Murray sat on a stool in front of his locker in the visitor's clubhouse at Veterans Stadium before Game 5 of the 1983 World Series. His wrists were hurting him, and so was his batting average. In Game 1, he had been embarrassed by Phillies rookie pitcher Charlie Hudson, who had struck Murray out and showed him up at Memorial Stadium by pumping his fists and going through a show on the mound after he got Murray out. He would be facing Hudson again that night, but his mind was on more than his own personal quest for redemption.

Rick Dempsey was getting his equipment ready so he could warm up that night's starting pitcher, Scott McGregor. He had a year's worth of aches and pains to deal with—137 games of squatting behind the plate—but he was feeling no pain. Dempsey had emerged as the hitting star of the Series. But he was thinking about the same thing Eddie Murray was mulling over quietly.

McGregor was going over the Phillies hitters in his head. He had already faced them once in Game 1, in which he pitched brilliantly but lost 2–1. If he could have been anyone that night, it would have been Don Larsen in 1956—because McGregor wanted to pitch a perfect game, if that was what it took to win this game. He was thinking that because he was also thinking about something else—the same thing that Eddie Murray and Rick Dempsey were thinking about.

Nearly every man in that visitor's clubhouse had the same subject on his mind—history.

History hung over the 1983 Baltimore Orioles squad like a ghost over a graveyard. History was like a shot of adrenaline through their

1

bodies and a vice on their chests. History was their inspiration and their greatest fear.

It wasn't ancient history. It was the history that many of the players in that room had experienced firsthand during seven days in 1979 and three days in 1982 that drove this 1983 team—the culmination of the so-called "Oriole Way"—to this point in October 1983.

In 1982, the Baltimore Orioles came from eight games behind in the American League East in the middle of August to tie the first-place Milwaukee Brewers in the 161st game of a 162-game season. The entire season—from the first day pitchers and catchers reported in mid-February to a crisp early October day in Baltimore—came down to just one game in Baltimore, before 50,000 screaming hometown fans at Memorial Stadium.

The Orioles lost 10–2.

"When we lost that last game in 1982, there wasn't a guy on that ball-club that didn't believe that we would come back and win in 1983," Murray said, reflecting on that disappointing day in October.

It may have been the loss in 1982 that inspired these players from the day they reported to spring training in 1983, but it was the fear of 1979 that ate at their guts as they waited to play Game 5 of the World Series.

In 1979, the Baltimore Orioles led the Pittsburgh Pirates three games to one in the World Series, with Mike Flanagan, a 23-game winner and the AL Cy Young Award recipient, taking the mound for Game 5. It seemed like a lock. The Orioles lost 7–1. Then they lost 4–0. What had been a 3–1 Series lead now came down to a seventh game between the two teams. Who would pitch for Baltimore in Game 7 in 1979? Scott McGregor.

The Orioles lost 4–1.

"We were disappointed for quite a few years," Dempsey said. "Finally, we got another chance to get back there. When we were up 3–1 in Philadelphia, there wasn't a sound in that clubhouse. Everyone was thinking the same thing: that we were not going to let what happened in 1979 happen again. It was an eerie quietness. We had thought about it for four years."

History, in the form of tradition, was always very important to the Orioles organization. It is how the Oriole Way of doing things—training players how to play the game the same way, and the right way, from rookie league ball all the way to the major leagues. It had become one of the richest traditions in baseball, yet the Orioles did not have a long and storied past, like the Yankees or the Dodgers. The Orioles came and went around the turn of the century—from the 19th to the 20th—and didn't exist in Baltimore again until one of the worst franchises in the history of baseball was sold and moved, about 50 years later.

The origins of a Baltimore Orioles baseball team date back to 1883, when a second version of the Lord Baltimores, playing in the American Association, changed the name of the club to the Orioles, after the official Maryland state bird. The franchise joined the National League in 1892 and fielded one of the great 19th-century baseball teams, managed by Ned Hanlon and boasting such legendary baseball men as John McGraw, Dan Brouthers, Hugh Jennings, and Wee Willie Keeler on the roster and managed by Ned Hanlon. They won three National League pennants from 1894 to 1896. But the franchise folded after the 1899 season.

Two years later, the Orioles were revived and joined the American League. But it was a short life, and after two seasons the team moved to New York and became the Highlanders. That team would later change its name. They became the New York Yankees—a historical fact that stuck in the throats of Orioles fans years later when the Yankees became the Orioles' most bitter rival (and they remain so).

Another version of the Orioles—a minor league club—began play in Baltimore in 1903, this one in the Eastern League and then in the International League from 1912 to 1953. Early on, the owners considered moving the franchise out of town. Those early 20th-century Orioles were managed by Jack Dunn and briefly featured a young Baltimore native, a big kid pitcher named George Herman "Babe" Ruth. The Babe had grown up just a few blocks from the current home of the Orioles, Camden Yards. (In fact, the tavern owned by Ruth's father was on the site of the new ballpark.)

Baltimore would remain a minor league baseball city until Bill Veeck was forced to sell his dismal St. Louis Browns, a major league team, to a group in Baltimore led by Mayor Tommy D'Alesandro. They moved the franchise and played in a renovated Memorial Stadium in 1954. That was the first year of the existing Orioles franchise in Baltimore.

The team struggled in those early years, losing 100 games in its first season (54–100), finishing 57 games out of first place behind the Cleveland Indians, who won 111 games that year. The Orioles didn't have a winning season until 1960, when the team went 89–65 and finished second. But the club was on its way to developing a strong farm system that would be the envy of other major league teams. They slid back to a losing record (77–85) in 1962 but would have only one more losing season (76–85 in 1967) over the next 24 years.

With Brooks Robinson leading the way, the Orioles began building the gold standard for an American League franchise through their minor league system and key trades. They put together a star-studded pitching staff—with Dave McNally, Wally Bunker, Steve Barber, and a young Jim Palmer—and fielded such standout position players as first baseman Boog Powell, second baseman Davey Johnson, and center fielder Paul Blair. They then made the most important trade in the history of the franchise, acquiring outfielder Frank Robinson from the Cincinnati Reds on December 9, 1965, for pitchers Milt Pappas and Jack Baldschun and outfielder Dick Simpson.

Everything changed for the Orioles after that. Frank Robinson—considered to be on the tail end of his career by the Reds—had a Triple Crown season in 1966, leading the American League in batting (.316), home runs (49), and RBIs (122). More importantly, he led the Orioles to their first AL pennant, as the team finished first with a 97–63 record. Then the Orioles shocked the sports world by sweeping the defending world champion Los Angeles Dodgers and their two aces, Sandy Koufax and Don Drysdale, in four straight games.

That 1966 world championship season was a watershed year for the Orioles and for baseball. The Yankees were suffering through their second straight losing season after nearly 40 years of dominating baseball, and the Orioles had suddenly emerged as a nationally recognized franchise, beginning their own version of a dynasty. The core of that 1966 club would play in three more World Series in the next five years.

They reached the fall classic again in 1969, this time as the big favorite, winning the most games ever in franchise history (109–53) and winning the newly created American League Eastern Division (the first season the two leagues broke into two divisions) by 19 games. While

Hank Bauer managed the Orioles to the 1966 World Series championship, he lost his job two years later, and a feisty little manager from the minor league system named Earl Weaver took over.

Baltimore swept the Minnesota Twins in 1969 in the first American League Championship Series ever held, with a combination of great pitching (Game 1 a 4–3 extra-inning win and Game 2 a 1–0 shutout by Dave McNally) and an 11–2 beating in the third and deciding game. It was on to the World Series in Weaver's first season as manager.

It was the Orioles who were now the favorites, a turnaround from their last World Series appearance, and they found themselves in the same position that the Dodgers had been in during the 1966 Series— losing to an underdog team. But the New York Mets were not just any underdog. They were one of the all-time underdogs, the Amazing Mets, who had been one of the most famous and popular losers in baseball history. A team with a roster of good players—Tommy Agee, Cleon Jones, Bud Harrelson—didn't seem to compare to the likes of Frank Robinson, Boog Powell, and Brooks Robinson. But the Mets had a great young pitching staff, led by Tom Seaver and Jerry Koosman, and turned in one of the biggest upsets in World Series history by defeating the Orioles four games to one. Baltimore won the first game, a 4–1 victory by Mike Cuellar over Seaver, the Mets ace who had won 25 games that season. But the Mets pitching shut down the big Orioles bats over the next four games. Koosman edged McNally 2–1 in Game 2; Gary Gentry shut down Palmer and company 5–0 in Game 3; the Mets won Game 4 in 10 innings, 2–1; and Koosman came back to win the clincher 5–3, as Jones caught a fly ball from Davey Johnson for the final out, leaving the Orioles the dumbfounded—and numbed—losers.

Elrod Hendricks, the longtime bullpen coach of the Orioles, was a catcher on that 1969 team. He remembers how the loss ate at them all winter. "When we lost to the Mets, we couldn't wait to get to spring training the next year," he said. "All winter we thought about those games we lost."

When the Orioles came back in 1970, they played like a team on a mission. They nearly matched their 1969 win total, finishing with 108 victories, and took the AL East title by 15 games. And just like in 1969, they swept the Twins in three straight in the ALCS. They then faced a

Cincinnati Reds team in the World Series that was in the early stages of the Big Red Machine, featuring such big-name stars as Pete Rose, Tony Perez, and Johnny Bench.

This time the Orioles, still driven by their 1969 failure, were not going to let the Reds have the chance to gain the upper hand. They won the first game 4–3 (a Palmer victory), with home runs by Hendricks, Boog Powell, and Brooks Robinson, who, although already recognized as the best third baseman in baseball and perhaps of all time, used the nationally televised Series as a stage to showcase his unforgettable diving plays at third base.

Baltimore went on to win Game 2 6–5, then exploded in Game 3 with home runs by Frank Robinson, Don Buford, and McNally, the winning pitcher, in a 9–3 victory. Down 0–3, the Reds came back to win Game 4 in another one-run game by the same score as Game 2, 6–5. Now the Orioles found themselves up three games to one in the Series—a position that would both haunt and inspire them in years to come. "We wanted to close it down in Game 5," Hendricks said. "We didn't want to let the Reds back up. We didn't want to lose it again after 1969."

They didn't. In a repeat of Game 3, the Orioles pounded Reds pitching in a 9–3 win, clinching their second World Series championship in five years. Cuellar got the win, with home runs by Merv Rettenmund and Frank Robinson. The defeat of the Reds was particularly satisfying for Frank Robinson, since it was the franchise that he had starred with in the early sixties but that had dealt him away in 1965 when management determined he was an "old 30"—or was too much of a problem to deal with, depending on the story you believe.

The Orioles remained the class of baseball and the most dominant franchise in the game the following season, making their third straight trip to the World Series in 1971. They won the AL East by 12 games, with a record of 101–57, giving them a three-year regular-season record of 318–164. And they managed to make baseball history with four 20-game winners—McNally (21–5), Cuellar (20–9), Palmer (20–9), and Pat Dobson (20–8). Again they swept their opponent in the ALCS. In the three years the championship series had existed, the Orioles had yet to lose a series game, going 9–0. This time they won Game 1 by a 5–3 score, Game 2 5–1, and Game 3 5–3. Who did they defeat? The team that would unseat the Orioles for league dominance very soon, a young Oakland Athletics team led by a brash slugger by the name of Reggie Jackson—a future Oriole.

Baltimore faced a different team for the third straight time in the World Series—the Pittsburgh Pirates, a team led by one of the most exciting and charismatic players of his time, Roberto Clemente. His presence on the field and at the plate was too much for the Orioles to handle, and he proved to be the difference over seven games, batting .414 and leading the Pirates to the World Series championship in seven games. Baltimore had won the first two games, and, with their pitching staff, appeared to be on their way to a second straight Series championship. But when the Series switched to Pittsburgh, the Pirates won the next three straight at home. The Orioles won Game 6 in 10 innings because they treated it like Game 7, starting Palmer and using Dobson and McNally in relief. But despite an outstanding pitching performance by Cuellar in Game 7, the Orioles went down in defeat 2–1, thanks to a better pitching performance by Steve Blass and a home run by Clemente.

The defeat would mark the end of two eras, neither of which was expected. One of them was far more tragic—the death of Clemente a year later on New Year's Eve 1972. He was aboard a plane that crashed shortly after takeoff from Puerto Rico on a mission to bring supplies to earthquake victims in Nicaragua.

It also marked the end of the legacy of this great Orioles team, though no one knew that was coming, either. The Orioles finished in third place with an 80–74 record in 1972 (a strike-shortened season). They bounced back with 97 and 91 wins in 1973 and 1974, but their ALCS dominance was a memory. They were beaten by Oakland in five games in 1973 and four games in 1974, and during that time the team that had been so dominant since 1966 began to fall apart. Frank Robinson was traded to the Los Angeles Dodgers after the 1971 season, and it was clear they missed his bat and his presence. Dobson and second baseman Davey Johnson were dealt to Atlanta in 1972, although Johnson was ably replaced by Bobby Grich. Boog Powell was moved to Cleveland in 1974, and McNally, with 181 career wins for the Orioles, was traded to Montreal after the 1974 season in a deal that would eventually help the Orioles rebuild and create another era of excellence, as they acquired a young outfielder named Ken Singleton.

Baltimore hardly collapsed in 1975, winning 90 games and finishing second in the AL East. And they followed that up with 88 wins and another second-place finish in 1976. But Hank Peters, the new general manager who had taken over for Frank Cashen, made a trade that would lay much of the foundation that led to their 1979 and 1982 successes and disappointments. In June 1976, the Orioles traded Elrod Hendricks, Grant Jackson, and Doyle Alexander to the Yankees for pitchers Rudy May, Dave Pagan, and Tippy Martinez, and two minor leaguers named Scott McGregor and Rick Dempsey. Other young players, such as Al Bumbry, began to blossom during this transition, and the much heralded farm system was producing such talented position players as Eddie Murray and Rich Dauer and such promising pitchers as Mike Flanagan and Dennis Martinez.

Much of this group came up together in the 1977 season, the first year of the new-age Orioles, and they helped Baltimore win 97 games, 2½ games behind the Yankees. Murray emerged as one of the game's brightest young stars, hitting 27 home runs, driving in 88 runs, and batting .283.

It was another watershed year in Orioles history, because just as it signaled a new crop of stars, it also marked the end of one of the most glorious eras of Baltimore baseball—it would be Brooks Robinson's last season. Born in Little Rock, Arkansas, the third baseman had become the most popular figure in Orioles history and took his place, along with Baltimore Colts quarterback Johnny Unitas, as one of the city's sports icons. He began his career briefly in Baltimore in 1955 and went on to become one of the greatest third basemen of all time. Over 23 seasons, Brooks Robinson batted .267 with 268 home runs and 1,357 RBIs. But while he was a solid—and clutch—hitter, it was his glove that made him a national figure, particularly his play during the World Series. He won 16 straight Gold Glove awards, from 1960 to 1975, and committed just 263 errors in 9,165 chances for a lifetime fielding average of .971. It seemed like he was at third base for the Orioles forever. He played in 97 percent of the team's games from 1959 to 1976 and finished with 2,896 games in his career, all with Baltimore.

But as Brooks Robinson left, the new Orioles took over, including a talented young player named Doug DeCinces at third base. DeCinces would never receive the respect he deserved in Baltimore because of the pressure of following the legendary Robinson, and he would be traded in 1982. But he was part of the new Orioles that showed promise in 1977 and 1978, leading up to what appeared to be the culmination of that new crop of Orioles in 1979, when they won 102 games (the most in all of baseball). Baltimore unseated the two-time world champion Yankees and took the AL Eastern Division crown. They faced the California Angels in the ALCS, beating them in four games, and seemed poised to bring Baltimore another World Series title when they faced the Pittsburgh Pirates, who had a much tougher road to the 1979 postseason. The Orioles had won the AL East by eight games, while the Pirates hadn't won the NL East until the final day of the season. But Pittsburgh swept the Cincinnati Reds in the NLCS, behind the leadership and the bat of Willie "Pops" Stargell.

Going into the Series, the Pirates appeared to have the momentum and the emotion, with their "We Are Family" theme song. But the Orioles had the pitching, and pitching usually wins in the postseason. They were led by Flanagan, the American League Cy Young Award winner, who went 23–9 that season; McGregor, with a 13–6 mark; and Palmer, who went 10–6 in a down year but was still considered the class of the American League, coming off four straight 20-win seasons. At the plate, they backed up their strong pitching with the bats of Singleton (35 home runs, 111 RBIs) and Murray (25 home runs, 99 RBIs) and a supporting batting cast that included Gary Roenicke (25 home runs) and the fleet Al Bumbry (.285 average, 37 steals). But statistics didn't tell the story of the dominance of the 1979 Orioles. These young players, who had come together through trades and the minor league system, had matured as a group and, under Weaver, learned a discipline about playing the game that was admired throughout baseball.

Bob Lemon, the Yankees manager who was fired during the season and replaced by the man he had replaced the year before, Billy Martin, during one of the many bizarre George Steinbrenner managerial moves that would nearly destroy the Yankees franchise, wrote a pre-Series analysis of the Orioles for *The New York Times*:

> Don't ask me for any secrets on how to beat the Orioles, because I don't know of any. If there was an easy way, then

Baltimore wouldn't have the best record in baseball this year. All I can say to the Pirates is, you better have two things going for you when you play the Orioles. First, your pitching has to be up. Second, you have to be able to cope with their pitching. In other words, whether you're pitching against the Orioles or hitting against them, playing the Orioles is no day at the beach. They're just a real steady ballclub, probably the steadiest in baseball right now. They don't have any weaknesses, as far as I can see. They score runs, and they don't allow very many. Even without the designated hitter, they will be strong at the plate.

One more thing. Don't look for the Orioles to beat themselves, which a lot of clubs do. They almost never lose by making mistakes, physical or mental. By mental mistakes, I mean throwing to the wrong base, not backing up a play, not hitting the cutoff man. They don't beat themselves. But if you make a mistake, they'll take advantage of it. You can count on that. They make all the plays, know all the fundamentals. Earl Weaver demands it.

The Pirates were no slouches. They were led by Stargell and one of the best players of his time, outfielder Dave Parker, who totaled 25 home runs and 24 stolen bases that season. They also featured such professional hitters as Bill Robinson (24 home runs, 75 RBIs) and Bill Madlock (.298 average, 14 home runs, 32 stolen bases), as well as Omar Moreno (77 stolen bases), who created havoc on the base paths.

The Orioles should have taken the weather as an omen of things to come. The opening game at Memorial Stadium was rained out. When the Series did finally open, many expected the damp coldness to result in another postponement. The field was also in rough shape because the NFL's Colts were in Baltimore and also playing at Memorial Stadium. But Commissioner Bowie Kuhn ordered the game to go on.

Flanagan took the mound against Bruce Kison before a crowd of 53,735, and, from the start, it looked as if it would be a rout. Baltimore scored five runs in the bottom of the first inning. With the bases loaded, John Lowenstein hit a ground ball that second baseman Phil Garner appeared to turn for a double play. But Garner's throw went over short-stop Tim Foli's head and into left field. Two runs scored, and then Murray trotted home on a wild pitch by Kison. Two more runners would score before the Pirates finally got out of the inning. But Pittsburgh gave a preview for the theme of this Series—and what lay ahead for Baltimore—when they came back to score four runs and nearly take it away from Flanagan, who hung on for the complete-game victory. "We didn't look good in the first inning, but we thought we would be able to come back," Pirates manager Chuck Tanner said. "We've been down by five runs before and we've come back." That belief would serve the Pirates well.

The Pirates came back to beat Jim Palmer in Game 2 by a score of 3–2. In the top of the ninth inning, with the score tied at 2–2, Manny Sanguillen drove a pinch-hit single to right field, scoring Ed Ott with the go-ahead run on another cold, rainy night in Baltimore before a crowd of 53,379. The game came down to two key plays at the plate, and the Orioles lost both of them. Parker threw Murray out at the plate in the sixth inning with the score tied at 2–2, and Singleton was unable to get Ott at the plate when he scored on Sanguillen's hit. After the game, the Orioles got the following message: Roberto Clemente was still making their lives miserable, even from the great beyond. Sanguillen told reporters the Pirates were dedicating their play in the Series to Clemente. "Anything we do, we're going to do for him," he said.

That inspiration, combined with taking the home-field advantage away from the Orioles and going back to Pittsburgh for Games 3, 4, and 5, appeared to put the Pirates in control of the Series. They were anything but, it turned out, as the Orioles did not seem to be haunted by the ghost of Clemente. With McGregor on the mound, Baltimore's offense opened up and beat Pittsburgh 8–4 in Game 3 at Three Rivers Stadium. Rain continued to plague the Series, and there was a 67-minute delay in the third inning. The Pirates led 3–0 at the time. But after being outhit 22–12 in the first two games, the Orioles lineup—which Weaver made significant changes to after the first two games, using a primarily right-handed unit against left-hander John Candelaria—exploded for eight runs on 13 hits. Nearly everyone in the lineup chipped in. Kiko Garcia, playing shortstop in place of Mark Belanger, contributed the most, going 4-for-4 with four RBIs and two runs scored. Benny Ayala, getting a rare start in left field, went 2-for-2 with a home run and two RBIs. Singleton went 2-for-5 with an RBI, and Rick Dempsey also went 2-for-5. Roenicke and Rich Dauer also had hits, but two of the big bats, Murray and DeCinces, went hitless. McGregor got the complete-game victory.

"It was one of those lineups that got us here in the first place," Weaver told reporters after the game. "It was designed to score runs. Nothing unusual. We did it all summer."

The small bats continued to deliver the big hits in Game 4. Dennis Martinez got the start for Baltimore but had a disastrous outing, giving up four runs on six hits in just 1⅓ innings. But the Orioles battled back from a 6–3 deficit by scoring six runs in the top of the eighth inning to beat the Pirates 9–6 and go up three games to one. Garcia led the eighth-inning comeback with a single to right, followed by a left-field single by Singleton. Murray grounded out, but DeCinces walked. Pittsburgh manager Chuck Tanner brought in reliever Kent Tekulve, and Weaver countered by sending up John Lowenstein, a left-handed hitter, to pinch hit. Lowenstein doubled down the right-field line and drove in two runs, cutting the Pittsburgh lead to 6–5. Billy Smith, the switch-hitting second baseman, came up as a pinch-hitter and cajoled a walk. Pinch-hitter extraordinaire Terry Crowley came to the plate and doubled to right field, scoring two more runs and putting Baltimore on top 7–6.

Then Weaver surprised everyone by letting reliever Tim Stoddard hit, and here was the proof, it seemed, that the Orioles were destined to be the 1979 World Series champions. Stoddard, the game-winning pitcher, singled to left, scoring another run. It was Stoddard's first professional baseball hit and the first time anyone ever got his first hit in a World Series game. Al Bumbry drove in the final run of the inning and the game. With a 3–1 lead, it was hard for the Orioles to think about any outcome other than winning the 1979 World Series. The attitude in the Orioles clubhouse before Game 5 of the Series would have quite an impact on everything that team would do in the future.

"When we were up 3–1 against the Pirates in the 1979 Series, with Palmer, Flanagan, and McGregor pitching for us, I'm thinking to myself, 'This is over,'" Dauer said.

It was far from over, though they did come close. With Flanagan pitching, the Orioles had a 1–0 lead going into the sixth inning of Game 5. But the left-hander, coming off his complete-game victory, was tired, and he gave up two runs on a sacrifice fly by Stargell and an RBI single by Madlock. Flanagan left the game, but Stoddard, Tippy Martinez, and Don Stanhouse were unable to stop the Pirates hitters, who went on to score five runs. Tanner brought in Bert Blyleven to relieve Jim Rooker in the sixth inning, and he held the Orioles hitters scoreless the rest of the way. Pittsburgh won 7–1 before a crowd of 50,920 at Three Rivers Stadium.

There was no panic yet in the Orioles clubhouse. "We were going back to Baltimore, and we had Palmer pitching," Dauer said. But left-hander John Candelaria proved to be the hot pitcher, throwing six shutout innings while Dave Parker hit a tie-breaking single to lead Pittsburgh to a 4–0 win in Game 6 and tie the Series at 3–3. The Memorial Stadium crowd of 53,379 appeared stunned at how futile its team now seemed to be, and the confidence that had filled the Orioles clubhouse was now gone. Murray was hounded for his failure to get a hit in his fourth straight World Series game. Palmer complained about Benny Ayala's presence in left field and his failure to run down a Garner hit for a ground-rule double. Earlier in the Series, Palmer had openly debated Weaver's gamble of using Ayala, a right-handed hitter against the left-handed Pirates pitcher, in the outfield. After Game 6, the outspoken Palmer told reporters, "I think most people think it should have been caught."

The momentum was now with the Pirates, the sentimental favorites for their comeback and for their fun-loving "We Are Family" team theme, promoted by their respected leader, "Pops" Stargell. It was all over now. Pittsburgh won Game 7 in Baltimore 4–1, beating McGregor and using four pitchers—Jim Bibby, Don Robinson, Grant Jackson, and Tekulve—to hold the Orioles to just one run. Stargell hit a two-run home run and wound up as the Series Most Valuable Player, batting .400 over the seven-game Series. As the Pirates celebrated at Memorial Stadium before a crowd of 53,733, the Orioles sat quietly in their clubhouse, in shock at their total collapse. Murray went hitless again and failed to deliver with the bases loaded and two out in the bottom of the eighth inning, flying out to Parker in right field. "Our bats just went flat—that's all there is to it," Weaver said. "It had nothing to do with experience or inexperience."

Looking back, Dempsey believes the Orioles were simply not the better team. "They were a better ballclub than we were at that time," he said. "We played over our heads to get there, but we were capable of doing that because we had an energy level that no one could rival. We could really get up for games and for series.

"We knew we had blown that Series," Dempsey continued. "A lot of things went against us in those three games. We hit some balls really good, but the Pirates turned double plays on balls that should have been base hits. They seemed to inch by in every one of those last three games. We didn't get any breaks, and they got the momentum. They were a high-intensity ballclub, too, and we just couldn't get anything going against them."

They didn't get it going in those final World Series games, but surely they would be back. After all, this was a team on the rise. That's what Weaver must have believed. Speaking to reporters before Game 6 of the 1979 World Series, Weaver told reporters he would retire after the 1982 season. He said he had planned to retire after his contract ran out after the 1980 season, but decided he wanted to manage two years past that "so I can be comfortable until I get my baseball pension." It may have been money that drove Weaver to keep managing, but he—and his players—felt confident that those remaining years would surely result in a World Series championship for this new era of Orioles. It would also be the final validation for Weaver, who had won his only World Series title with the team led by Brooks and Frank Robinson, a team that, while managed by Weaver, was not as strongly influenced by him as this group of players was.

But that string of World Series appearances never came. The Orioles won 100 games in 1980, which should have been good enough for a return to the Series, but they finished second in the AL East behind the Yankees, who won 103 games. Then came the bizarre strike season of 1981, which found the Orioles finishing second in both halves of the divided season. Then came the 1982 campaign, and the wild final series of the season that proved to be influential on the 1983 championship squad.

The Milwaukee Brewers had pulled ahead of the Orioles in the AL East by 7½ games by mid-August. But Baltimore pushed hard to catch up, winning 30 of their last 40 games before a final weekend showdown against the Brewers at Memorial Stadium. Four games behind Milwaukee, the Orioles swept a doubleheader 8–3 and 7–1, then followed that up with an 11–3 victory on Saturday. The Orioles were one game behind Milwaukee on the final day of the season, playing at home, with Jim Palmer on the mound facing Don Sutton. They felt overwhelming pressure to win it for Weaver, who was retiring at the end of the season. "In that last game, we had our ace going, Palmer, and I thought we were going to win it," Tippy Martinez said. "After all, by that point, who would have thought we could win five straight from Milwaukee at that time?"

Again, the Orioles came up short, taking a 10–2 beating, though it was closer than the score showed. They were down 5–1 in the eighth inning, when, with two outs and Lowenstein and Cal Ripken Jr. on base, Terry Crowley, pinch hitting for Dempsey, singled to left, scoring Lowenstein and cutting the Brewers lead to 5–2. Weaver seemed on the verge of working his pinch-hitting magic again. Joe Nolan was sent in as another pinch-hitter, and drove a fly ball deep to the left-field corner. It appeared that it would fall in for a hit, which would have scored two more runs. But left fielder Ben Oglivie dove and snared the ball for the third out, ending the rally. The Brewers broke the game open in the top of the ninth, bringing a disappointing end—or so it seemed—to the managing career of Earl Weaver.

The sellout crowd of 51,642 fans at Memorial Stadium stayed long after the game to cheer and pay tribute to a tearful Weaver, who came back on the field, followed by many of his players. With the team's blue-collar mascot, cab driver Wild Bill Hagy, standing on the mound to lead the cheers, Weaver joined in on those Orioles cheers with Hagy and the crowd. It was an emotional evening, but at the end of the night reality set in: the team that had showed so much promise when they came together five years earlier, and had been one of the winningest teams in baseball over that period, had no World Series rings to show for their efforts.

"That was a sad day," Dempsey said. "We should have won that last game, but Robin Yount hit two home runs and it got away from us. We had been pretty far back, and we came back to tie it. We beat Milwaukee something like seven of the last eight games we played them. Here we were, tied for first with one game left, and they had Don Sutton on the mound and we had Jim Palmer, who hadn't lost a game since May. We thought it was in the bag.

"I'll never forget the shot Joe Nolan hit down the left-field line," he said. "Ben Oglivie ran down the line and slid into the fence and made the catch. That was a key moment in the game. . . . Just like in 1979, in those three World Series games, we couldn't get a break in that last game of 1982. We hit some balls good, but it wasn't in the cards. It was doubly disappointing because it was Earl's last game."

Lowenstein said he went into a state of depression after that loss to the Brewers. "That year, 1982, was a psychological disaster for me, and it took about 10 days for me to get over it," he said. "To come that close and not get in, it wiped everything out for a week. It was there for us. What if Oglivie hadn't caught that ball? It would have been a different game. But great plays are what make great seasons for great teams. With Cakes [Palmer] on the mound, I thought there was no way we were going to lose. But Robin Yount killed us."

The Weaver era appeared to have ended, but his players remained behind. Time was running out for them as well, though. They sensed it, and all winter the disappointment of coming close yet again, and the fear that their run was coming to an end, made these players want to take the field in 1983 as soon as possible. "One thing that really helped us in 1983 was what happened in 1982, when we came up short," Singleton said. "We had played so great down the stretch, and to have that last game get away was so disappointing. I think as a group it made us even more determined when we started the next season. Also, we were getting older as a team, and it looked like our last chance."

Pitching coach Ray Miller sensed the urgency among the players when they reported to spring training. "You felt like everyone expected that we were going to win and get to the World Series," he said.

Not just get there. They had done that before. If 1982 was the fuel that drove the Orioles in 1983, it was 1979 that seared into their memories as they sat there in the visitor's clubhouse at Veterans Stadium before Game 5 of the 1983 World Series.

"Everyone in there was very aware of 1979," Bumbry said. "We weren't going to let that happen again."

They filed out of the clubhouse and through the tunnel to the dugout, ready to finally fulfill their destiny.

2 | A New Man in the Dugout

Pitchers and catchers reported to Miami Stadium for spring training in February 1983 like they had done every year for the previous 15 seasons. But there was one thing that was very, very different—the manager.

Earl Weaver was gone.

"It was strange not having Earl there after we were with him for so long," Rick Dempsey said.

Fortunately for the Orioles, they had a familiar face to ease the strangeness. They already knew the new manager well, and the new manager knew the Orioles' Miami spring-training home well.

Joe Altobelli once played in the Orioles organization for seven seasons, five of them with their Rochester farm club. He played for a hard-nosed manager there named Earl Weaver. Later, Altobelli managed the Triple-A Rochester team from 1971 through 1976, mentoring a group of young players named Eddie Murray, Rich Dauer, and Mike Flanagan, as well as other Orioles prospects.

"I had been to spring training for the club many times before," Altobelli said. "When I was the manager in Rochester, I always went to spring training with the major league club. Everyone was familiar to me, even the writers. When I managed in Rochester, I used to go to Baltimore for about six games a year to watch. So it was like a homecoming for me. I knew the surroundings, the organization, and the people in it."

That was one of the reasons that owner Edward Bennett Williams and general manager Hank Peters hired Altobelli in November 1982. But it wasn't the only reason. If familiarity was the basis for the managing job, then one of the two other candidates, both from the coaching staff—Cal Ripken Sr. and Ray Miller—would have gotten the job. But neither had major league managing experience. Altobelli did, managing the San Francisco Giants for three seasons, from 1977 to 1979. After a losing season of 75–87 in 1977, Altobelli led the Giants to an 89–73 record in 1978. But then they suffered another losing season (61–79 in 1979), and he was fired.

The favorite among the players was Ripken—or Senior, as he was called. The father of Cal Jr. and Billy Ripken was one of the most influential figures in the history of the Orioles franchise. Managing in the club's minor league system from 1961 to 1974, Ripken, perhaps more than anyone else, established the Oriole Way of playing. Senior ran spring training for the Orioles, making sure the workouts were organized and run like a train on a schedule. He had managed nearly all of the players on that 1983 roster; they were Senior disciples. He joined the major league club as a coach in 1975 and was Weaver's right-hand man on the staff. He was also Weaver's choice to replace him as manager but, surprisingly, Williams passed him over in favor of Altobelli.

Although the players and staff respected their owner, it appeared to mean little to Williams, who treated the coach shabbily. After passing over Ripken Sr. to manage the Orioles in 1982, Williams did finally hire him to manage the 1987 team, when the franchise was on the verge of collapse on the field. Senior went 67–95, and after starting the 1988 season 0–6, he was suddenly fired by Williams. Frank Robinson was hired to replace Senior, and the team went on to lose its next 15 games, starting the season with an 0–21 record.

Altobelli was working as the Yankees third-base coach and appeared to be a compromise candidate between Williams and Peters, who reportedly favored bringing in John McNamara. He had been fired by the Cincinnati Reds in the middle of the 1982 season, and was a close friend of Peters. But Williams had another choice in mind. It wasn't Altobelli. And until then, no one knew who Williams desperately wanted to succeed Weaver and manage the 1983 Orioles, because the story that was reported at the time was not really what was happening behind the scenes.

Former Orioles great Frank Robinson was managing the Giants at the time Weaver retired and the Orioles job was open. After Altobelli was hired, Robinson said publicly he was disappointed that the Orioles did not approach him about the managing job, even though he was still managing in San Francisco at the time.

"Did I want to be manager of the Baltimore Orioles?" Robinson said when asked by a Baltimore reporter while in town for a baseball seminar. "Well, that's a tough one to answer. I don't know if that's for me to answer. Perhaps you should talk to Hank Peters about that. It really wasn't up to me. . . . As far as I know, the Orioles never asked the Giants for permission to talk to me. Maybe the success I had in San Francisco led to the Orioles' decision not to pursue me. I really don't know. But somehow I feel that people, maybe even the Orioles, got the impression that I wasn't interested in the job. That wasn't the case. Don't get me wrong. I have two years left in a contract to manage San Francisco and I'm quite happy there. I feel we've turned the franchise around, and it's exciting to be a part of that. But I still would have given the Orioles the courtesy of listening to them if they had come to me about the job. And I certainly would have given a lot of consideration to accepting the job if I thought it was the right thing for me."

What Robinson didn't know at the time was that the Orioles did ask the Giants for permission to talk to him about the managing job—and the Giants refused, never even telling Robinson about the inquiry. "They did ask to talk to me," said Robinson 20 years later, sitting behind his desk during spring training at the Montreal Expos camp in Viera, Florida. "I didn't know it until later that they did ask, and the Giants refused. The Giants told me that later. I was let down. At least they could have told me and then let me make the decision. I don't think that was right. At least make me aware of it. That was very disappointing for me."

Williams loved big names, and Frank Robinson was a big name. Williams would finally get his big name, and Frank Robinson would get his chance to come home and manage the Orioles five years later, but he would not be inheriting a championship team. The 1988 team he inherited lost 107 games. Frank Robinson would last just three years before being fired during the 1991 season with a 230–285 record. He would remain in the front office as an assistant general manager, but was let go just before the 1996 season when Pat Gillick was hired as general manager. Robinson remains estranged from the organization, still bitter about the way he was treated by current owner Peter Angelos when he left the franchise.

After the Frank Robinson debacle, Williams settled on Altobelli. But that decision was a slap against Weaver, who was still working for the organization as a scout and consultant. There was a history between Altobelli and Weaver, who had kept Altobelli off his major league coaching staff, seeing him as a threat.

Weaver was clearly not pleased by the passing over of Senior and offered a lukewarm endorsement of the hiring. "It was entirely up to Mr. Williams and Mr. Peters," he told reporters, carefully choosing his words. "They selected the man they wanted to work with, the man they thought who would best do the best job. Rip has 25 years in the organization. But Joe's from out of the organization, too. . . . What are you going to say except that Rip has been with the major league club, so why go anyplace else?"

And Weaver's nemesis, Jim Palmer, also publicly questioned the choice of Altobelli, telling reporters that either Senior or Ray Miller might have been better suited for the job. He said Weaver's endorsement of Senior killed any chance he had for the job because of a power struggle between Weaver and Peters. "The kiss of death was when Earl said Cal ought to be manager, especially when Earl said if Cal had any problems he could call him," Palmer said.

Not that Palmer was particularly looking for Weaver to have any influence on the team. He had some harsh words for Weaver during a public relations appearance less than two months after Weaver retired. "The greatest thing that happened to Earl was to be manager of our teams in 1969, 1970, and 1971, because we won and it made him out to be one of the best managers in baseball," Palmer said. "But I think his claim to fame was that he didn't mess up those teams. I think that caused Earl to lose a lot of his introspection. I think he began to think he was the reason we were winning. It wasn't Frank Robinson, it wasn't Brooks Robinson, it wasn't me, it wasn't Davey Johnson—it was Earl."

In case anyone wasn't paying attention to Palmer, everyone was reminded of one of the main reasons the Orioles had been such a winning franchise since 1966 on January 12, 1983, the day that former Baltimore third baseman Brooks Robinson was elected to the National Baseball Hall of Fame. Brooks Robinson made it in on the first ballot, the 14th player at the time to do so. He was the most beloved baseball figure in Orioles history, and right up there with Johnny Unitas as a Baltimore sports icon. He was considered—and still is by many—to be the greatest third baseman of all time (only Mike Schmidt has been successfully argued as his equal or better, and that is primarily because of Schmidt's home run power). His election was just another confirmation of the excellence of the Orioles organization, and he remained the face of the franchise as a television analyst for many years after retiring, including the 1983 season. He would later cut his ties with the club and has rarely been seen around Camden Yards under the regime of owner Peter Angelos.

Brooks Robinson may have been the face of the franchise, but the voice was still Weaver, even in retirement. The former manager lived just a few miles from Miami Stadium, and either his presence in camp, when he showed up in his role as an advisor and scout, or his lack of presence would hound Altobelli throughout training camp. Many of the stories that came out of Miami centered around both subjects, including Weaver's golf game. "Weaver retired as manager of the Orioles after 14½ eminently successful years, preceded by 21 seasons as a minor league player and field leader," columnist John Steadman wrote. "What he wanted was to spend the rest of his life on a golf course and he has found what he believes is his Valhalla right here on earth, the Country Club of Miami." That conclusion was a dubious one, because, as history would prove, Valhalla did not last long for Weaver.

The papers were still full of the Weaver-Palmer love-hate festival. Weaver was not about to let Palmer get away with the comments he made during the off-season without his chance to hit back, and he told *The Miami Herald*, "Palmer's going to win. I just wish he'd quit trying to be smart and funny. We had fun with statements going back and forth, but they never looked the same in the paper."

No, they did not, and the whole Weaver circus certainly created additional pressure for Altobelli, who didn't need any more pressure after inheriting a team that had come close over the past few years—within one game in 1979—to winning a World Series championship but failed to do so.

Altobelli may not have been Weaver's choice, but he was a breath of fresh air to the players who had grown tired of the tension of playing for Weaver. "Joe was a very calming influence on our club," Dempsey said. "We had a good team, and we knew that. It felt good not to have that feistiness that Earl seemed to put into every game.

"Earl was a tough guy for the umpires to get along with," Dempsey said. "He was also very demanding of the ballclub and of himself as well. That was great when we were all young and learning how to play the game. But by this time we were a solid, veteran club, and what we really needed was somebody to sit back and coordinate things and go from there. Joe Altobelli fit that bill."

The new manager was not about to make any major changes. He kept the coaching staff intact and ran the team the way it had been run for so many years under Weaver—the Oriole Way. "I knew the Oriole Way of playing and preparing for the game," he said. "That's how I learned as a young manager. It was a fine way to play baseball."

The Oriole Way worked so well and was so instilled in that group of players that they believed they could operate on their own. "In a lot of ways, we were a self-managed team," Dempsey said. "Everyone knew their roles so well."

Elrod Hendricks looks back on that 1983 team with admiration. "It was fun watching them go about their business day in and day out," he said. "I think back on all my years of coaching, and that was the one year that I had the least amount to do as a coach because they were such a veteran team. Basically, you left them alone and let them play."

One change the Orioles players would have welcomed was to not have to return to their Miami complex for another year. Miami Stadium was once a fine minor league ballpark with a colorful past befitting the Casablanca personality of Miami. The stadium opened in 1949 featuring a game between the Havana Cubans and the Miami Sun Sox in a Class B Florida International League contest. The facility had been built by Jose Aleman Sr., a government official in Cuba in the late forties. He was forced to leave after an aborted attempt to lead Cuban troops in an attack on the government of Dominican Republic strongman Rafael Trujillo. Reportedly, he fled the island with an estimated $19 million in U.S. currency taken from the Cuban treasury. He had already owned a piece of the Miami Sun Sox. He then purchased the majority share and used his money to build the new stadium. At the time, it was a state-of-the-art ballpark. It hosted such baseball greats as Joe DiMaggio, Ted Williams, and Jackie Robinson (the Dodgers trained there briefly) in exhibition games, and the great Satchel Paige pitched for the minor league Miami Marlins in the late fifties.

But it was much more than a baseball stadium. Aleman, an opponent of Cuban dictator Fulgencio Batista, supported a young revolutionary by the name of Fidel Castro. He stored rifles, bazookas, and grenades for Castro in the stadium, and he also allowed the rebels to come to Miami and use the ballpark as a training ground and sleeping quarters. In 1987, the Miami City Commission changed the name of the ballpark from Miami Stadium to Bobby Maduro Field, named after one of the legendary figures in Cuban baseball. Maduro owned the great Havana Cubans and Havana Sugar Kings minor league clubs in the late forties and early fifties. Maduro would eventually leave Cuba and become a special assistant to baseball commissioner Bowie Kuhn.

Thirty years after it served as a place to train rebels, the stadium wound up in the middle of an urban war zone, in the center of a neighborhood that had been the focus of unrest since the 1968 Liberty City riots. Players feared for their safety and that of their families coming and going from the complex. And fears were particularly heightened as they arrived for spring training in 1983, on the heels of riots in the nearby Overtown section of the city after a Hispanic police officer shot and killed a black youth. Cars were burned, stores were looted, and nearly 30 people were injured. "It seems like it gets worse every year," Rich Dauer said before coming to camp. "I won't allow my wife or baby girls to come see spring-training games. It's too dangerous around that stadium." Palmer, upon leaving the complex and entering the parking lot one day, told a reporter, "Well, my car is still there. That's what I consider a good day."

Scott McGregor remembers it as being a particularly unique place to play. "Playing in Miami, we were always the visiting team," he said.

"Everyone usually came to see the other team. We didn't have a real following in Miami. The Yankees were more popular, Boston was more popular.

"The fans would bet on anything there," McGregor said. "It was like playing winter ball. They were always betting or fighting or doing all kinds of stuff in the stands. It was interesting. The stadium was right in the riot zone, too, so our cars were getting broken into. So we started renting cars—let them break into the rental cars."

Eventually the Orioles would leave town after the 1990 season—31 years after they first came to Miami—but have never truly found a permanent training home since then. They were vagabonds in 1991, training in a minor league complex in Sarasota but traveling around the state, playing all away games. They moved to St. Petersburg in 1992, and then from 1993 through 1995, they trained in Sarasota before the exhibition season and moved to St. Petersburg when the playing schedule began. They eventually took over the Yankees training facility in Fort Lauderdale in 1996 after the Yankees moved to their new spring home in Tampa, and they have been there ever since. However, the club has kept looking for a new place because the Lauderdale complex is antiquated and does not allow the team to house both the major and minor leaguers, as most spring-training facilities do these days.

Overall, the Orioles made very few changes in spring training in 1983—certainly not in the starting pitching rotation, which was well established with Palmer, Mike Flanagan, McGregor, Dennis Martinez, and newcomer Storm Davis, who had come up from Rochester during the 1982 season and went 8–4 with a 3.49 ERA. There was no room for a young pitcher named Mike Boddicker, who, for the third straight spring, was sent back to Rochester before the season began.

The outfield situation wasn't quite as settled. "Disco" Dan Ford came from the California Angels to the Orioles in a trade before the 1982 season, in exchange for one of the most popular players in the clubhouse, third baseman Doug DeCinces, and pitcher Jeff Schneider. Ford had trouble adjusting to the Oriole Way of doing things and didn't quite fit in on the conservative club. He struggled during the 1982 season, batting .235 with 10 home runs and 43 RBIs in 123 games, and became the target of boos from fans at Memorial Stadium.

When Ford came to spring training in 1983, he reported with a determination to try to turn things around. "It was important to fit in on the Orioles," he said. "That was one of my main problems in 1982. When I got there, guys were telling me about the Oriole Way. I said, 'The Oriole Way? I thought baseball was played the same every place you go.' They said, 'We do things a little different here. We want you to do this, we want you to be that.' I said to myself, 'Uh-oh, I'm in trouble.' It took me a little while to get the hang of things.

"I didn't have a very good year in 1982, and I think when we lost it at the end, the talk that winter was that one of the reasons we lost was because Dan Ford didn't play very well. I was the first person that Altobelli called to talk to that spring."

Most of the positions on that 1983 team were set. But that doesn't mean there wasn't a battle for a piece of turf between one of the old guard and a new player. Part of the intrigue of spring training was the battle that went on in center field between Al Bumbry and John Shelby.

Alonza Benjamin Bumbry was a special man. Just before he was to begin his professional career in June 1968, Bumbry, who was in the Virginia State R.O.T.C. program, was called to active duty as a second lieutenant. He was sent to Vietnam and served as a platoon leader, returning 11 months later and earning a Bronze Star. He was discharged from duty as a first lieutenant in May 1971 and returned to professional baseball—a career that was hardly second nature to Bumbry.

The 5'8", 175-pound native of Fredericksburg, Virginia, did not even start to play baseball until his senior year in college. He went to Virginia State on a basketball scholarship after averaging 32 points a game at Ralph Bunche High School in King George, Virginia. Orioles scout Dick Bowie had talked Bumbry into trying out for baseball while in college, and in the one season he played at Virginia State, Bumbry won the Central Intercollegiate Athletic Association batting title with a .378 average and was All-CIAA in both basketball and baseball.

Bowie signed Bumbry, and he went to Stockton to play 35 games of minor league ball before being called up to active duty. He batted just .175 in those games, but when he returned in 1971 and played in Aberdeen, South Dakota, Bumbry batted .336 with 34 stolen bases and 68 runs scored in 66 games. He started the season with Ashville in 1972, and after batting .347 in 26 games with 10 steals and 26 runs scored, Bumbry moved up to Triple-A Rochester and hit .345 in 108 games with 83 runs scored and 22 stolen bases. He batted .364 in nine games with the major league club to finish the season, and, with his speed and hitting, showed enough to Weaver to make the team out of spring training in 1973. He made an impressive rookie debut, batting .337 in 110 games, leading the league with 11 triples, and stealing 23 bases. He would continue to be a solid leadoff batter, peaking in 1980 with a .318 average, 205 hits, 29 doubles, nine triples, 118 runs scored, nine home runs, 53 RBIs, and 44 stolen bases.

"When I was young, I didn't play much," he said. "I played basketball. When the Orioles signed me and I got to the minor leagues, I didn't have a lot of experience. Back then it was nothing for a guy to have five or six years in the minors. But then in 1973, Earl decided he wanted to take another position player north and one less pitcher. I had done well in spring training, and he told me, 'You're the guy.' That's how I got there."

He may have been Earl's "guy," but it took some getting used to for Bumbry to play for Weaver. "Earl was so vocal, and always driving, driving, driving," Bumbry said. "Earl was always on you, and it was difficult at first for me to play for Earl because he was so volatile and demanding in the way he wanted us to play. Then I learned his ways and got to understand him better, and what his expectations were, and then I didn't have a problem with Earl. But it took a while for me to grasp his style and what he wanted. He wanted us to play the game hard and smart. You were getting paid a good salary, and he wanted you to earn your money.

"But it was a treat to play for Joe. He was more calm and laid-back. And by the time Joe took over, we had guys who could pretty much handle themselves. We had learned from Earl about what needed to be done and when it needed to be done during a game. And there wasn't a whole lot of difference in the way Earl used players and the way Joe used players. People had roles on the team, and they accepted those roles and prepared themselves to fill those roles when they were needed."

Bumbry knows about preparing himself. He worked hard to become a good hitter, but he worked even harder to become a good outfielder. He started in left field, but when the Orioles traded Paul Blair after the 1976 season, Bumbry moved to center field. On a team managed by

Weaver, center field was very important. The manager was a big believer in strength up the middle, and a good, fast center fielder was key to the success of the Orioles' quality starting pitching.

"Bumbry made himself into a good center fielder," Elrod Hendricks said. "He worked harder than anyone I had ever seen. When he got done hitting in batting practice, he would run out to center field and chase everyone away and try to catch every ball off the bat. Any ball that would be hit out that way, he wanted to get. He would tell people, 'Out of my way, I'm working here.' Palmer and Flanny and Scotty would love to get out there and shag fly balls during batting practice, but he would tell them to get out of his way, go down the line and play someplace else. He worked hard to play center field."

Bumbry said it was his way of working on his game. "Players respected me for that," he said. "They gave me a tough time about it, but you ask those pitchers that I played behind. They would rather have me out there working like that, because when I was in center field, I ran everything down. Shagging balls was a great way to practice. Those guys would move out of the way if I was out there working. It was a sign of respect."

By the end of the 1982 season, though, Bumbry, at the age of 35, was on the down side of his career. He batted .262 that season, scoring just 77 runs and stealing just 10 bases. He would turn 36 three weeks into the 1983 season, and there was a young, talented center fielder in the minors that appeared ready to make the jump to the major leagues.

John Shelby was not a self-made baseball player like Bumbry. He had played the game since he was a young boy, in Little League, Babe Ruth League, and Connie Mack programs. He won three letters in baseball and was the team Most Valuable Player at Henry Clay High School in Lexington, Kentucky, in 1976. He played one year at Columbia State Community College in Columbia, South Carolina, batting .358, and was selected in the first round by the Orioles in the 1977 draft.

Shelby began his career with the Orioles' farm club in Bluefield in 1977 and moved up to Rochester by the 1981 season. Although he was not a self-made ballplayer, he did have to learn how to play center field, despite being a natural for the position. "I signed as a right-handed-hitting shortstop and made it to the majors as a switch-hitting outfielder,"

Shelby said. "I had one manager in particular, Lance Nichols, who was dedicated to me being a switch-hitter, and it was a struggle in my first year, which was my third year of professional baseball. But I got an opportunity to play.

"One of the things that was always stressed in the Orioles was pitching and defense, and I knew that me playing in center field was a key position. My first day of camp in Bluefield, when they told all the infielders to go to the infield and the outfielders to go to the outfield, I went in with the infielders and they told me to go to the outfield. You always heard about being strong up the middle. I took a lot of pride in playing center field.

"Switch-hitting started in the instructional league, down in Clearwater. I was taking batting practice and jumped on the left side, and I hit a couple of balls pretty good. Little did I know our hitting instructor, Ralph Rowe, was sitting up in the booth watching the whole time. He asked me if I had ever switch-hit before, and I got nervous. I said no. I think I got one at-bat in the instructional leagues. The next year they asked me to do it in spring training. It was a tough battle. When I made the club in 1980, it really clicked for me."

In 1979 Shelby led the Florida State League in at-bats and strikeouts, and he was playing every day. Toward the end of the season, he said, he began to progress, so he set a goal for himself. "My goal next year was to make the Double-A club, but actually my goal was to hit over .201," he said. "I know that sounds bad, but the way I was hitting that year, my goal was to hit over .200. I hit .201. I went away that year in 1979 with my goal accomplished. I made the Double-A team the next year, started out on the bench, then after a few weeks our manager, Jimmy Williams, put me in and my hitting seemed to carry over from 1979. I wound up with a 21-game hitting streak, and led the team in triples, and tied with Cal Ripken for doubles. But somehow they gave him an extra double. We had a doubles race, and I know we tied at the end of the season and he knew we did, but when the media guide came out, he had led the team in doubles. But I got put on the major league roster when I went to winter ball that year. Playing in Double-A gave me confidence, and turned it around for me. You always heard that Double-A was the level that could make you or break you if you had a chance to make it to the major leagues."

Shelby had a standout 1982 season in Rochester, batting .279 in 133 games with 16 home runs, 52 RBIs, 92 runs scored, and 34 stolen bases. Then, after being called up to Baltimore at the end of the season, Shelby continued his strong hitting performance, batting .314 in 26 games.

"When I got called up in 1981 from Rochester, I just observed. It was a thrill just getting called up," Shelby said. "I had veterans come up and tell me, when you're not out there, just stay on the bench and watch. That couple of weeks at the end of that season, most of it was observation, watching how the big boys play. I was really in awe of that, watching superstars from other teams and how they went about their business, took batting practice, and all that. To see it live in front of you was impressive. It was a big learning experience for me.

"When I got called up in 1982 for the pennant stretch, I fit in and played a major part. I didn't feel like I was overwhelmed then. I really didn't feel a lot of pressure. The veterans really talked to the young players there. I know we won it in 1983, but I don't think I've ever experienced anything like the final series of the 1982 season. Nothing I've ever experienced has been close to that."

Shelby's offense in Rochester and Baltimore in 1982 impressed the Orioles, but they also saw his value as a fielder. "John Shelby was a natural center fielder with a strong arm," Hendricks said. "He got good jumps and had very good angles."

The competition between a veteran and a rookie on a team can often lead to bad feelings and divisiveness in the clubhouse, but, to his credit, Bumbry stepped up and welcomed Shelby. He called Shelby aside at one point during spring training and said, "I see what is going on. We're not going to let this thing get in between us. I'm pulling for you to make the ballclub. You can help this team. Let's not let this affect us."

Shelby said that really impressed him, but then, that was the Oriole Way—for the team. "That really showed me something, coming from a guy whose job I was in line for," Shelby said. "I had a great deal of respect for him for doing that."

During that 1983 season, Bumbry played in 124 games, batting .275, and Shelby played in 126 games, batting .258. Both contributed to the team's championship success.

Another job that was up for grabs was a place on the roster for a pinch-hitter—also important under Weaver's style of platooning players. There was just one left-handed pinch-hitting spot open, and it came down to Jim Dwyer and longtime Oriole and fan favorite Terry Crowley, one of the premier pinch-hitters of his era. The 36-year-old Crowley was the odd man out, despite the fact that he had hit .357 in spring training.

Altobelli called Crowley into his office at Memorial Stadium just before the start of the 1983 season. He was sitting at his desk, and said to Crowley, "Terry, this is very tough for me. I'm hoping I don't have to do this. We're trying to work a deal, and I'm still here right now hoping the phone will ring and something will change."

But the phone didn't ring, and instead Altobelli picked it up and dialed the number of owner Edward Bennett Williams. He told Crowley, "EBW wants to talk to you."

Crowley took the phone, with Williams on the other end. "I just want you to know how sorry I am we have to do this, and that you will always be an Oriole to us," Williams said. "You have a job with the organization for life."

Altobelli's decision to cut Crowley just before the start of the season left the Orioles clubhouse as quiet as a funeral home after the final Sunday workout at Memorial Stadium, and Crowley was near tears when reporters asked him about the decision. He had come up in the Orioles organization, selected in the 15th round of the 1966 player draft. He played with the major league club from 1969 to 1973 before being traded to Texas in the winter of 1973 and then to Cincinnati before the 1974 season began. After two seasons with the Reds and a brief stay with Atlanta, Crowley returned home to Baltimore in 1976 and stayed until he was released.

"It was a shame because I knew it was a really good team that was primed and ready to win," Crowley said. "I had given it my best shot in spring training. It came down to me and Jimmy Dwyer as a left-handed hitter off the bench, and he was four or five years younger than I was. It was a solid organizational move. I got an absolutely fair chance to hit. I had a legitimate chance, and showed them what I could do, and they made their decision. It would have been harder for me if I had gotten just 12 at-bats and just one hit or so, and they had made their judgment on that basis. That would have made it worse for me. I knew coming into spring training . . . what the numbers were. Jimmy Dwyer was a good hitter and did a tremendous job for them, and is still one of my good friends in baseball. I could live with it."

Crowley had been offered a job by general manager Hank Peters as the organization's minor league hitting instructor. But just before he decided to take the job, the Montreal Expos called and signed Crowley. He appeared in 50 games, but he batted just .182 and retired after the season. "I ended up sitting around for a while and got rusty, and then when I hooked up with Montreal, I really couldn't get it going," Crowley said. "But Montreal was very good to me. I made some good friends up there, too."

In his years with the Orioles, Crowley batted .253 with 322 hits in 1,272 at bats, 153 runs scored, 44 doubles, 40 home runs, and 194 RBIs. He ripped 108 career pinch-hits, 11th all-time. Crowley has since served twice as the Orioles' hitting coach, once from 1985 to 1988 and then again from the winter of 1998 to the present.

Another change in the organization occurred that would turn out to be historic, though no one realized it at the time. Longtime Orioles announcer and future Hall of Famer Chuck Thompson was leaving the radio booth and switching to television. He would be replaced by a relatively unknown 31-year-old announcer coming from Boston, where he had been the second announcer on the team calling Red Sox games—Jon Miller. He would become an announcing legend for the Orioles, with his play-by-play skills and sharp wit, and was one of the most popular figures connected with the franchise. Miller became the top national baseball announcer in the game, the lead man on ESPN broadcasts with his partner, Hall of Fame second baseman Joe Morgan. Miller left after the 1996 season in a contract dispute with Peter Angelos and is now calling games for the San Francisco Giants.

Despite the changes at the helm and in the broadcast booth, the Orioles would return to their familiar home for the 29th season. Memorial Stadium, on 33rd Street, had become a very familiar sight to national television audiences over the years because of all the postseason play the team had been involved in. It also had a national reputation as a house of champions because it was also the home of those legendary Baltimore Colts teams under Johnny Unitas and the most recent version of competitive, exciting teams led by quarterback Bert Jones. But, unlike the Orioles, the Colts had fallen on hard times under the ownership of Robert Irsay. What was once called "the largest outdoor insane asylum" by sportswriters for its enthusiastic football fans no longer sold out for NFL games. The team, under Irsay's bizarre direction, became a perennial loser. Little did Baltimore sports fans realize that 1983 would be the last season the Colts would play at Memorial Stadium. After the season, the Colts would move in the legendary midnight run of Mayflower vans leaving their training complex.

Since 1979, the Orioles had begun to take over the city, changing the fan devotion from football to baseball. By the time 1983 would come to a close, the transformation would be complete. But another battle would continue. Just as Irsay had lobbied for a new stadium, so had Williams, the Orioles owner, though he would not be heavy-handed. He had been laying the groundwork for a new stadium and, thanks in part to the fear Baltimore and the state of Maryland felt from the loss of the Colts, would eventually get what he wanted. However, Williams would not be alive to see his new ballpark, Camden Yards, built near the city's top tourist attraction, Inner Harbor.

Camden Yards would open to rave reviews in 1992, kicking off an entire generation of stadium and arena construction. But Memorial Stadium had something that Camden Yards has yet to enjoy—playing host to a World Series championship team. When Joe Altobelli and his Orioles team took the field in 1983, it would be Memorial Stadium's last championship season.

3 | The Roller-Coaster Ride Begins

I t never helps to lose on Opening Day. It is just one game, but it is a symbolic game. Though officially spring arrives on March 21, Opening Day is often seen as the welcoming of spring and a farewell to winter. It is the game that has fans excited about their team's prospects. It is the game that will attract more media and dignitaries than any other regular-season game most teams will play.

And when you are a new manager replacing a legend in a city where fans are accustomed to winning, it is an important symbolic game because, as they say, you only get one chance to make a first impression.

Joe Altobelli did not make a strong first impression.

They should have known it was not the Orioles' day when Brooks Robinson threw out the first pitch and it bounced about 15 feet short of home plate.

They should have known it was not the Orioles' day when they announced to the 51,889 fans in sold-out Memorial Stadium that the team had changed the seventh-inning stretch song from one the fans had adopted as their own—John Denver's "Thank God I'm a Country Boy"—to some new theme called "That Magic Feeling." The boos rained down loud and long.

The hometown team booed on Opening Day—not a great way to start the Altobelli era.

A parachutist dressed as the Orioles mascot—the black and orange bird—nearly crashed into the outfield bleachers and wound up landing in the parking lot outside the stadium, as Baltimore Mayor William

Donald Schaefer and owner Edward Bennett Williams stood on the mound where the parachutist was supposed to land.

Before the game, they released three thousand balloons to symbolize the 30 years the Orioles had been in Baltimore. The way things were going that day, you can be relatively sure that some seagulls in the Chesapeake Bay died from that balloon release.

The Orioles lost 7–2 to the Kansas City Royals. Dennis Martinez was the losing pitcher, and he only got the start because Jim Palmer had bowed out of the assignment a few days before, saying he had lower back problems. Martinez had started the 1982 Opening Day game against the Royals as well, and was gone by the fourth inning, though the Orioles would come back to pummel Kansas City that day 13–5 thanks to a grand slam by Eddie Murray, Cal Ripken's first major league home run, a home run by Dan Ford in his debut as an Oriole, and one more homer by Gary Roenicke.

That was the Orioles' third straight Opening Day win. There would be no big bats to save a fourth straight victory. And it was the Orioles' gloves that betrayed them, a terrible sin for a team that took such pride in its defense.

Cal Ripken committed an error with two outs in the seventh inning that allowed Amos Otis and Hal McRae to follow with RBI hits off reliever Storm Davis. And the guy who could least afford to make an error on Opening Day before the Baltimore fans did. Dan Ford, the target of Orioles fans' wrath for his dismal play the year before, failed to catch a pop fly in the top of the first inning. He tried a basket catch, but the ball hit him on the elbow, resulting in a roar of boos from the home crowd before the Orioles even got to the plate to start the season.

Ford did manage to salvage the day for himself by going 2-for-4. He cracked a single and a double, scored both Orioles runs, and forced an infield error by hustling to first in the sixth inning, drawing cheers from the fans. He felt good about at least saving face with the fans, particularly after the beating he took from the hometown crowd in 1982. "Last year was the worst, the most aggravating year of my life in baseball, even worse than Little League when you cry after you strike out," Ford told reporters. "I want to change a few opinions about Dan Ford." Before the season was over, Ford would do just that.

While Ford redeemed himself, the Orioles didn't, and George Brett supplied enough hitting to give Kansas City the win when he hit a two-run home run in the top of the third inning that broke a 1–1 tie. Brett also had a double, and normally a two-hit day by a hitter as great as George Brett might not be noteworthy. However, it was another indication that this was not the Orioles' day, since Brett was coming off a 4-for-32 slump in spring training.

Dennis Martinez was gone after the sixth inning, having given up four runs on six hits and two walks. The game did prove to be an indication that Martinez was in for a very rough year. He had emerged as a quality starting pitcher since his first full season with Baltimore in 1977, when he went 14–7. In six major league seasons, he owned an impressive 82–57 career record with a 3.75 ERA, including a 16–12 record in 1982.

But Martinez was suffering from alcohol abuse that would nearly destroy his career, and, though it wasn't known publicly at the time, the effects of losing that fight would take its toll on him in 1983. Martinez would find himself dropped from the starting rotation at times and toiling in the bullpen. He finished with a 7–16 record and was on the verge of seeing his career end.

His teammates knew something was wrong with him. "Dennis had a great arm, but he had a lot of problems then," Gary Roenicke said. "You could see he wasn't quite with it. I would be out there playing at times while Dennis was pitching, and he would have strike one and strike two on a guy, then hang a pitch, and the guy would whack it."

Altobelli knew Dennis Martinez well and perhaps saw what was coming, despite Dennis' talent. "Dennis pitched for me in the minors," Altobelli said. "I used to have to kick him in the tail sometimes because he would get guys out so easily. He would sometimes toy with them in the seventh or eighth inning, and I would go out there and chew him out. 'Hey, I want to go home and eat! Let's go!' I would say to him. He was very tough on hitters when he was at his best. But he was having a tough time that year, and he was blaming everyone for his downfall. But he really changed his life around, and since then has apologized to me several times for the way he was acting back then."

Dennis Martinez was hitting rock bottom when the Orioles were rising to the top that season. After the Orioles won the 1983 World

Series, he was arrested on December 3, 1983, and jailed for drunken driving. He would enter the chemical dependency unit of Shepherd Pratt Hospital three days before Christmas and begin the fight to turn his life around. He would continue to struggle in Baltimore on the field before being traded to the Montreal Expos in 1986, and it was there that all of it clicked again for Dennis Martinez—his life was renewed away from the ballpark and his talent was rediscovered on the field. He went 11–4 in 1987 and would go 134–94 over the next 12 years with the Expos, Cleveland Indians, Seattle Mariners, and Atlanta Braves before retiring in 1998 with a career mark of 245–193—the most career wins of any Hispanic pitcher in the history of major league baseball.

The highlight of his comeback came on July 28, 1991, when Martinez retired all 27 Los Angeles Dodgers he faced in a 2–0 Expos win to record the 13th perfect game in major league history.

Ken Singleton was an Orioles teammate who knew Dennis during the bad and good times of his career. "Dennis was really battling his alcohol problems back then," Singleton said. "He was an enigma. You didn't know what to expect. You didn't know which Dennis would show up. I think Dennis resented the fact that some of the other guys got a little more notoriety than he did, and he felt he was just as good.

"I got to know Dennis better when I was broadcasting Expos games. He was a lot more approachable then. I was the broadcaster on his perfect game."

Dennis took the time with many of his old Orioles teammates and cohorts to explain what he was going through at the time. "Dennis was dealing with things then that I wasn't aware of," fellow pitcher Storm Davis said. "Years later, when I was with San Diego and he was with Montreal, he took me to lunch and explained to me what had been going on."

Maybe some people didn't know what was going on with Dennis Martinez on that Opening Day of 1983, but nearly everyone knew what was coming after the loss—the Weaver questions. The little man's presence remained so big, club officials even joked about it. "Obviously we can't win without Earl," general manager Hank Peters told reporters. "What other conclusion could you draw?"

The questions would remain for some time, as the Orioles, though winning, played up-and-down baseball. They were down on Opening Day.

They were up in the second game of the season two days later, beating Kansas City 11–1 on a chilly day. It was the sort of win that would reflect the team effort the Orioles had all season. They had 14 hits, with leadoff hitter Al Bumbry setting the tone. He went 2-for-3 with two walks, four runs, and one run driven in, along with a stolen base. Ford went 2-for-5 with an RBI. Cal Ripken also went 2-for-5 with one run scored and one RBI. Eddie Murray went 1-for-4. John Lowenstein went 3-for-4 with three RBIs. Rich Dauer went 2-for-4 with an RBI and two runs scored, and third baseman Leo Hernandez went 1-for-4 with an RBI and a run scored. Also, while Singleton and Rick Dempsey went hitless, Singleton walked and scored a run and Dempsey drove in one run with a sacrifice fly.

The Orioles wouldn't stay home for long. After the two games at Memorial Stadium, they traveled to Cleveland for the Indians' home opener, and the two games they played in Cleveland were nearly a replica of their first two games to open the season. The Orioles lost the first game 8–4, with the bullpen taking the loss for the Orioles. Scott McGregor, making his first start of the season, pitched well enough to win, giving up two runs over six innings pitched—both in the first inning—and the score was tied at 2–2 after six, thanks to RBIs by Ford and Murray. But Sammy Stewart, after pitching a perfect seventh inning, let the game get away in the bottom of the eighth, walking three and giving up two runs. Tippy Martinez didn't fare much better, surrendering four runs on three hits and one walk. In all, Cleveland scored six runs in the eighth inning, allowing Rick Sutcliffe to get the win. Nine years later, Sutcliffe would be the Opening Day pitcher for the Orioles in the first regular-season game ever played at Camden Yards. He'd win that one as well.

But the Orioles came back the next game and trounced the Indians 13–2. Murray led the attack by going 4-for-5, scoring four runs, and driving in four runs with a double and a home run. Lowenstein, batting behind Murray, went 2-for-4 (a double and a triple) with three RBIs and one run scored, and both John Shelby and Joe Nolan also drove in runs. The Orioles starting pitcher didn't need all those runs. On this day, Dennis Martinez, the Opening Day loser, was on his game, giving up just two runs on four hits over eight innings. He didn't have his best control, walking six, but he kept the damage to a minimum. Tim Stoddard came in for the ninth inning to finish the game. His performance (two walks) hinted at the possibility that the bullpen—the same group that had been so solid for the Orioles for five years now (Sammy Stewart, Tim Stoddard, and Tippy Martinez)—might be a source of problems for the Orioles this year.

As things turned out, there was nothing to worry about. Before all was said and done, the bullpen would turn in one of the most consistent and reliable performances in Orioles history.

Baltimore was now 2–2 going into the first big series of the season, though no one knew at the time it was a big series. After all, they weren't playing a division rival like the Yankees or Blue Jays, or even the previous year's nemesis, the Brewers. It was a team from the American League West, but a team that the Orioles would build a rivalry against throughout the year that would culminate in a hard-fought postseason series.

The Chicago White Sox had been a franchise that was unlike the Orioles, in that winning was the exception, not the rule, over recent years. But they hired a young, intense manager with a law degree, of all things, by the name of Tony LaRussa after firing Don Kessinger in 1979. LaRussa, along with general manager Roland Hemond, had turned the team around, from a 70–90 season in his first full year in 1980 to a winning record of 87–75 in 1982. They were on the verge of becoming one of the best teams in baseball in 1983, with a pitching staff equal to or better than Baltimore's—La Marr Hoyt, Britt Burns, Richard Dotson, Floyd Bannister, and even the veteran Jerry Koosman—plus the big bats of Harold Baines, Carlton Fisk, Ron Kittle, and Greg Luzinski.

The fates of the Orioles and the White Sox would be intertwined all season. "The White Sox turned out to be a big rivalry for us," Gary Roenicke said. "We had some wild games with them, and Comiskey Park was a tough place to play. They were a very good home team."

Stoddard said playing the White Sox was almost like the Orioles looking in a mirror. "We were similar in a lot of ways," he said. "We both had great pitching, power, and defense. We played each other close the whole year, in a lot of intense games."

Ford didn't particularly enjoy going to Comiskey Park. "The fans were right there in the outfield, and they could easily reach over and interfere," he said. "Those were tough games."

He had to go to Comiskey Park for these two games, though, and they were two raucous, memorable games that the teams split between them. The Orioles' wild 10–8 win in the first game was particularly noteworthy because Baltimore had gone 0–6 at Comiskey Park in 1982 and had lost 10 straight games there.

It was Mike Flanagan versus Britt Burns, but it was no pitching duel. Burns lasted just 1⅔ innings before he was chased away by Orioles hitters who scored seven runs on him on seven hits—including home runs by Shelby and Roenicke—and two walks. Flanagan nearly matched him run for run, lasting just two innings and surrendering six runs on six hits—including home runs by Tony Bernazard and Tom Paciorek—and two walks. Bernazard would deal Flanagan a much more serious blow a few weeks later. Baltimore led 3–0 after the top of the first, and it appeared that would be enough for Flanagan, who was coming off a 15–11 season in 1982. He shut out the White Sox in the bottom of the first, and the Orioles made things even easier for Flanagan by scoring four more runs in the top of the second to give them a 7–0 lead. The Orioles thought they were home free. "When we got seven runs, I figured we had the jinx broken easily," Dempsey told reporters, referring to the losing streak at Comiskey Park.

The White Sox wouldn't fall so easily, though. They came back to score five runs in the bottom of the second and two more in the bottom of the third, tying the score at 7–7. Chicago took an 8–7 lead in the bottom of the sixth, but among all the Baltimore big bats on that day, the one that would deliver the biggest hit was one of their weakest hitters—Dempsey. His clutch double in the top of the seventh inning would score two runs and give the Orioles a 10–8 lead, after Bumbry had tied the game with an infield single—a foreshadowing of the Orioles' success in the most clutch of times. Stewart, pitching 3⅔ innings in relief, would get the win.

Dempsey's double was a wind-driven shot that fooled right fielder Harold Baines—a White Sox icon who would have his No. 3 retired by the club after he was traded to the Texas Rangers for a young prospect named Sammy Sosa. Baines would later spend parts of six seasons with the Orioles (he was a hometown hero from St. Michael's, Maryland, on the Eastern Shore) and become a fan favorite in Baltimore as well.

"I'll bet I've hit that same ball 50 times over the last couple of years, and it's been caught every time," Dempsey told reporters after the game. "I've probably hit 10 of them at him [Baines]."

It was a big hit for Dempsey, who had been taking some heat for struggling in their first few games. He had to carry with him on the road a plastic orange bat wherever he went with "3 K's" written on it—the punishment his Orioles teammates required for anyone who struck out three times in one game. Dempsey struck out three times in each of Baltimore's previous two games. The award was designed by Murray during spring training. "Rick needed a confidence booster, and he got one," Altobelli said, now managing the first-place 3–2 Orioles in the AL East.

That didn't last long. The Orioles, in another wild contest, lost the next game two days later to Chicago, 12–11, in what turned out to be the longest nine-inning game in club history at the time—three hours and 56 minutes, primarily because of a 35-mph wind that swirled around Comiskey Park and played havoc with the ball.

Scott McGregor faced Dotson, but again the vaunted starting pitching for both teams would be irrelevant. McGregor gave up eight runs on 10 hits and two walks in 4⅔ innings. Dotson gave up four runs on seven hits, with home runs by Ripken and Dauer, and two walks in 5⅓ innings. After Baltimore scored in the top of the first to take a 1–0 lead, Chicago came back to score two runs and take a 2–1 lead in the bottom of the first, then added another run in the second inning for a 3–1 lead. The White Sox' big inning came in the fifth, when they scored six runs. Kittle was a one-man team at the plate, belting two home runs off McGregor and driving in six runs for the game, including the game-winning two-run single in the bottom of the eighth inning. The White Sox led 12–9 going into the ninth, but the Orioles showed the sort of confidence they carried with them throughout the year by battling back to score two runs before losing 12–11. Shelby drove in one run with a double, and Ford followed with an RBI single. But Ripken, facing the fifth Chicago pitcher of the game, Kevin Hickey, and the tenth overall between both teams, popped up to first baseman Mike Squires to close the game.

Altobelli figured some games aren't meant to be won. "I must give credit to the players for today's game," he said afterward. "I think they played well under very difficult circumstances. It was a cold winter day.

I'm happy it's over, but I'm not happy with the outcome. With 11 runs you would like to win, but it doesn't bother me. This was not your typical ballgame."

The contrast between Weaver and Altobelli was never more startling than after a game like this one against Chicago—a big game, even in April. Weaver would have gone ballistic over such a loss and would not have been talking about giving credit to anyone. Altobelli took it in stride.

"Earl was a constant complainer, constantly wanting more from everybody," Dempsey said. "He was not an easy person to get along [with], on or off the field. He had this way of doing things, and he got everybody on one page against him. We have to prove every day that we were a better ballclub than he made us out to be. Earl got everyone to play together as a team, but we all did it to show Earl that we were better than he said we were.

"Earl took some tremendous abuse from us off the field. When we got on the buses to go to the airport or hotel after a game, and Earl had been screaming at everyone, something like, 'Jesus Christ, please make the ball hit the outfield grass one fucking time,' we would get tired of that. One time we came back from being down something like ten runs and won the game by five runs. We got on the bus, and Earl would be up front laughing, so some guys would start mimicking him laughing, and one guy after another would start saying, 'Jesus Christ, please make the ball hit the outfield grass one fucking time.' He would look back and get mad, wondering who said it, and we would all laugh under our breath. Earl took some abuse, but that was the way the ballclub worked. That was our only way of getting back at him, to make fun of him on the bus after we came back and won a game where he had been complaining that we couldn't play anymore."

There was nothing like that with Altobelli. "I treated the players like professionals, and that was a team full of professional players," he said. "They didn't let anything bother them, so they didn't need me to yell at them when they lost. They knew it, and knew what went wrong, and knew what to do about it. They were capable of taking that loss and moving on, forgetting about yesterday whether they won or lost, and that is a big compliment to a baseball player."

Altobelli and Baltimore would return home with a 3–3 record, and the seesaw early season would continue. Jim Palmer had been complaining of back stiffness before the start of the season and begged off the Opening Day start; he was replaced by Dennis Martinez. But the three-time Cy Young winner, near the end of his career, made this start in game seven of the 1983 season. The 37-year-old right-hander showed he still had enough to handle the Cleveland Indians for at least five innings, shutting them out in the first game of a doubleheader, with no walks and five hits, for his first win of the season. Lowenstein and Dauer drove in two runs for the 2–0 victory, with Storm Davis and Tippy Martinez preserving the staff shutout by throwing three innings of scoreless ball.

Win one, lose one. The pattern continued. The Orioles lost to the Indians in the second game that day, 7–4. Dennis Martinez got blasted again, giving up five runs in 3⅔ innings, evening their record again, this time at 4–4. Fortunately for the Orioles, they had a life preserver early in the season who would keep them afloat. His name was Mike Flanagan.

The left-hander from Manchester, New Hampshire, was one of the most respected and well-liked pitchers ever to throw for the Orioles, and he was a favorite of the writers as well for his sense of humor and quips. Quoted many times, he had such treasured lines as: "I could never play in New York. The first time I came into a game there, I got in the bullpen car and they told me to lock the doors."

Flanagan was respected and admired by his teammates not only for his pitching ability and warm personality, but for his New England toughness as well, a trait he showed early in his baseball career. He had missed his entire senior year in high school with a sore elbow, but he came back to pitch in the Cape Cod League that summer and went on to pitch at the University of Massachusetts for two years.

Like many ballplayers, Flanagan was a tremendous all-around high school athlete. He played both baseball and basketball at Memorial High School in Manchester, and was such a standout basketball player that he was named one of the top five players in New Hampshire high school basketball in the seventies. He would go on to play basketball at the University of Massachusetts on the freshman team there, and he once played in a freshman-varsity scrimmage against a pretty good basketball player himself—Julius Erving.

Despite his success at Massachusetts, with a 12–2 record in two seasons, and leading the Yankee Conference in strikeouts in 1972, with 89, and in ERA in 1973, at 1.72, he was not drafted until the seventh round by the Orioles in June 1973. Teams had fears about the elbow problems he had in high school. (Flanagan had been drafted by the Houston Astros in 1971 coming out of high school but decided to go to college instead.)

Flanagan spent three years in the minor league system, playing for Miami, Asheville, and Rochester, posting a record of 35–16. He was brought up to Baltimore with the September call-ups in 1975 and went 0–1 in two appearances, though his ERA was just 2.70—three runs in 10 innings pitched. The following season, after starting out 6–1 at Rochester, Flanagan was called up to Baltimore and finished the year there with a 3–5 record and a 4.13 ERA. But he had shown enough to convince Weaver to take him north from spring training for the 1977 season, and he paid back that faith with a solid 15–10 record and a 3.64 ERA.

The following season, Flanagan showed that he was a workhorse that could be counted on by throwing 281 innings, making 40 starts, and going 19–15 with a 4.04 ERA. The 1979 campaign was Flanagan's crowning achievement—his Cy Young season. The left-hander posted a 23–9 mark, leading the American League in victories, with a 3.08 ERA in 39 starts. He led the Orioles to the AL pennant and into the World Series. He was also named the AL Pitcher of the Year by *The Sporting News*. But he would find his toughness put to the test starting in 1980, when he began developing arm problems. He went 16–13 in 1980 in 37 starts, with a 4.12 ERA, and the arm soreness worsened the following year when he made just 20 starts, going 9–6 with a 4.19 ERA. He had made 157 consecutive starts—dating back to June 1977—before being pulled out of the rotation on August 23, 1981, after tearing a muscle in his left forearm while throwing a strike to Cliff Johnson in a game against Oakland. He had been experiencing stiffness in his arm since May, and he would not appear in another game until the end of September.

There was a lot of concern that he might not ever be able to recover from his arm troubles. Flanagan struggled for about two-thirds of the 1982 season, with an 8–10 record on August 13. But he fixed whatever was ailing him after that, winning seven of his last eight decisions. He was one of the leading forces behind the Orioles' run on the division-leading Brewers at the end of the 1982 season, finishing the year with a 15–11 record and a 3.97 ERA.

Flanagan continued his success in 1983. He won his first start and then, after the Orioles' 7–4 loss to the Indians to even their record at 4–4, put Baltimore back over .500 with a complete-game 6–1 victory, thanks to two RBIs by Murray and runs driven in by Ford, Bumbry, and Jim Dwyer. Throughout the Orioles' early seesaw season, Flanagan would be the one reliable constant to keep the club from falling into a losing streak. He was an important symbol for the team, because he was so tough. "Flanny was just a bulldog," Dempsey said. "He was ready to pitch whenever you needed him. He was a power pitcher at one time, and through the course of his career he learned how to make adjustments."

McGregor came back the next game and beat the Indians 4–1, and Storm Davis, backed up by Sammy Stewart coming out of the bullpen, made it three in a row with a 4–2 victory on a long home run by John Lowenstein in the opening game of a series against the Texas Rangers—more than 10 years removed from being the rival Washington Senators. The Orioles were now using Washington as part of their new and expanded fan base under the ownership of Williams—and Orioles fans feared that he would someday try to move the team to his home base of Washington.

The Orioles had a three-game winning streak, but unless someone watched the 4–2 win over Texas on television, listened to it on the radio, or read about it in the newspapers the next day, very few people in Baltimore would have known. The Orioles had made a huge leap in attendance at Memorial Stadium starting in 1979, drawing 600,000 more fans than the previous season and finishing the year with a record-setting attendance of 1.6 million. They beat that in 1980 by drawing 1.7 million, and, after the strike-shortened season of 1981 (when they drew about 1 million fans), bounced back in 1982 by drawing 1.6 million fans again. Those were big numbers at the time, although they paled in comparison to the 3 million–plus fans the Orioles would draw to Camden Yards for nearly 10 seasons after the ballpark opened in 1992.

Those numbers were startling when compared to the attendance for a team in first place in the AL East, coming off a remarkable stretch run the season before, with a city full of expectations of going to a World Series in 1983. On this day in April, even though it was just the 11th game of the season, 6,305 fans were in the stands at Memorial Stadium. Granted, it was cold—very cold, as snow had fallen the day before. But that low of a number for a Baltimore Orioles game—particularly when the team was competitive—at Camden Yards was unheard of, no matter what the weather was. Even more remarkable was that the game lasted just two hours and seven minutes. It was rare in those days, even just 20 years ago, for a nine-inning game to last three hours or more, as is the case today.

The win streak ended with Dennis Martinez taking the mound against Texas, which blasted Baltimore 11–2. Jim Palmer did his job in the series finale, holding Texas to two runs over eight innings pitched, and, after fourteen innings, the Orioles broke a 2–2 tie to win 3–2. They were sky-high after that win, but the team began to follow a disturbing trend. As they embarked on a West Coast road trip, the momentum of the extra-inning win didn't carry over, as they lost an extra-inning game, 6–5 in 11 innings, to the California Angels in Anaheim. Surprisingly, Flanagan was on the mound, though he did not suffer the loss after surrendering three runs on six hits and three walks in five innings pitched. The Orioles now had an 8–6 record.

The next game, though, was a lock for the Orioles. It was Scott McGregor against the Angels, and that usually meant a Baltimore win. This game would not take place before a crowd of 6,300—more like 63,073, the largest ever to see the Orioles play, as Angels fans were pumped up about their team's chances that season. But their chances were slim to none with McGregor on the mound, as he held the Angels to just one run, even though the Angels got nine hits, in a 3–1 win over Tommy John, who also pitched a brilliant complete game in defeat. It was McGregor's 13th win in his last 14 starts against the Angels. "I beat the Angels quite a bit," McGregor said. "I guess they didn't like to see me. I don't know, for whatever reason, maybe being from California. . . . I loved their mound and their stadium." McGregor was born in Inglewood, California, and grew up in El Segundo.

McGregor's good start—2–0 in April—should have been a good sign for the Orioles. Before 1983, April had been the only month over

McGregor's career in which the pitcher had a losing record (4–8). But the Orioles, now with a 9–6 record, lost the following game 7–3 to the Angels. It was Dennis Martinez taking his fourth loss of the season, as he gave up five runs on nine hits over five innings.

Now, the Orioles getting off to a slow start was nothing new. But getting off to a slow start without Earl Weaver in the dugout *was* something new. While many of the players welcomed Altobelli's laid-back style, nerves were starting to show over the roller-coaster start, and players started to sound off, which was uncharacteristic for this Orioles squad.

The first to do so was Dennis Martinez, who was a wreck after suffering four losses in April. He had some clashes with Altobelli when they were in Rochester, and he also had personal problems that had affected his personality, made him remote from his teammates, and put a first-class chip on his shoulder. Dennis told reporters that he wasn't being used right, and he lashed out at everyone. He was upset at the pitch selection, particularly against Rod Carew, who had four hits against Dennis. "If they don't think I can pitch myself, why don't they trade me?" he said. "They have a reason to keep me here. It's because I'm a winner. They never leave me alone. They can advise me and tell me what I'm doing wrong. That's good. But when I pitch, leave me alone and let me pitch my game. It's no good that every time they have to tell you what to do. I'm the guy. It's my fault. They say, 'We tell him he is supposed to do this and he doesn't do it . . . his concentration . . .' They always complain about that. That can hurt you. They confuse me. They say challenge them and throw a lot of slow stuff. That doesn't make sense at all."

He also blasted Dempsey for his work behind the plate. "I've always had trouble with Dempsey," Dennis said. "I don't have anything against him, but I can never feel good when he is behind the plate. . . . Dempsey is one of the other guys. He says to throw this pitch, and I say no. He doesn't go with the pitcher. He goes with the manager. Why does he do this?

"They might ruin my career and they don't even know it."

Dennis' attack seemed to unleash some frustration that had been brewing among some players. The next day, the Orioles traveled to Oakland and lost 4–3 with Palmer on the mound. The veteran hurler struggled over the 3⅔ innings he pitched, allowing four runs on seven hits and four walks. And while the bullpen held the Athletics scoreless over the final 4⅓ innings to keep their team in the game, the Orioles were unable to reach Oakland's bullpen for the go-ahead runs after scoring two runs in the seventh and one in the eighth.

The loss dropped the Orioles out of first place in the American League East and set in motion another day of very un-Oriole-like reactions. Storm Davis came into the game after Palmer, and Tippy Martinez pitched as well. But Tim Stoddard sat in the bullpen and was stewing up a storm. Like Dennis Martinez the day before, Stoddard, who had made just six appearances, pitching 6⅔ innings (with a 1.35 ERA), spoke his mind. He particularly ripped Altobelli for using Tippy and not Stoddard in the game. The 6'7", 250-pound right-handed reliever got into a heated argument with Altobelli after the game in the manager's office in the visitor's clubhouse. He told reporters, who could hear the argument, about it. "I told him I don't want to pitch here no more," Stoddard said. "If he is not going to use me, I don't want to stay here."

The soap opera continued the next day. Altobelli defended his actions, responding to both Dennis and Stoddard. "I can understand why Dennis was frustrated," Altobelli said. "He was 2–2 with about the same ERA at this time last year, and now he is 1–4 and a little frustrated. But he can't keep blaming everybody else. He can't blame the manager, the catcher, and the pitching coach. He has to go out there and pitch."

As far as Stoddard was concerned, Altobelli had some harsh words for the reliever. "It isn't like he [Stoddard] is a world beater or anything," Altobelli said. "He's a guy coming off an injury." Stoddard missed the last month of the 1982 season after suffering torn ligaments in his right knee. "I don't mind a guy wanting to pitch," Altobelli said. "I'm surprised he didn't know what I was doing. If there is anything added to that, I'd rather he came to me with it.

"I confronted Tim. I'll probably confront him again. I guarantee he won't do this to me again."

Pitching coach Ray Miller was extremely blunt about Stoddard. "It was the dumbest thing I've ever seen in baseball," Miller said. "Seventeen games into the season and he says he doesn't want to pitch for this team? Especially when Tippy goes out and retires the side on seven pitches.

That makes it twice as stupid. . . . It was obvious to everyone in the ballgame but Stoddard what was going on.

"They didn't like Earl because he was intimidating. A couple of more things like this and they will end up with a manager who is intimidating."

Seventeen games into the season and the Orioles were sounding more like the Bronx Zoo Yankees than the businesslike group of players who had exemplified the Oriole Way for the past five seasons. And the worst was yet to come. In a few days, Jim Palmer would be put on the disabled list. Now the Orioles had lost the heart and soul of their pitching staff, a three-time Cy Young Award winner, and were left with pitchers bickering with the manager. It seemed like panic was right around the corner.

4 | A Change in the Heart of the Order

With the team seemingly on the brink of falling apart over dissension in the clubhouse, the Orioles got what they needed from the man who continued to keep the team's head above water early in the season. Facing Oakland, Mike Flanagan blanked the Athletics over five innings, and Sammy Stewart completed the job for a 6–0 shutout, keeping the Orioles, now 10–8, from slipping down to .500. Flanagan had suffered a groin pull in his previous start against the Angels, but he recovered well enough to get through five innings, which allowed him to remain undefeated (9–0) in his career at the Coliseum. Rich Dauer drove in two runs for Baltimore. The team went to Seattle next, and the standout pitching continued. Scott McGregor won his third game of the season, against no losses, in a 9–1 beating of the Mariners that put the team back in first place in the AL East. Ken Singleton led the charge, driving in four runs and breaking out of an 0-for-13 slump with a single and a double. The losing pitcher was a big right-hander named Jim Beattie, who would be hired 20 years later by owner Peter Angelos to run the Orioles front office, along with Flanagan.

Singleton, in the twilight of his career, got most of his playing time these days in the designated hitter's role, after spending much of his career playing a solid right field at Memorial Stadium. He was a first-round draft choice of the New York Mets in 1967, but was traded to the Montreal Expos in 1972 along with two other Mets prospects, Mike Jorgensen and Tim Foli, for outfielder Rusty Staub. Singleton blossomed into a major league hitter and fan favorite in Montreal during his three seasons there, with his best year in 1973, when, playing in all of Montreal's 162 games, he batted .302 with 23 home runs, 103 RBIs, and 100 runs scored. But he was traded to Baltimore in December 1974, along with pitcher Mike Torrez, for Orioles pitching great Dave McNally, pitcher Bill Kirkpatrick, and outfielder Rich Coggins. Though Singleton was not a product of the so-called Oriole Way, he fit right in with his intelligence and professionalism—and his impressive numbers. Over 10 seasons with Baltimore, Singleton hit 182 home runs, drove in 767 runs, and batted .284. His best seasons were 1979, when he hit 35 home runs, drove in 111 runs, and batted .295, and 1980, when he smashed 24 home runs, drove in 104 runs, and batted .304. He was nearing the end of his career in 1983 after hitting 14 home runs, driving in 77 runs, and batting .251 in 1982. Though, unlike many of the Orioles, Singleton did not play for Joe Altobelli in the Orioles minor league system, he became a favorite of the new Orioles manager. "Kenny Singleton was one of the most professional players I have ever managed," Altobelli said. "He was a pleasure to manage."

John Lowenstein said Singleton had a single-mindedness about his play that drove his teammates. "He was determined," Lowenstein said. "He had a special drive that allowed him to accomplish the things that someone else might not have. He was a hell of an outfielder, and would be ready to play every day. Little things didn't bother him."

Singleton, now a broadcaster with the Yankees, looks back on his days as an Oriole with much pleasure. "We had some very good teams during the 10 years I played with the Orioles," he said. "The 1983 team might not have even been the best. But we had a bunch of guys who played hard and did whatever they had to to win—work the count and get on base any way they could."

That team concept was a little shaky early on. Dennis Martinez lost again in his next start, 6–2 to Seattle, and, with a 1–5 record, was a liability more than an asset in the starting rotation. Tim Stoddard finally got into a game, though, and held the Mariners scoreless in mop-up duty in the bottom of the eighth at the Kingdome. The Orioles' starting pitching was about to suffer another blow. Jim Palmer, scheduled to start the second game of the series, had to bow out because of back problems. Palmer took some heat for missing the start—he was accused of suffering from a case of Kingdome Syndrome. Palmer had made it clear in the past how much he hated the dark, dreary, domed stadium, but he reacted angrily to suggestions he was begging out simply because he didn't want to pitch in the Kingdome. "That's crap," Palmer told reporters. "That got started because Earl told everyone I didn't want to pitch here. The way I feel, it wouldn't matter if we were playing in Yosemite Park. I haven't felt normal all season."

Here it was, a month into the season, and Weaver was still the subject of conversation and debate. A few days later, there would be no debate about Palmer's health and no suggestions about Kingdome Syndrome or any other imaginary malady.

Palmer's replacement, Storm Davis, picked up the slack in the emergency start, holding the Mariners to two runs in 5⅓ innings pitched to get his first win of the season. Tippy Martinez tossed 3⅔ shutout innings in relief for an 8–2 win, giving Baltimore a 12–9 record. Singleton continued his hot hitting, with a three-run home run off the grand old spitballer, Gaylord Perry. If Palmer didn't like the Kingdome, Singleton loved it. It was his 12th home run in the stadium, more than any other opposing hitter. The Orioles now headed back home, having survived the month of April with a winning, if erratic, record and some controversy. Overall, though, things were not that bad for Joe Altobelli. They were still in first place in the AL East. "Three games over .500 is not that great, but it's not bad compared to a year ago [when the Orioles were 6–12 for the month of April]," he said. "Being in first place isn't too bad, either."

But in case he got too satisfied or forgot the shadow that hung over him in the manager's seat, Joe Altobelli got a reminder on the plane back home from Seattle, when a flight attendant asked him, "Is Earl Weaver on this flight?" Altobelli replied, "I think he's in the back somewhere."

It was a light moment, one that Altobelli could use, because he was about to get some very bad news—but not before Flanagan extended his record to 4–0 with a 4–2 complete-game victory over California (even with a nagging stiff hamstring) in the first game of this homestand. The crowds were starting to grow—20,837 for this one—and they saw a much better game than the Orioles fans who came to Memorial Stadium for the following game. It was a pitching breakdown from top to bottom, a

16–8 loss to the Angels. McGregor gave up seven runs, five of them earned, in four innings. Stewart followed and surrendered three runs in 1⅔ innings. Stoddard didn't do any better, allowing two runs in 2⅓ innings. Tippy Martinez made it a full staff embarrassment by giving up four runs in just one inning pitched.

Baltimore was now 13–10 and about to suffer another pitching break-down, this one a devastating one. The 37-year-old Palmer was moved to the disabled list, suffering from back spasms that would not subside. "I don't want to go on the disabled list," he told reporters. "But I want to get well, too. I want to do what is best for the club. . . . It's a question of whether it is best for me to be ready during the important part of the season, or take some risks now. I feel like I've taken some risks already, but it hasn't worked out. . . . It behooves me to go out there as many times as I can because of my contract." Palmer had a clause in his con-tract that said he had to make at least 29 starts or pitch at least 203 innings for his option for the next season to be picked up. "It would be selfish of me to go out there just because of the contract," he said.

Storm Davis would take Palmer's place in the rotation, but then that meant the Orioles had to find someone to fill the long-relief and spot-starting role that Davis had filled. They put in a call to Rochester for a familiar face, at least in spring training—Mike Boddicker. The 5'11", 170-pound right-hander, born in Cedar Rapids, Iowa, was signed by the Orioles in 1978 after playing for three years at the University of Iowa—one as a third baseman and two as a pitcher. He started with the Orioles rookie team in Bluefield, West Virginia, in 1978, playing alongside another prospect named Cal Ripken. After impressing Orioles minor league officials by giving up just two runs in 19 innings pitched, Boddicker moved through the system quickly. He went 4–3 with a 1.94 ERA in 10 appearances for Double-A Charlotte. He finished the same season with the organization's Triple-A club in Rochester, where he allowed one run and won the one game he appeared in there. It seemed like Mike Boddicker was on the fast track to Baltimore.

It turned out that he was stuck on a slow-moving train that couldn't leave the station in Rochester. He spent most of the next four seasons with the Red Wings, despite being called up to Baltimore for September call-ups in 1980, 1981, and 1982. Every spring, before the team would head north, there was Palmer and McGregor and Flanagan and Dennis Martinez, and now Storm Davis. He had hit the pitching version of the glass ceiling. By the end of the 1982 season, Boddicker had an impressive minor league record—52–37 with a 3.30 ERA. Boddicker knew what he was up against, but that didn't make it any less frustrating. "My situation was that I had four Cy Young winners ahead of me in Baltimore," he said. "I figured if I kept pitching well down in the minors, sooner or later I would become a minor league free agent and somebody would want me. I figured I could bide my time as long as I could pitch well."

Pitching coach Ray Miller recalled that Boddicker was not a favorite of Weaver's. "I loved Boddicker, but Weaver never did," Miller said. "Weaver used to say, 'He doesn't throw hard enough.' Weaver was used to those big guys who had four great pitches and a good fastball, and Mike was an off-speed guy. I thought he should have made the team two years before, and he didn't.

"Back then, we had a maturation process within the organization. If you're an off-speed guy, you don't just come up and win right away. You have to learn not to overthrow and realize what you have is good enough. One spring we came up with a change-up for Boddicker. He was a curveball-sinker pitcher. We called it a 'foshball,' sort of like a split-finger that he twisted, and it turned into a great change-up. That really got him going. In the past, when he couldn't get his breaking ball over, he had to throw his fastball, and it wasn't strong enough. From then on, when he got into situations where he should throw a fastball, he threw a change-up and the batter would either swing and miss or hit it on the ground, and then we had the great defense to back him up."

Altobelli recalled reluctantly sending Boddicker down in the spring of 1983, and he also remembered Miller developing the "foshball" pitch that made Boddicker so effective. "We were going to go with a 10-man staff to open the season," Altobelli said. "I had three guys to pick from, and Mike was one of those guys. I called all three in at the same time and said, 'The one guy that I am going to keep out of you three is a guy that will have to pitch every seven or ten days and come in and throw strikes. So I'm not doing you any favors. You might be better off going down to Rochester and starting every fourth or fifth day, so that when somebody goes down, you can come up not having lost any time or regularity.' So I sent Boddicker down, but I liked the way he pitched and I knew he would be back.

"Ray Miller gets some of the credit for the way he pitched. He came up with that 'foshball,' which was really a change-up that broke down. A change-up is a hell of a pitch, and when you have one where the bottom drops out, it is really special."

Boddicker got the call, but he was told very clearly that his stay would be a temporary one. "Don't give up your apartment in Rochester," general manager Hank Peters told Boddicker. "As soon as Palmer is back, you're going down again."

Boddicker began working out of the bullpen, and Dennis Martinez took the mound after that terrible 16–8 beating by the Angels. He started in the first game of a three-game home series against Oakland, and he turned in a solid complete-game performance in a 9–2 victory, with home runs by Dan Ford and Cal Ripken, who drove in four runs before a crowd of 44,252 at Memorial Stadium. They followed that up with a second win, this one a little shakier, but an 8–6 victory nonetheless, as Flanagan earned his fifth win without a loss for the season. The starting left-hander survived a rough outing, giving up five runs in 5⅔ innings pitched, but he left with an 8–5 lead, thanks to home runs by Singleton and Rick Dempsey. Sammy Stewart and Tippy Martinez finished out the game in relief, allowing just one more run.

But the Orioles failed to extend their 15–10 record and sweep the series, losing 1–0 in the Sunday finale in a rain-delayed game known as "Mudders Day," since it fell on Mother's Day and because the weather was so dismal. The rain ignited controversy between the two teams, as tempers ran high with four rain delays and a five-hour, 42-minute contest. Brawls nearly broke out on the field and in the stands as well. The Orioles argued that the game should have been called, and Oakland manager Steve Boros played the game under protest, charging that Altobelli had waved to head groundskeeper Pat Santarone not to cover the field when the final delay was called. Altobelli claimed he did no such thing. "What does he know?" Altobelli said, referring to Boros. "I could have been waving at someone in the stands."

It was funny at times, and it was scary at times. Oakland led 1–0 in the eighth inning on a Wayne Gross home run. And after Ripken struck out with two men on and two out in the bottom of the eighth—with the field in terrible shape and the rain falling hard—it appeared third-base umpire Joe Brinkman called the game. "Every other time he [Brinkman] stopped play, he stayed out there to direct the groundskeepers," Altobelli said. "This time he was gone. I thought the game was over, and nobody gave me any indication it was not."

General manager Hank Peters also ripped the umpiring crew. "I never saw a game handled like that," he said. "The tarp was on when it should not have been, and not on when it should have been."

Cal Ripken Sr. thought it was over as well, and that sent him into a rage. He argued that if the game was being called after the Orioles made their third out, it should have been called during the at-bat, when conditions were just as bad. If the game was called while the Orioles were still in their at-bat, it would have been suspended and finished at a later date—not going down yet as a loss. Ripken Sr. had to be physically restrained from going after Brinkman after a vicious argument with the umpire. The fans were in an uproar as well, and some near the Oakland dugout got into a nasty verbal war with A's star Rickey Henderson, who had to be held back from going into the stands after the fans.

Happy Mudders Day.

The Orioles lost again the next time they took the field, and this time Jim Beattie got the better of them with a 6–4 win for the Mariners. It was the first time that Beattie had beaten the Orioles in five years. McGregor took the loss, lasting just three innings while giving up four runs, and the pattern continued for the Orioles—a win, a loss, a win or two, then a loss, as they managed to tread water just above .500—still good enough to lead or be around first place in the AL East.

Dennis Martinez was a lot like the team then—up and down, although more down than up. But he was up in his next start, stopping Baltimore's losing streak at two games, thanks to some big run support in a complete-game 13–2 win over Seattle. The leadoff combination of Al Bumbry and John Shelby drove in three runs and scored two with a double by Shelby and a triple by Bumbry, and Dan Ford homered and drove in three runs as well. The John Lowenstein–Gary Roenicke platoon displayed its effectiveness, too. Lowenstein started the game and went 1-for-2. He was replaced by Roenicke, who also went 1-for-2 but drove in three runs.

It was not all hitting, though, that made an Orioles offense. The modern-day New York Yankees did not invent patience at the plate. That was one of the characteristics of these Orioles teams as well. In this win over Seattle, Ripken and Dempsey both walked twice, and Singleton walked three times. In all, the Orioles walked nine times in the game. It takes not only bad pitching to do that, but patient, disciplined hitters as well.

Remarkably, even with a 13–2 score, the game took less than three hours—2:59, a quick game by today's standards.

The Orioles, who were now 16–12, would win the series finale against Seattle. But what makes that game particularly worth noting is that Flanagan pitched in it. At that point in the season, any game Flanagan was pitching had a chance to be a masterpiece, because the left-hander was off to the best start of his career. This was one of those masterpieces, a complete-game 1–0 shutout over the old master, Gaylord Perry, the lone run driven in by a Ripken double. The win—his 15th career shutout—gave Flanagan a 6–0 record and put the Orioles back into first place in the division.

What did he attribute his early season success to? A groin pull. The injury made him change his delivery and become more of a pitcher. "It worked out in a strange way, because when he came back, he couldn't throw as hard, but it helped him as a pitcher because he couldn't over-push, and he stayed within himself," Ray Miller said.

And Flanagan would pitch when he was hurt. His legendary toughness was one of the reasons he was so admired by his teammates.

"Flanny was my idol," Storm Davis said. "He wanted the ball and he took the ball. I had a lot of admiration for Mike because he would do that."

It wasn't just his fellow pitchers who admired Flanagan's grit. "You knew Mike was going to put his heart and soul into it every time he went out to pitch," Roenicke said. "It looked like Flanny was going to have a Cy Young year."

McGregor marveled at his teammate's toughness. "He always seemed to have something physical going on," he said. "One year he blew his Achilles out. The year he won the Cy Young, he lost the whole muscle behind his left shoulder. He was a gladiator."

He may have been a gladiator, but the Orioles would soon see that he was not indestructible.

The Orioles left Baltimore in first place for a short three-game road trip to Arlington, Texas, to face the Texas Rangers, a team they dominated the season before, winning 9 of 12 games. They won again, 8–1, in the first game of the series, with Davis winning his second game of the season. Lowenstein and Singleton both homered (Singleton tripled as well, and both of them drove in three runs each), and Ford had two doubles. Baltimore was now 18–12, its largest margin over .500 that year, and seemingly ready to break away from the pack. But things got strange. Then they got worse.

The second game of the series was a wild one, but the Orioles came out on top, 14–11. It was McGregor's second straight difficult outing, as he was hammered for seven runs and 11 hits in four innings. But he was bailed out by the Baltimore lineup—Bumbry/Shelby (4-for-7, two runs scored), Ford (2-for-6, three RBIs), Ripken (2-for-5, two RBIs), Eddie Murray (2-for-5, three RBIs), Lenn Sakata (2-for-3, two RBIs), and Dempsey (3-for-5, two RBIs). The Orioles used five pitchers, with Tippy Martinez getting the win, pitching one inning of relief and giving up one run on three hits, and Stoddard getting the bizarre save: he was the only Orioles pitcher who did not give up a run in the game.

It may not have been pretty, but Baltimore was now 19–12 and cruising.

Then the team hit a bump—a big 300-pound bump in the form of umpire Ken Kaiser.

Kaiser was a former bar bouncer and professional wrestler. In the ring he had worn a black hood, carried an ax, and was known as "The Hatchet Man." He was a colorful umpire as well. One story goes that in 1981, when New York Yankees manager Billy Martin was suspended but still telephoning instructions to the dugout, Kaiser took the phone from a player's hand and said, "You're disconnected, Billy!" Then he ripped the instrument from the dugout wall. He was from Rochester, and got his start there, and it was there that he began a long and very testy relationship with a young Orioles prospect named Eddie Murray.

Kaiser and Murray had butted heads since their days in the minor leagues. He had kicked Murray out of a game in Oakland over a balk call in 1982, and their feud came to a boiling point on May 13 of this season in Texas. It made for great theater.

In the bottom of the first inning against the Rangers, Larry Parrish came to the plate for Texas. He checked his swing on one pitch from Dennis Martinez, and home plate umpire Rick Reed called the pitch a ball. Dempsey appealed the call to Kaiser, who was umpiring first base and upheld Reed's call despite Dempsey's arguments. Kaiser, expecting Murray to join in, stood near the first baseman, folded his arms, and stared at Murray. The first baseman simply folded his arms and stared back. It was funny, and it made Kaiser go ballistic.

"You're mimicking me," Kaiser screamed at Murray.

He ordered Murray to unfold his arms, which Murray refused to do, and then, remarkably, Kaiser threw Murray out of the game.

"I never said a word to him," Murray said after the game. "How in the world could he throw somebody out for that? He's so bad it looks like he was trying to stick it to us. He should not be allowed to umpire a game against us."

He may not have said anything to Kaiser before he was ejected, but he had a shot for the umpire as he left the field. "Who the hell would want to mimic you?" Murray said to Kaiser.

Twenty years later, Murray's ejection is still a source of amusement for his teammates and his old manager—who came out and argued a close call at the plate and then was thrown out of the game, also by Kaiser.

"You were a hell of an umpire in Triple-A ball," Altobelli said to Kaiser. "What the heck happened?" And with that, Kaiser tossed Altobelli.

"I knew he and Eddie had a thing going," Altobelli said. "I knew Kaiser from his time in Rochester. Heck, I was the guy that talked him up when the [International] league asked me about him when he was umpiring there. I thought he was a great ball-and-strike umpire behind the plate. But you know what happens to some guys. It happens to ballplayers and umpires, I guess. They take their success for granted and get an attitude."

Elrod Hendricks agreed. "We all knew how Kaiser was," Hendricks said. "He could be a good umpire. He was a damn good umpire in the minor leagues and the first few years he was in the major leagues. But as time went on, he got lazier and didn't care, and did what he wanted to do, and he didn't want to move.

"Eddie had trouble with people who didn't give 100 percent. So he just did what Kaiser did, and folded his arms."

Singleton thought it was amusing that Altobelli and Murray were kicked out together. It was sort of an Oriole tradition with Weaver. "When Eddie got ejected, Earl usually did as well," he said. "We called them father and son ejections. Earl felt that we really lost a chance to win when Eddie got kicked out of a game."

The Orioles lost 2–1, and you could easily make a case that it was Kaiser who cost them the game. Not only did he kick out their best run producer in the first inning, but he wound up making a call at the plate that gave Texas the winning run, just one inning after tossing Murray. In the bottom of the second, with two outs and Pete O'Brien at first base, Jim Sundberg hit a line drive down the left-field line and into the Orioles bullpen, which was on the field in foul territory and not enclosed. Lowenstein ran the ball down and threw it to Ripken, who turned around and threw it to Dempsey, with the ball arriving just ahead of O'Brien. Dempsey caught the ball on the bounce in front of the plate, and O'Brien slid around him. Dempsey tried to block O'Brien while he tagged him. Kaiser made the call, and he called O'Brien safe. Bucky Dent followed with a single underneath Ripken's glove into center field, and Sundberg scored to give the Rangers a 2–0 lead. Dempsey argued the call, and then Altobelli came out and was thrown out by Kaiser.

Later that season, Kaiser did an interview with *The Evening Sun* in Baltimore, and the umpire defended his actions. He said if he believed Murray was mimicking him again, he would eject him again. "Anyone would," Kaiser said. "I was probably too lenient; 75 percent of us would have run him before I did. I took three steps back, and he did. I dropped my arms, and he did. Then I folded my arms, took three steps back, and he did the same. I waited 37 seconds to eject him. [Texas pitcher] Frank Tanana said it was the bushest he had ever seen in 12 years."

Kaiser said his family in Rochester took abuse for the Murray ejection. "I had to take my boy out of school in Rochester for two days because of what kids were saying, plus my wife had to take a day off because of the flak she was taking," he said. "She went to work and there was a sign put up that said, 'Strike Three.' People don't realize that we are human, too."

He also took some shots at Orioles such as Dempsey, Dauer, Ray Miller, and Altobelli, who had been critical of him. "Dempsey didn't have enough guts to block the plate on the safe call I made," Kaiser said. "Dauer is a cheap shooter who backs everything Eddie does, I guess. As for Miller, I'd be mad, too, if I had two Cy Young winners and couldn't win a title. Altobelli? He has to back his players."

In 1999, the Players Association released the results of a survey rating major league umpires in both leagues, and Kaiser received the lowest grade. Two years later, after the umpires union meltdown and baseball's crackdown on bad umpires, Kaiser was gone, out of the game.

Kaiser wasn't the only umpire the Orioles clashed with. Dauer believes that umpires in general were harder on the Orioles than other teams. "I don't think umpires like us very much," he said, "and I think that may have stemmed from the little guy himself," referring to the combative Weaver.

The Orioles soon forgot about their Kaiser problem. Two days later, back in Baltimore, they would have a much more serious issue to deal with.

They returned home to Memorial Stadium and were supposed to start a series on Monday against their rivals, the White Sox. But the game was postponed because of rain, which made a unique story in itself, because it meant that owner Edward Bennett Williams finally got a chance to use the much-ballyhooed rain insurance he had purchased from Lloyds of London during the off-season. The Orioles already had two rainouts so far in 1983, but the insurance kicked in with the third date lost, because the policy had a two-date deductible.

So they faced the White Sox in a twi-night doubleheader on the following day. They felt pretty good about winning the first game. After all, Flanagan, with his 6–0 record, was pitching. He had not lost a start at home since June 30, 1982, and had a record of 13–1 in his last 19 starts at Memorial Stadium. The second game of the doubleheader was scheduled to feature the debut of an Orioles starter that year—Mike Boddicker, who had been limited to 1⅔ innings of bullpen work since his call-up after Palmer went on the disabled list.

After Flanagan retired the first batter he faced in the game on a fly ball to right, Tony Bernazard came up and hit a weak ground ball. Flanagan tried to come off the mound to field it, but he caught his spikes and twisted his left knee. He had to leave the game, but Stewart came in and pitched 5⅔ innings. Tim Stoddard finished it to get a win, as the Orioles, with the score tied at 2–2, put five runs on the board in the bottom of the seventh off starter La Marr Hoyt. Ford, who had three hits, drove in pinch-runner John Shelby with the go-ahead run. Ripken walked, and Murray drove a shot that scored Ford and gave Baltimore a 4–2 lead. Roenicke, batting for Lowenstein after left-hander Jerry Koosman came in to relieve Hoyt, blasted a three-run home run to break the game open and get the win.

Baltimore would win the nightcap as well, as Boddicker pitched a five-hit shutout in a 5–0 win. It was his first start since he was called up in 1980, and he wound up losing that one. Leo Hernandez and Dempsey both homered, and Jim Dwyer went 3-for-3, scoring one of the five runs. The sweep put the Orioles one game ahead of the Red Sox in the division and gave Baltimore a 21–13 record.

But all anyone wanted to talk about after the game was Flanagan's injury. "It was a freak accident," Flanagan said. "I think I just caught my spike and just twisted my knee. I felt sharp pain immediately. What is encouraging is that I was able to get up, but we'll have to wait and see what the tests show."

Everyone was worried that he had torn ligaments, but Ford, who had suffered torn knee ligaments in 1979, offered his personal amateur diagnosis to reporters. "If it had been torn, he wouldn't have been able to walk off the mound like he did," Ford said. "When I asked him about it, he said it popped back into place and was feeling better. It's definitely a good sign that he walked off."

Dr. Ford should have stuck to his day job.

He underestimated how tough Flanagan was. The pitcher was able to walk off the mound with an incomplete tear of the medial collateral ligament. He would not need surgery, but the doctors were saying it would be eight to ten weeks before Flanagan could pitch again. Remarkably, this was the first time that Flanagan would go on the disabled list in his major league career.

"Eight to ten; it sounds like a prison sentence," Singleton said.

It might as well have been. Flanagan joined Palmer on the disabled list, and with Dennis Martinez pitching erratically, the starting rotation appeared to be very shaky. Plus, Flanagan was such an important leader of the staff and in the clubhouse that it appeared the loss might take the heart right out of the team.

"That was a big blow to us," Altobelli remembered.

Pitching coach Ray Miller perhaps felt the loss more than anyone because he had such admiration for his pitcher. "Flanny was such a gamer," Miller said. "I remember one start he made the year before. Weaver, you couldn't tell him that somebody had a pitch count. I would go over in the fifth inning or so and tell him that Flanny had 85, and he would say, 'I don't want to hear that; he will be all right.'

"So there would be two outs in the ninth inning, and I would turn to him and say he has 120 or so. Weaver said, 'Go tell him we will go one inning at a time, and if he gets in trouble we'll be out there.' I told Flanny that. The ninth inning, tenth inning, eleventh inning goes by, and I keep telling Flanny, if you get in trouble, we'll be there. It was still tied with two outs in the eleventh with bases loaded and a right-handed pinch-hitter coming up. Weaver said, 'Go out there and tell him to throw this guy all change-ups.' Now Mike never said anything when I went to the mound. I walk to the mound and he looks at me, sweat dripping off him, and he says, 'I want to know one thing. When the fuck is in trouble?' But he got out of it, and then next inning Earl put on a double steal, with [Doug] DeCinces on third and [Mark] Belanger on first, and DeCinces stole home to win the game."

It should have been a memorable day for Boddicker—pitching a five-hit shutout against a team like the White Sox and beating a pitcher like Hoyt. But the Flanagan injury overshadowed the moment. "I remember the five-hit shutout," Boddicker said. "But I remember Flanny getting hurt more than winning that game."

But this was a quality team, built by a quality organization, and it was that organization—unknowingly in the final stages of its glory years—that would give the Orioles enough confidence to believe that they could still compete. And they would look to the man who had completed the doubleheader sweep in only his second major league start to step up and pitch like a veteran Orioles starter. The club purchased the contract of left-handed reliever Dan Morogiello to fill the roster spot. They would continue the season with a starting rotation of McGregor, Davis, Dennis Martinez, and Boddicker. Stewart was considered the fifth starter, but much of the time that season, the club wound up going with a four-man rotation.

Altobelli was prophetic about how they would handle the loss. "It's an old baseball cliche, but it is still true that when you have an injury, you never know what you might fall into," he told reporters. "Wally Pipp had a stomachache and the Yankees found Lou Gehrig."

"We had come to believe that whenever things like injuries did occur, like when Flanagan tore up his knee, there was always somebody there to step up and make a contribution," Bumbry said. "While it was disappointing, we felt that Boddicker could step up because that was the way things went for the Orioles then."

Dempsey, who knew the pitching staff as well as anyone, said there was no sense of panic when Flanagan was lost. "We didn't lose our confidence," he said. "We bit our lower lips and dug in. We still had a good ballclub with depth and guys like Boddicker who we thought could fill in."

Stoddard said the pitchers also felt that Boddicker would do the job. "We knew we were going to miss Flanny, because he was one of the greatest left-handed pitchers in baseball at the time," he said. "But it appeared he would come back before the season was over. We still had a solid staff, even though Flanny was one of our main guys. Boddicker came in, and it was a credit to the Orioles farm system and to him that he just filled right in. When he finally got the ball, he wasn't going to give it back up to anyone."

He wasn't going to give it back because it took him so long to get it. Boddicker was 25 when he got his final call-up, and would turn 26 before the season was over. "We had Boddicker buried down in Triple-A for years, the poor guy," McGregor said. "He already knew all of us very well by the time he came up that year because he had been in the system for so long. He was old by the time he got there.

"But he just stepped in and fit right in. That was how it was in those days. Steve Stone came over just as a so-so pitcher and jumped in with us and won the Cy Young Award. It was sort of like what has happened with Atlanta's pitching staff. There was just a kind of osmosis."

Elrod Hendricks, who had seen so many Orioles come through the system, agreed that Boddicker "fit right in like he had been there forever," and Boddicker said it was easier to adjust because he felt so confident about the team surrounding him. "Everybody contributed on that team," he said. "Everybody knew their role and what they were supposed to do. A guy would have a bat in his hand two hitters before he was called up to pinch hit."

Looking back at how Boddicker did fit in, Dauer bemoaned the loss of that magnificent farm system that made the Orioles so good for so long. "That was the thing about the Orioles that is missing today," he said. "Because they had such a solid minor league system, and because of the teachings of the coaches throughout the system, guys were prepared to play when they were called on to step in. We were all taught one way. The guys who came up were pretty near as good as the guys they were replacing who were hurt. We had guys who were developed through the system and, if they were on another team, they probably would be starting in the big leagues. Back in those days, when we went to spring training, maybe there was one spot open on the team.

"When someone came up, they were part of the team immediately. You weren't an outcast. Now that started to change shortly after that season, when we started to get into the free agent market and traded away guys. But there is no doubt that the personality of a team over 162 games will win you some games and keep you out of slumps. We weren't the best team on paper. If you went around position by position, first and shortstop, with Eddie and Cal, were pretty hard to beat. But as far as me and some of the others, there were better guys throughout the league, but not better guys who played together. And when we had a new guy who came in, that was when that personality paid off for us. They became part of that team personality."

Boddicker would become a life preserver for the Orioles in 1983. He finished the season with a 16–8 record and 2.77 ERA, and would go on to have a successful 14-season major league career with the Orioles, Boston Red Sox, Kansas City Royals, and Milwaukee Brewers, finishing in 1993. Boddicker retired with a career record of 134–116 and an ERA of 3.80. He was the last pitcher the Orioles farm system developed into a quality starter until Mike Mussina came along in 1992. And Boddicker would pay off for the Orioles farm system long after he was gone. He was traded to the Red Sox during the 1988 season in a deal that included a young, struggling outfield prospect named Brady Anderson, who would go on to become one of the top leadoff hitters in the game for the Orioles, scoring 1,056 runs, hitting 209 home runs, driving in 761 runs, and stealing 315 bases over 14 seasons with Baltimore.

It was once a magnificent farm system, so strong that years later it was still paying off, albeit in dwindling dividends. But minor leaguers weren't the only players who the Orioles called on to fill roles. The 1983 team was not entirely home grown—far from it. The Orioles had traded for a number of the players on that roster, and one trade they made the year before had appeared to backfire on them at the time. But in 1983, Dan Ford made it pay off.

5 | Disco Time

His nickname was "Disco," because he came from California and had a little more style and flair than the conservative Baltimore Orioles clubhouse was used to.

Darnell "Disco Dan" Ford never really became the player the Orioles had hoped they were getting when they traded Doug DeCinces and pitcher Jeff Schneider to the California Angels for him on January 28, 1982. He lasted just four more years with the Orioles and hit a total of 21 home runs and 104 RBIs in 279 games. But for one year—1983—it seemed like every hit Dan Ford got was an important one, and those hits may have very well made the difference between another year of what-ifs and a championship season.

Ford was born and raised in Los Angeles. He played baseball as a kid along with a generation of great African-American ballplayers who emerged from the city during that time, under the direction of former Negro Leagues pitching great Chet Brewer, the godfather of black youth baseball in Los Angeles. One of those players Ford played with and knew well was Eddie Murray. "I knew Eddie all of our lives, and all of his brothers," Ford said.

He played baseball at John C. Fremont High School and was drafted by Oakland in the first round in 1970. He moved quickly through the Athletics farm system while putting up solid numbers, batting .290 and averaging 14 home runs a year for four seasons. After batting .273 for Triple-A Tucson with 12 home runs, 65 RBIs, and 16 steals in the minors in 1974, he was traded to the Minnesota Twins in October 1974 along with pitcher Dennis Myers in a deal for first baseman Pat Bourque. Ford continued his steady play as a rookie with the Twins, batting .280 with 15 home runs, 59 RBIs, and 72 runs scored in 130 games.

Ford appeared to be a talent on the rise. In his second season with the Twins, he hit 20 home runs, drove in 86 runs, scored 87 runs, and stole 17 bases. But after driving in 82 runs and batting .274 in 1978, he was traded to California that December for catcher Danny Goodwin and first baseman Ron Jackson. He became a major contributor to the Angels' drive to the American League Western division title in 1979 with a career year, batting .290 with 21 home runs, 101 RBIs, and 100 runs scored. And he made a big impression on the Orioles, as Ford hit home runs in the first innings of Games 1 and 2 in the ALCS against Jim Palmer and Mike Flanagan. Even though the Orioles won the series three games to one, Ford led the team in home runs (two) and RBIs (four) in the series.

It was never as good for Dan Ford in California again. He never fully recovered from off-season knee surgery going into the 1980 season. He played in just 65 games, batting .279 with seven home runs and 26 RBIs. And it didn't get much better in 1981, as he still struggled with knee problems and other injuries. He made more news for his off-the-field activities, solidifying his "Disco Dan" image by posing for a centerfold for *Playgirl* magazine. He also got into two fights during the year, one with Cleveland pitcher John Denny, who plunked Ford in the ribs after the outfielder had gone 7-for-9 against the Indians in the two previous games. He also fought with Oakland catcher Mike Heath, who tried to take Ford's bat, claiming it was corked. The Angels had their fill of Dan Ford, and they made the deal to land DeCinces—a very unpopular trade in the Orioles clubhouse. DeCinces, though, had problems with Orioles fans because of the pressure of trying to replace Brooks Robinson at third base.

"When we traded Doug for Dan Ford, everyone in the clubhouse was wondering what the heck we were doing," Rich Dauer said. "Doug was a popular teammate and a heck of a player. Nobody knew how hard it was to step in and take over for Brooks. Doug had a lot of talent and he had a great career, but people didn't realize how hard it was for him to take over for the biggest player to have ever played in the city at the time."

Ken Singleton thinks DeCinces was dealt in part because of his union activities. "DeCinces was a very popular player on the team, and he was one of the labor leaders on the team, and I think that is one of the reasons he was traded after the 1981 strike season," he said. "Mark Belanger was also traded or let go, and he was another labor leader on our team. I think that was one way the owners got back at the Players Association then—moving player reps around."

Ford felt like his presence was a big change for the team to handle. "I think when I came over, I disrupted things a little bit," he said. "I remember Benny Ayala saying, 'Danny Ford, he took three people's jobs.'

"I said to him, 'How did I do that?'

"He said, 'When Kenny [Singleton] was out in right field, I would be the right-hand pinch-hitter. [Terry] Crowley would be the left-hand pinch-hitter, and someone else would come in and fill a role, too. When you came, Kenny Singleton became the designated hitter, and he is a switch-hitter. So he took two jobs, and you took another one.'"

It didn't help that Ford had a terrible season in Baltimore in 1982, batting just .235 in 123 games with 10 home runs and 43 RBIs, plus struggling in the outfield. He became the target of abuse from fans, and he said his teammates felt that his failure to produce that year cost them a trip to the 1982 postseason. If Dan Ford had played like they expected, they wouldn't have needed a final game of the season against Milwaukee to decide the winner of the AL East.

"It took a while for Dan Ford to adjust to us," Gary Roenicke said. "There was a way of doing things on the Orioles. It wasn't 'me' or an 'I.' It was a 'we.' We played so much as a team, and we got along. Nobody acted like he was a big star."

Dauer said he remembered that the loss of DeCinces made it tougher for Ford to become part of the close-knit group the Orioles had. "Dan didn't fit in right away," he said. "We had lost Doug, and Dan had a different style of his own. We had to break him down a little bit. But as time went on he became more and more of what we considered to be an Oriole-type player. He eventually fit in and contributed."

Ford admitted it took some time for him to feel comfortable—and for his teammates to feel comfortable with him. "When I got there, guys were talking about the Oriole Way," he said. "They said we do things a little different here. It took me a little while to get the hang of things."

Ford took some kidding from his teammates for his batting stance. "He had this awkward stance, like his whole butt faced the pitcher, and guys would kid him about it," Tippy Martinez said. "He would say he saw the ball better that way. He would put those arms up like a praying mantis. He was a little bit of a showman."

Elrod Hendricks, though, said many people didn't realize the problems Ford was dealing with physically that year. "He played hurt a lot that season, and to his credit never begged out of playing," Hendricks said. "He could have easily sat out a lot of games because of his knees. I watched him ice those knees down after every game. But he had a lot of big hits for us in 1983. Boy, did he ever."

One of the bigger hits came against Chicago on May 18, the day after the Orioles swept the White Sox in a doubleheader. Even though they were in different divisions, these were big games, and this one, coming on the heels of losing Flanagan, was particularly big.

As the game went on at Memorial Stadium, it didn't look particularly winnable, though. It was 0–0 through eight innings, but it didn't seem as if the Orioles were going to be able to reach Chicago starter Richard Dotson. While Storm Davis had shut out the White Sox for 7⅓ innings, he had given up three hits. Dotson, through 7⅓ innings, had not given up any hits—zero, a no-hitter—until Ford came up with one out in the bottom of the eighth inning. He lifted a fly ball just into the right-field seats to give Baltimore a 1–0 lead, which Tippy Martinez would preserve to get the win. Ford's hit would be the only one for the Orioles. It was the second straight shutout for Baltimore.

"This is a very long way from last year," Ford told reporters after the game. "It's something that I had to do for myself, establishing myself as an everyday ballplayer, and a good everyday ballplayer."

It really was a long way from the year before. Ford's heroics were now making him a fan favorite, particularly in right field.

Dotson said he didn't think he made a bad pitch to Ford. "I had a good fastball and I pretty much stuck to it," he said after the game. "I figured if they were going to hit me, they were going to hit me with my fastball." He had so much confidence in his fastball that he didn't seem particularly worried about his control. Dotson walked seven batters, but he figured the way he was pitching, no one was going to drive anyone home. Ford drove one runner home—himself.

"It wasn't a bad pitch," Dotson said. "Earlier in the game I was throwing it by him [Ford had struck out twice]. This was a pitch out over the plate and he hit it, got it up. I thought, 'Well, it's a home run,' just like that. . . . I knew I had a no-hitter. I wasn't concerned that much. The score was nothing-nothing and I was worried about losing the game."

Later on that night, Ford happened to run into Dotson and his father in a Baltimore hotel. "We were in an elevator together," Ford said. "His father said, 'You're Dan Ford, the guy that broke up my son's no-hitter, and then he wound up losing the game 1–0.'

"I said, 'Yup, I'm the one.'"

Ford wasn't done, either, though the White Sox would not be the victims. Chicago was leaving town, battered and bruised. They had not scored a run against Orioles pitching in 24 innings, had lost eight of their last nine games, and had scored just 23 runs over that nine-game span. The Orioles would also be leaving town for a four-game series in Toronto against their division rivals, the Blue Jays. And even though the team had suffered a devastating loss when Flanagan was hurt, they were on a roll, having won seven of their last eight games and sitting on top of the AL East with a 22–13 record and a three-game lead on the Boston Red Sox.

This wasn't the Toronto with the state-of-the-art SkyDome. These were the days of the old, outdoor, no-sliding-dome Exhibition Stadium, and it was a cold, rainy night that greeted the Orioles for the first game of the series. But this was Dan Ford's 31st birthday, and the way he was going, how could they lose?

They couldn't, and remarkably it was Ford who won it again with another game-winning home run in a 2–1 victory. Ford's two-run home run came in the top of the eighth inning; it was nearly midnight because the game had been delayed two hours by rain. Ironically, Ford's second straight game-winning home run saved him from being the goat. He had drilled a double off the left-center-field fence in the top of the first inning, but he was thrown out when he made a base-running mistake and tried to stretch it into a triple. There was just one out, and Cal Ripken and Murray were coming up behind him when he made the second out of the inning at third base, leaving nobody on base.

Baltimore got another great pitching performance, as Scott McGregor allowed just one run on six hits and no walks in 8⅓ innings pitched. The Orioles had now won eight out of nine games and owned a 23–13 record. What seemed like a team on the brink of chaos a month before was now cruising along.

And then things got ugly.

Baltimore lost the next day 7–5, with Dennis Martinez getting knocked around, giving up five runs in just 3⅓ innings. Not that Ford didn't try to be the hero three games in a row, hitting yet another home run. But there was too much of Dennis Martinez to go around and not enough of Dan Ford.

The pitching staff depth, with the loss of Palmer and Flanagan, came into play in the third game of the series against Toronto. The Orioles were forced to start Sammy Stewart. He had spot-started before in his career—23 times over five seasons—but it was not an ideal situation for their long reliever. He wasn't long for this game, as Toronto reached Stewart for four runs on eight hits in four innings. He left with the score tied at 4–4, but the Blue Jays scored two runs off Dan Morogiello, and while this was going on, Dave Stieb was shutting down the Orioles, who mustered just four hits off the Blue Jays starter.

Suddenly, the Orioles had become a version of the team they had just beaten up on at Memorial Stadium. They couldn't score any runs and were facing some hot pitching. This time it was Jim Clancy who shut out the Orioles for the second straight game, a 5–0 win. Mike Boddicker couldn't match the zeros, but the rookie pitched well, giving up just three runs in seven innings—good enough to win on most days with this Baltimore lineup. But not yesterday and not today.

Baltimore left Toronto with a record of 23–16, having lost three straight, and stuck in its first slump of the year. What had been an up-and-down season had gone from a good run of going up to a run of falling down. They had arrived in Toronto hitting .285 and averaging six runs a game. Against the Blue Jays, they batted .180 and averaged 1.8 runs per game. John Lowenstein was stuck in an 0-for-19 slump, leaving 14 runners on base; Rick Dempsey was 0-for-12; John Shelby was 2-for-19; and Eddie Murray, the heart of the order, was 3-for-19 and hadn't homered in 27 games.

"To me, it does look like their hitters are starting to get in a slump," Clancy said after the game. "They aren't too aggressive. You can tell that by the way they are swinging. They aren't confident. They are swinging at bad pitches."

Altobelli tried to be philosophical about it. "We're going home and we're still in first place," he told reporters.

Not for long.

Things weren't any better back home. The Minnesota Twins—a team the Orioles were 8–4 against the year before, a team that held a substantial 257–199 lifetime mark against Baltimore—embarrassed the Orioles with a 12–4 pummeling. Davis didn't make it out of the third inning, allowing four runs in 2⅓ innings pitched. Before it was even over, Baltimore was no longer in first place, with the Red Sox moving ahead of them.

Orioles pitchers gave up 13 hits and four walks, while Twins starter Frank Viola pitched well enough for a complete-game win. Ripken and Roenicke homered against Frank Viola, but they would have needed a lot more than four runs this day. They would need more than four runs the next day, too, as Baltimore lost its fifth straight, 6–1, as Twins hitters battered McGregor for five runs on eight hits in six innings, and Bobby Castillo held the Baltimore hitters in check.

This loss would make the papers, meaning it would wind up as much more than simply the fifth loss in a losing streak. Owner Edward Bennett Williams had something to say about this loss: "This is the worst we've looked in my short tenure with the club," he told reporters. "We look like we're in a coma. We're not doing anything."

Yes, they were. They were falling fast, and nobody was stepping forward to stop the fall. They had hoped Palmer was about to come off the disabled list. But Palmer, who had been on the disabled list for three weeks because of back spasms, now had developed bicep tendinitis and was ordered by doctors not to throw for three days. He had been scheduled to start against the Royals when the Orioles made the trip to Kansas City.

But first they had the Twins to deal with. Baltimore lost its sixth straight, 7–4, as the Twins completed their first sweep ever of the Orioles at Memorial Stadium, where, before this three-game series began, the Orioles had gone 13–1 in their previous 14 games. They had not lost there to the Twins since 1980. Dennis Martinez would have been pitching his way out of the rotation by now, as ineffective as he had been, this time allowing six runs on six hits and two walks in just 1⅔ innings. But they had little choice but to keep putting him out there given the lack of pitching depth due to injuries.

The nightmare continued in Kansas City. Boddicker, their savior, couldn't stop it, surrendering six runs on five hits and three walks in 3⅔ innings in an 8–2 defeat for their seventh straight loss. In the AL East, where the Orioles, Yankees, Red Sox, and Tigers would be crowded close to each other for much of the year, Baltimore, with a record of 23–20, had now fallen all the way to fourth place, even though they were just two games out of first.

The frustration level was rising high. Dempsey and the Royals' Willie Wilson got into a beef after Dempsey tried to throw U. L. Washington out on a steal attempt. The catcher thought that Wilson, who said he was trying to bunt, was interfering with him. They had words at home plate.

"If you stick that bat out again, I'll kick your butt," Dempsey told Wilson.

Wilson looked back, and Dempsey said, "I hear you want to kick my ass. Come on, let's go."

Dempsey and Wilson had a history dating back to 1976, when Dempsey was the player-manager of a team in the Puerto Rico Winter League that Wilson played for. "He was always getting into fights," Wilson told reporters after the game. "He went out to the mound one time and punched a pitcher because the pitcher wouldn't come out of the game. I decided then I wanted to leave the club because I didn't want him to come out and try to punch me.

"I felt like punching him in the face out there," Wilson said, referring to their home-plate argument. "But that's dirty baseball, and I'm not a dirty person. Besides, I won't waste my energy fighting a .210 hitter."

Both benches cleared as the two jawed at each other, but no punches were thrown. "The only thing he can do is shoot off his mouth and run," Dempsey told reporters. "He doesn't want to do anything. He told Dan Ford I was crazy and he wanted to kick my butt, so I invited him to try it. . . . In Puerto Rico, he was a big baby. I had a tough time even getting him to the ballpark."

Panic was in the air. General manager Hank Peters made the trip to Kansas City to huddle with Altobelli and try to figure out how to stop the losing. After the game, Altobelli talked to his players, but again, it was no Earl Weaver rant. He just told them to relax, that they were pressing, and he still had faith in them. "We're three games over .500, right in the thick of it, so why think negatively?" he said, which must have surprised some of those Orioles players who were so used to Weaver's outbursts.

Someone finally appeared to stop the free fall. Murray, who had not clubbed a home run in 31 games, finally hit a shot, and so did Roenicke, in a 7–4 win over the Royals, behind Storm Davis and Tippy Martinez. They moved up to third place with the win, and followed that with a second straight victory, this one 1–0. Murray was now on a roll, delivering a solo home run, which was good enough for McGregor, who gave up just two hits. Still, the Orioles had only three hits themselves, and concerns over the offense were still in the forefront.

Those concerns were well grounded. The Orioles were shut out in the series finale by the Royals, 4–0. Dennis Martinez took another loss, and his record was now 3–9, with eight innings pitched, 10 hits, three walks, and four runs. In their last 15 games, Baltimore was 6–9 and had just six hitters batting over .200 during that stretch.

Still, with a 25–21 record, Baltimore was just one game out of first place. The Orioles would manage to win their next series, going to Minnesota and taking two out of three from the Twins. They would return to Baltimore with a 27–22 record, but in the topsy-turvy AL East, they were in fourth place, with 1½ games separating the Orioles, Yankees, Red Sox, and the first-place Blue Jays—who the Orioles were about to face at Memorial Stadium. This time, Dennis Martinez was the old Dennis, holding Toronto to two runs over seven innings for a 3–2 win. Boddicker—who was becoming the Orioles' most consistent starter—won the next game 6–4, with home runs by Murray, Al Bumbry, and Lowenstein, who went deep in consecutive innings. Davis lost the third game of the series 5–2, but McGregor came back to win the final game—a rain-shortened 8–1 victory, backed by Ripken and Leo Hernandez home runs. Baltimore was now 30–23 and back in first place. Meanwhile, Palmer was working toward coming back, having pitched in a simulated game and batting practice. In an interview, Palmer said he was feeling the pressure of trying to come back as soon as possible. "You bet there is overt pressure," he said. "I know two days after [Mike] Flanagan was hurt, Hank Peters called him and told him that the club really needed him back as soon as possible. I get calls from Edward Bennett Williams. There is always pressure on me because of who I am."

Of course, there are all sorts of pressure. There is the pressure a three-time Cy Young Award winner feels to come back and help the team. Then there is the pressure of a rookie pitcher being called up to make his first major league start for a first-place team against a division rival. That is the pressure Allan Ramirez felt when he was brought up from Rochester on June 6 to start two days later against the Milwaukee Brewers.

Ramirez, born and raised in Victoria, Texas, had been a promising young right-hander—he had gone 16–8 for Double-A Charlotte in 1980—but was coming off a tough season in Rochester in 1982, going 6–10 with a 4.86 ERA after developing tendinitis. But he had pitched well in spring training and was solid if not spectacular in Rochester, with a 3–3 record, a 3.78 ERA, and team highs in complete games and strike-outs. Now he was being called on to keep the Orioles back on the winning track and to beat the defending American League champions.

In a way, the story of Allan Ramirez is the story of the 1983 Orioles. There were the stars, the Murrays, the Ripkens, and outstanding pitchers such as McGregor and Flanagan. But it was the spare parts here and there, the role players who made up the 25-man roster, that made the difference for this 1983 championship team.

The Red Wings were home in Rochester when the 26-year-old Ramirez got the word. "[Rochester manager] Lance Nichols called me into his office and told me I had been called up," Ramirez said. "I told my wife, then I called my parents when I got back to our apartment, and my wife called her parents.

"At the time, I wasn't pitching great, but I wasn't pitching bad, either. It was a surprise to me. I got on the plane the next day and flew to Baltimore after I got the news. Lance told me I would be starting against Milwaukee. All I could think of was all those big hitters in Milwaukee. What a way to start."

This would be the first time the Orioles faced the Brewers since losing to them on that heartbreaking final day of the 1982 season. But this was a different Brewers team. Their Cy Young Award winner from the previous year, Pete Vukovich, was out for the year, and slugger Gorman Thomas had been traded. Dennis Martinez won the series opener 6–4, with home runs by Roenicke and Murray, who was now on a tear, plus RBI triples by Ayala and Dauer. The next day, Ramirez would start.

General manager Hank Peters called Ramirez into his office when he first got to Baltimore. "The two hardest things about major league baseball are getting called up and then staying there," he said. "You've already achieved one. Let's see if you can achieve the other."

There were many times when, if you were pitching in the Orioles minor league system, you wondered if you would ever even achieve the first step—getting called up, given the starting rotation in Baltimore. "When we were in the minors, and see Jim Palmer, Mike Flanagan, Scott McGregor, Storm Davis, and then Mike Boddicker, we would be back in Rochester thinking, 'We're never going to break into that rotation,'" Ramirez said. "We were just biding our time in Rochester. They were Cy Young Award winners. When I got up there, just being in the same clubhouse with them, it was like a dream. And they were great guys. You couldn't meet a better bunch of guys. They took me in and tried to help me as much as they could and really put me at ease."

Ray Miller and Dempsey met with Ramirez to go over the Milwaukee lineup, and so did Palmer. "Jim came by my locker and sat down and told me what each hitter liked and didn't like," Ramirez said.

All that preparation didn't seem to help. Ramirez, going up against veteran Don Sutton, walked leadoff hitter Paul Molitor. After getting Rick Manning out on a fly ball to left, he walked Robin Yount and Cecil Cooper to load the bases. Ted Simmons slapped a single to right, scoring Molitor and Yount to give Milwaukee a 2–0 lead. "I was very nervous," Ramirez said. "The adrenaline was flowing. My stomach was hurting. I was throwing way too hard and the ball was flying everywhere. Ray came out to talk to me. I could see in the bullpen they had somebody warming up already [Morogiello]. I thought to myself, 'My God, I'm not even going to get out of the first inning.'"

He did get out of the inning, though, without any more damage, as Ben Oglivie grounded into a double play. Ramirez walked two more hitters in the top of the second, but settled down and didn't give up any more runs, coming out of the game after seven innings with the score tied at 2–2, thanks to a two-run home run by Ken Singleton in the bottom of the seventh. The Brewers took a 3–2 lead on a single by Oglivie off reliever Tippy Martinez in the top of the eighth, but Baltimore came back to score five runs in the bottom of the inning. With two outs, Dauer singled to score pinch-runner John Shelby, and then Ripken followed with a two-run home run. After Milwaukee reliever Tom Tellmann walked Murray, Lowenstein homered to give Baltimore a 7–3 win. Ramirez didn't get credit for the victory, but he did his job—he kept the team in the game. "I had realized that those hitters were going up there to hit the ball, and with the great infield and out-field we had, I learned to let those guys play behind me," he said. The Orioles, back on a winning run, swept the series the next day, but this one was no masterpiece. The Orioles committed six errors, tying a club record, and gave up seven runs—only two of them earned. Nevertheless, they pounded out 15 hits for a 10–7 win, giving them a 33–23 record and a three-game division lead.

The Orioles left town for Boston and a six-game road trip, and got off to a good start with a 3–0 shutout win by Davis. Roenicke homered, and Singleton tripled to lead the Baltimore offense. Davis gave up just three hits, and they followed that up with a 10–6 win for their sixth straight victory—all against division opponents. Good news followed. Palmer would be reactivated, though the plan was for him to start working out of the bullpen.

The Orioles lost the final game of the series in Boston, 7–6, but they were now winning a series at a time. Most managers will tell you that it's best to approach a season not one game at a time, but one series at a time. If you can win most of the series against your opponents, you will usually win at the end of the year. They went to Milwaukee, and this time Ramirez got his first major league victory, a 3–2 win, while facing Sutton for the second straight time. The Orioles got home runs by Ripken and key doubles by Ford and Bumbry. Tuesday's game was rained out, but not before Dempsey got to do his rain-delay comedy act on the field, to the delight of the Milwaukee fans. He comically re-created Yount's two-homer performance from the final game of the 1982 season, wearing a

Yount jersey with towels stuffed under it to create the big-belly clown effect. "Nothing Dempsey does surprises me," Yount said later.

The Orioles could afford to laugh at their past nightmares. Everything seemed to be working for them now. They defeated Milwaukee 11–8 to assure them of another series win, and this was an inspired victory, coming in the tenth inning after Baltimore was down 7–0 after six innings. They scored five runs in the top of the seventh, led by a three-run home run by Ripken. They tied it in the top of the eighth with runs driven in by Singleton and Shelby, who had a big game with three hits, two RBIs, two walks, and a stolen base. Then Joe Nolan led off the top of the tenth inning by beating out a grounder and reaching second on a throwing error by Cecil Cooper. Dauer moved him over with a bunt, and Shelby sliced a single to right to score Nolan for the game-winning hit. Ripken added two more with a double that just missed being his second home run of the game. Murray brought home the eleventh run with a sacrifice fly, and Tippy Martinez allowed one run in the bottom of the eleventh before closing out the game and getting the win. "A win like this shows you're never out of a game," Singleton said, which was the attitude of this Orioles squad.

It wasn't all good news, though. Palmer made his debut as a reliever, and it wasn't particularly smooth; he gave up two runs on four hits in three innings. But the plan was for Palmer to ease his way back into the rotation with more bullpen work. "There is no sense rushing back, because the team is playing too well," he told reporters.

The best laid plans, though, unraveled when two things happened— the team started to struggle, and Storm Davis got laid up with the flu. The Orioles suffered a tough 2–1 loss in 11 innings to Milwaukee, wasting a remarkable pitching performance by McGregor, who in 10 innings gave up just one run on five hits and one walk. He left in the top of the eleventh with the game tied at 1–1, but Tim Stoddard gave up a home run to Rick Manning for a Brewers walk-off win.

It was a difficult loss, but the Orioles felt good going back home after a 4–2 road trip. Yet this team, which had been slowly building a respectable record, was now streaky. They lost the home opener against Boston 5–3 and followed that with a 3–2 loss, wasting another strong pitching outing, this one by Boddicker. The first loss on Friday, though, spelled more trouble for the Orioles, because it was another defeat for Dennis Martinez—his tenth loss of the season. He lasted just 1⅔ innings, giving up four runs on six hits. The only thing that was keeping him in the rotation was the fact that the team was so thin in starting pitching—and getting thinner. Davis had a severe case of the flu, meaning that Palmer would be pressed into starting duty much more quickly than he had expected. Altobelli talked about sending Dennis Martinez back out to pitch three days after his loss to Boston because there were fears that Davis might not be ready to start that day, the first game of a three-game series against their hated division rivals the Yankees. That was not the way Baltimore wanted to face New York for the first time this season.

This wasn't the only personnel problem for Altobelli. Leo Hernandez was becoming a liability at third base. With a pitching staff like the Orioles had, defense was a high priority—and always had been as part of the Oriole Way. Hernandez had already committed 12 errors, and his range toward shortstop was very limited. The Orioles were considering using Roenicke at third. He had started as a third baseman in the minor leagues, but it had been a long time since he played the position on a regular basis, and though he would offer more offense than Hernandez, the defensive questions would still exist. Third base would remain a problem for the Orioles until help came from the West Coast.

Meanwhile, Palmer was being forced to start the last game of the Red Sox series. "We need him to pitch, that's all," Ray Miller told reporters. "Storm is sick and Scott needs an extra day off coming off 10 innings."

Palmer said he had received a cortisone shot in his shoulder the week before, and the effects of that were working now. He said he felt better than he did when he went out in relief against Milwaukee a few days before. "I couldn't extend my arm that day," he told reporters. "It feels better now."

He had not started since April 26, but the veteran gave the team just what it was looking for—and more. He pitched 5⅓ innings of shutout ball against the Red Sox, allowing just three hits. Two solo home runs by Murray staked Palmer to a 3–0 lead. Although Tim Stoddard gave up three runs in relief, the Orioles added three more, and the 37-year-old Palmer came away with his 265th career victory, which stopped the Orioles' losing streak at three games. The win allowed Baltimore, now 38–27, to extend its lead in the AL East by two games over the Blue Jays.

Now the Orioles would face the Yankees, probably their greatest rivals. The Yankees had dealt this group of Orioles a tough blow in 1980, when Baltimore won 100 games only to finish second behind New York, which had won 103. Many players believe that, along with 1979 and 1982, 1980 could have been the difference between the great dynasty that this club could have put together and what they actually had to show so far from the group that first emerged with the rookie class of 1977—one AL pennant. This year, the Yankees were trailing the Orioles by 3½ games going into this series.

Singleton didn't look forward to facing the Yankees. "I hated playing against the Yankees, because they had all the money and had very good teams that were tough to beat," he said. "I grew up in New York, but I wasn't a Yankee fan when I was growing up. We always had big crowds for Yankee games. They were always big games, and there was a lot on the line." Ironically, Singleton is now an announcer for Yankees games.

It would be a strange season for the Yankees, a particularly bizarre one for the Bronx Zoo. This was the year of the "Pine Tar" game between the Royals and the Yankees on July 24. George Brett appeared to hit a two-run home run off Goose Gossage to give the Royals a 5–4 lead, only to have the home run erased when New York manager Billy Martin complained that Brett's pine tar had exceeded the 17-inch limit. The home run was reversed, sending Brett out of the visitor's dugout in a rage that has been shown thousands of times since on sports television clips. New York appeared to have won 4–3, but AL president Lee MacPhail overruled his umpires, declaring that Brett's home run should have been allowed and that the game would be resumed from that point almost five weeks later.

Two weeks later, New York's Dave Winfield hit a seagull in Toronto's Exhibition Stadium while warming up in the outfield before the fifth inning. He killed the bird and was arrested after the game on charges of cruelty to animals. He had to post $500 to get out of jail, but the charges were dropped the next day.

The Orioles had no such exotic problems. They were simply trying to keep winning while plugging holes in the pitching rotation. Davis made things easier when he recovered from the flu enough to start against the Yankees. He held them to two runs over 7⅔ innings for a 5–2 win, with Roenicke carrying the offense, slugging two two-run home runs. Roenicke was a solid major league hitter, but, first under Weaver and then under Altobelli, he became part of one of the best-known and most successful two-man platoon systems in baseball, as he and the colorful John Lowenstein became an outstanding two-headed left fielder.

Roenicke, who had been a first-round draft choice by the Montreal Expos in 1973, came to Baltimore in a December 1977 trade, along with pitchers Don Stanhouse and Joe Kerrigan, for pitchers Rudy May, Randy Miller, and Bryn Smith. In his first full season with the Orioles, Roenicke showed that he had everyday major league power, logging 25 home runs and 64 RBIs in 133 games. But Weaver began tinkering with platooning Roenicke, a right-handed hitter who would face left-handed pitching, with another solid-hitting outfielder, Lowenstein, a left-handed hitter who would play mostly against right-handed pitching. Lowenstein was a steal for the Orioles, who picked him up on waivers after he was released by the Texas Rangers in November 1978. Lowenstein had been a mediocre hitter through the first eight seasons of his career, primarily with the Cleveland Indians. But when he came to Baltimore, Lowenstein found his niche. He enjoyed a career year in 1982, when he hit 24 home runs, drove in 66 runs, and batted .320 in 122 games.

Roenicke never welcomed the platooning. He said that although it started with Weaver, it was Altobelli who began relying on it regularly. "I know a lot of people think it started in 1982, but if you added up both our [Roenicke's and Lowenstein's] at-bats, they were up over 700, so we had to both have played a lot of time [Lowenstein had 322 at-bats in 1982, while Roenicke went up to the plate 393 times]," Roenicke said. "But when Altobelli took over for Earl, he started the platooning all the time.

"I wasn't comfortable with it because that is pretty much all that I did the rest of my career. But we were such a dynamic and good team that I didn't want to rock the boat and complain about just me. We were victims of our own success."

Altobelli certainly thought it was a success. "Lowenstein and Roenicke was a terrific platoon combination," he said. "I couldn't have asked for better cooperation from either one of them. They knew exactly when they were going to hit and when they had to be ready. They knew how to play the game. I didn't have to say, 'Lo, get ready,' or, 'Gary, get ready.' They knew and they got ready."

The Orioles—particularly the pitchers—also praised the platoon system that, in a way, came to symbolize the concept that the sum of this team was greater than its individual parts. "Roenicke and Lo were the classic platoon situation," McGregor said. "They would get 35 home runs and over 100 RBIs together out of one position. Put a left-hander in and you had to face Roenicke, and with a right-hander you had to face Lowenstein. Now, Roenicke hated it because there were always more right-handers than left-handers, so Lowenstein got to play more. Roenicke was always saying, 'I've got to get out of here. I've got to get out of here and go play someplace.'"

Roenicke said he and Lowenstein handled the situation like professionals. "Our relationship was OK," he said. "John was a veteran, and I had been around for a while. We got along fine. That is what made that team special. We didn't have any problems like that; we had some good chemistry. Nothing to take away from Joe, but that 1983 team, it was pretty much a veteran team. Rip Sr., Ray Miller, and Joe managed the team, but we pretty much managed ourselves. It didn't take John and I long to figure out what we did. When a right-hander pitched, John played, and when a left-hander pitched, I played."

Lowenstein was more philosophical about sharing playing time. Then again, Lo marched to a different drummer—a colorful figure on a conservative team. He had a certain flair, as witnessed the day he was carried off the field at Memorial Stadium on a stretcher after a collision. He suddenly stuck his arm up in the air to signal he was OK, to the delight of the home crowd. It is part of Orioles lore now.

"Lowenstein was a little off the wall," Singleton said. "I had some good discussions with him about various things, and some of them were a little goofy. But he was a good man and a good teammate."

Lowenstein said they weren't just a two-headed platoon. Benny Ayala often made it a three-man combination. "At that stage in my career, I was comfortable with platooning because I didn't look forward to facing left-handed pitching, because I hadn't faced it for so long," Lo said. "I think the two of us, and the three of us with Ayala included, were the best three-headed monster in the game. If you look at the statistics we put up, they are pretty good numbers [34 home runs and 124 RBIs between Lowenstein and Roenicke in 1983]. I used to joke that we should split the MVP."

"We got along," Lowenstein said of his relationship with Roenicke. "We weren't drinking buddies or anything. But I don't know anybody on that team who didn't really get along. That's unusual for a team that wins championships, because often there are so many frustrations and emotions that go into winning a championship, and sometimes a lot of friction. There wasn't on that team. The only friction that might have existed was if Earl was the manager. But Altobelli was the manager, and I've always given Joe credit for maintaining the ship's course. Anybody coming in could have screwed that up. He was a big part of why we won."

It wasn't an easy ship for the manager to steer. It kept veering off course for periods of time in the first half of the season. After beating New York in the first game, the Orioles went up against Ron Guidry the next day and lost 5–2. They were back in a losing spin again. They dropped two straight to Detroit, the first one a 9–0 beating, with Dennis Martinez again embarrassed on the mound. He lasted just four innings and gave up six runs for his 11th loss. The defeat, coupled with a Toronto win over Seattle, put Baltimore in a tie for first place with the Blue Jays in the AL East. And now Ford, who had fallen off after his hot start to hit .156 in his last 19 games, was going on the disabled list due to an injury to his left knee that he had suffered three weeks before while diving for a ball in Minnesota. Ford would undergo arthroscopic surgery, and no one knew for sure when he would return. Baltimore called up outfielder Mike Young to take Ford's spot.

The Orioles lost their third straight, 9–3, to the Tigers, and the good feeling that had run through the organization after Palmer's last start disappeared after this one. He was charged with seven runs on 10 hits and three walks in 7⅓ innings pitched. It was their third straight loss, but with a record of 39–30, the Orioles remained in first place.

Storm Davis showed no lingering effects of any flu when he faced Jack Morris and the Detroit Tigers in the next game. Davis pitched a no-hitter through eight innings, but former Michigan quarterback Rick

Leach, pinch-hitting for Tom Brookens to lead off the top of the ninth, sent a Davis pitch over the wall for a solo home run, breaking up the no-hitter. Davis was shaken after that and couldn't finish the game. He walked pinch-hitter Johnny Grubb and then went two balls on Lou Whitaker before Altobelli had seen enough. He brought in Tippy Martinez to preserve a 3–1 win, which included home runs by Ripken and Bumbry.

The Orioles were in first place, with a 40–30 record, when they went up to New York to play the Yankees. And just like that, in 72 hours, they lost three straight to the Yankees by scores of 4–3, 7–0, and 4–3. The two 4–3 losses were particularly difficult for the club and for Tim Stoddard, who lost both of them. The first loss came in the bottom of the eleventh, as Butch Wynegar drove home the winning run against Stoddard, who had come in to pitch in the bottom of the inning. Goose Gossage, who struck out the side in the top of the eleventh, got the win. The same thing happened in the second 4–3 defeat, this one coming in the bottom of the twelfth on another game-winning hit by Wynegar off Stoddard, with Gossage getting the win.

It was June 30, the brink of the All-Star break, and the Orioles were now 40–33 and in second place in the AL East, two games behind the Blue Jays and just a half game ahead of the third-place Yankees. They needed a rudder to stabilize the ship, and they saw a way to do that by shoring up their defense—an Orioles trademark. So they called the "Watchman."

6 | The Watchman Cometh

The first time the Orioles got a look at their new teammate, Todd Cruz, he made a memorable impression. "He had about seven watches on his arm," Rich Dauer said. "We asked him what time it was."

It was defense time. Orioles management had decided that their pitching was taking too much of a beating from balls getting through and around third baseman Leo Hernandez, who had committed 13 errors and showed a troubling lack of range. So they went shopping for a third baseman and came away with a guy who was a pretty good shortstop and a little bit strange.

"We pick up a guy who was selling watches someplace," Scott McGregor said. "He was a piece of work."

Cruz's watch fetish preceded him. In July 1981, while with the White Sox, he was arrested for attempted breaking and entering and theft while on rehabilitation option in Edmonton. Police caught him in the men's section of a department store with dozens of watches stuffed in his pocket. He had been on a drinking binge and fell asleep in the store, only to wake up to see police dogs hovering over him. "I'm sorry, I'm sorry, I'm sorry," he reportedly told the police. Cruz said he was suffering from alcohol and personal problems.

He had other time problems as well. Cruz, playing for Seattle, was the target of Mariners manager Rene Lachemann's wrath for consistently showing up late to the ballpark before games. The Orioles, though, were willing to overlook all that for two reasons: first, they were convinced that given the peer pressure in the clubhouse for following the Oriole Way, Cruz would be forced to straighten up his act; second, Cruz could, as they like to say in the game, "pick it." He was a tremendous fielder and turned out to be an important piece of the Orioles' 1983 championship puzzle. "The biggest move we made was when we got Todd Cruz from Seattle," Altobelli said. "General manager Hank Peters made a great move there. Leo Hernandez, he was a little late in getting the ball to second base, and his range was a little shallow. Todd Cruz was playing shortstop for Seattle when we got him. We moved him over to third base. He had real good range and got rid of the ball real quick. He solidified our infield for the second half."

Cruz, who had come up in the Philadelphia Phillies organization, had been playing shortstop for the Seattle Mariners. But he was unhappy with the direction the team was heading, particularly after his friend and double-play partner, Julio Cruz, had been traded. "When Seattle got rid of Julio Cruz, we had been leading the league for the last year and a half as a double-play combination, with him at second and me at short," he said.

Cruz was either a free spirit or a loose cannon, depending on your point of view, even though he was considered a very talented ballplayer. The Mariners were his fifth team in six major league seasons, having already gone through the Phillies, Royals, Angels, and White Sox before going to Seattle.

Seattle management also had its fill of him after he criticized them in the papers. "They got mad at me because I called them liars, in round-about words," he said. "In trying to supposedly build a winning team, they got rid of [pitcher] Floyd Bannister first, then Julio, breaking up the best double-play combination in the league. Two weeks later, I was traded."

Cruz had no complaints, though. He was going from a last-place team to a first-place team, and, fittingly, he would join the Orioles in Detroit, where Cruz grew up as a baseball star at Detroit Western High School. When he arrived in the visitor's clubhouse, it was as if there were forces of karma at work. Not only was he going to play in front of home-town fans, but he would finally wear his high school uniform number—10—something he had also wanted to do. "I was drafted by the Phillies when I was 17, and Larry Bowa wore No. 10," Cruz said. "He was an All-Star shortstop, and I didn't want anyone to think I was trying to copy him. So I started wearing different numbers."

His new Orioles uniform was hanging in his locker with No. 10 on the back. "I didn't ask for it," Cruz said. "I just walked into the clubhouse and it was hanging in my locker. Somebody may have told them something, I don't now. That made me feel good, plus playing in my hometown. I think I gave away 272 tickets for the whole series to family and friends."

Cruz was elated about the trade and the uniform, but he was in for two quick shocks. First, he had to shave his goatee, which he had had for many years. Team rules—no facial hair. "They made me shave it before I played in that first game against Detroit," he said. "Ripken, Dauer, Murray, Bumbry, Roenicke, all of them were there to watch it."

He begged Altobelli for a temporary reprieve. "Can I shave it after the game?" Cruz asked. "I don't know how I'm going to feel about this. It's a little weird."

Altobelli said no, and Cruz shaved the goatee, though he wasn't happy about it. Something else, though, shook him even more. When he looked at the lineup card, he saw that the shortstop from Seattle was playing third base. He had played third in only 14 major league games over his career. "They didn't tell me I was going to be moved to third base," Cruz said. "I thought Ripken was going to move back to third [where he had played when he came up to Baltimore in 1981] and I would take over short. But before we went out for batting practice, I looked at the lineup card to see where I was hitting. I was hitting sixth or seventh. But then it had my position—5, third base."

Cruz went into Altobelli's office, where Cal Ripken Sr. and Elrod Hendricks were there with the manager.

"How come I'm at third?" Cruz asked.

"We're going to give the kid a chance to stay there," Altobelli said.

Cruz said he figured it wouldn't last long. "I thought it would be a month before I would be back at shortstop," he said. "Boy, was I wrong. Look what he [Ripken] did there." Of course, Ripken set a number of records at shortstop, including 2,216 consecutive games at the position out of the 2,632 consecutive games he played during his remarkable career.

Needless to say, it was the right move for the team. "Ripken was able to move over up the middle more, because I could cover the hole," Cruz said.

Ripken saw the difference when Cruz arrived. "In the first part of the year, we were going back and forth at third base," Ripken said. "It was an issue for us. But when Todd Cruz came over and was put at third base, he went from a shortstop with real good range to a third baseman with great range. Defensively, with the type of pitching staff we had, he was very instrumental in taking hits away from the hole and turning double plays. And offensively, he contributed a lot in certain games. He allowed me to play further up the middle. I didn't have to shade toward the hole a little bit. As a matter of fact, it became the exact opposite. If there was a pull hitter up, I felt that with his range to the left, he could cover so much ground there, so I only needed to cover to that ground, and then I could position myself further up the middle. I think both of us were able to cover more of the left side of the infield because he had some great range."

The move to third didn't seem to bother Cruz that much. "I figured it was OK," he said. "I had my old number. I was playing for a first-place team. And my dad played third when he played for the Tigers [in the minors]."

It certainly didn't affect Cruz at the plate in his first game with the Orioles. He had one of the more remarkable debuts. He drove in six runs with a three-run home run and a bases-loaded double, leading the Orioles to a 9–5 win, stopping their three-game losing streak, and cutting their deficit to just one game out of first place (41–33). He had entered the game batting just .190, and Tigers manager Sparky Anderson intentionally walked Jim Dwyer to get to Cruz, who answered with his three-run homer.

Cruz did the damage against his good friend, Detroit starter Milt Wilcox. "Uncle Miltie, we called him," Cruz said. They had dinner together that night in a Mexican restaurant called Armandos, across the street from Detroit Western High. Wilcox's mother joined them.

"How could you do that to my son, hit a home run against him?" she asked Cruz.

This was another example of Orioles magic—a .190 hitter turning in a Babe Ruth–like performance as soon as he put on an Orioles uniform. "Todd Cruz drives in six runs in his first game," McGregor said. "That's us, that was the way things were. We picked up guys and they produced. It just seemed to happen."

It wouldn't last, as Cruz wound up hitting just three home runs, driving in 27 runs, and batting .208 for Baltimore for the rest of the year.

But any offense he provided was gravy, because he delivered what he was supposed to—he brought the infield defense together. "We were always known as a defensive team, and I was going back between second and third," Dauer said. "When Todd got there, he just shut down third base. He was a tremendous defensive player and had a tremendous arm. He made some great athletic plays down there, and I think that is part of the reason why our pitching really took off down the stretch. Once you have a great defense, pitchers don't worry as much about making a mistake."

Storm Davis, who got the win in that 9–5 victory, confirmed that the pitching staff was elated to have Cruz behind them now. "I was thrilled when we got him," Davis said. "He solidified the infield. And he had a cannon for an arm."

It was a legendary arm, one so powerful that pitchers were warned to make sure they stayed low to avoid getting nailed with a throw, an arm so powerful that first basemen would complain about how hard the ball came in. "Eddie [Murray] would get mad at me because I would break his glove throwing the ball over," Cruz said. "He had two of them and would keep one on the bench. I would gun it over. I got some complaints from other guys, George Brett and Rod Carew, about bruising their hands. I would gun it and throw it straight to the base. Rod once told me, 'Stop throwing the ball so hard.' I said, 'This is not Little League. This is the big leagues. Catch the damn ball. I'll throw it as hard as I want.' What am I supposed to do, lob it over so I don't hurt his little pinky? If you have an arm, you show it."

While the club was happy about their new addition, it was still faced with a number of unanswered questions. Jim Palmer's status was on hold as he still suffered from a sore shoulder, and Dennis Martinez was still struggling. McGregor would beat the Tigers 7–2 the next day, but Detroit pounded Mike Boddicker for five runs in just 2⅔ innings and defeated Baltimore 10–1. The following day, with the score tied at 4–4 after four innings, the series finale was called because of rain.

Palmer went on the disabled list for the second time because of triceps tendinitis. The Orioles were hardly sinking going into the All-Star break with a record of 42–34 and in second place in the AL East, just one game out of first place. But the starting rotation was unsettling, and his teammates publicly wished he had tried to stick it out. "He could still give us a good five innings," Sammy Stewart told reporters. "We need an older pitcher in the rotation." Soon, Stewart would have bigger problems than Jim Palmer's status.

Two Orioles were named to the All-Star squad—Murray and Ripken (his first of what would be 18 straight midsummer classics), though neither player had been elected. The fact that the Orioles did not have one starter elected to the American League squad, yet were competing for the AL East title, is more evidence of how much of a "team" this squad was and not a unit that succeeded solely because of their super-star players.

Most players—those who aren't playing in the game—welcome the All-Star break for the couple of days of rest they get before the second half of the season begins. Sometimes, though, a player is better off without so much time on his hands. Sammy Stewart fell into that latter category. The reliever was arrested for driving while intoxicated early in the morning on the day play was supposed to resume with a home series against the Mariners. Stewart was stopped at about 5:30 A.M. by a state trooper who said he saw Stewart's car weaving from shoulder to shoulder on the Baltimore Beltway. Stewart said he had been at a friend's birthday party and before that was visiting his son, who suffered from cystic fibrosis, at the hospital.

The arrest came as no surprise to those who knew him. Stewart, a good old boy from Asheville, North Carolina, was well liked by his team-mates. But he enjoyed having a good time without the benefit of bound-aries, a flaw that sometimes led to trouble. "Sammy was a live wire," said bullpen coach Elrod Hendricks. "He would say, 'I'm a little tired, but give me the ball.' You could depend on Sammy to keep things loose. And he did an outstanding job on the field."

Ray Miller said, "Out of the bullpen, Stewart had as good of stuff as anyone in the league, a four-pitch pitcher."

Stewart was signed as a free agent after two years of community college in North Carolina. He had been drafted by the Royals earlier, but he did not sign. He wasn't drafted by anyone in the June 1975 draft, though, and signed with Baltimore after attending a major league tryout camp in Asheville. He moved up through the minor league system one step at a time, primarily as a starter—Bluefield in 1975, Miami in 1976,

Charlotte and Rochester in 1977, and Rochester again in 1978—until he arrived in Baltimore with the September call-ups. He made a great impression in his major league debut by striking out seven straight batters, setting a major league record for most strikeouts in a debut game. In 5⅓ innings, he struck out nine and beat the White Sox in the second game of a doubleheader. But though he made two starts that September, his future with the Orioles was as a long reliever. Over five seasons before 1983, Stewart pitched in 133 games—23 of them starts—and 499 innings.

"Sammy could literally throw every day," Storm Davis said. "He had a phenomenal recovery time. He could throw five innings and could turn around and throw two or three the next day. In my 13 years in the big leagues, Gene Nelson with Oakland was the only other guy I saw who could do that. Sammy would come in the game in the middle or late or whatever you needed him to do. He would throw strikes and get the ball over the plate and get people out.

"Sammy was a little bit different, and he enjoyed life," continued Davis. "But on the field he had as much talent as anyone there was out there. Whether you needed a starter or a closer or a long man or a set-up guy, Sammy had the kind of durability to do it all."

Stewart went 9–4 during the championship season, but lasted just two more seasons with Baltimore before he went to play for the Red Sox in 1986, then Cleveland in 1987. He left the game with a respectable career mark of 59–48. Life got worse for Stewart without baseball. In 1988, he was arrested in Chelsea, Massachusetts, and charged with cocaine and weapons possession. One year later, he was arrested for stealing $350 worth of merchandise from four stores in an Asheville mall. And in 1990, he was charged with second-degree kidnapping for holding his wife captive at their home. He suffered through the tragedy of having his two children die, and he is now out of touch with his old teammates. "Sammy, he has been through some wars," Rick Dempsey said.

Besides the Stewart arrest, the Orioles were dealing with a "mystery" illness that hit Tippy Martinez—it turned out to be appendicitis. It was not a good All-Star break for the Orioles. The loss of Martinez, who had already made 34 appearances that season and had 10 saves with a 5–3 record and a 3.17 ERA, would appear to be a devastating blow to the team. He was the life preserver that helped keep them afloat through the first half of the year.

Then a Palmer controversy hit the papers. Reports claimed that the terms of Palmer's contract dictated he would be a free agent at the end of the season, something that Palmer vehemently denied.

This was the backdrop of the Orioles' return to the field for the second half of the season, and they again lost the first game of a home series with Seattle, 3–0, to Jim Beattie. They followed that with another loss, 3–2, to the Mariners. This one—their third straight loss, dropping them to three games behind the first-place Blue Jays—was particularly disturbing for two reasons: Stewart, making his first appearance after his arrest, gave up the winning run in the top of the tenth inning; and Tippy Martinez went on the disabled list after undergoing an emergency appendectomy. "It's a big loss for us," a dejected Altobelli said. Allan Ramirez, who had been sent back down to Rochester when Palmer came off the disabled list the first time, was recalled from Rochester, as was reliever Paul Mirabella.

It sure seemed like a big loss, but upon reflection, Tippy Martinez's appendicitis may have saved the season for Baltimore. "The appendectomy probably saved his career," bullpen coach Elrod Hendricks said. "His arm was just starting to ache and bother him. It seemed like he was in every game. It was a blessing in disguise. When he came back, he picked up right where he left off."

McGregor agreed that the layup ultimately had a positive effect. "Tippy had that appendectomy, which probably helped him, because he was up every night, and this gave his arm a break and gave him the strength to go down the wire," he said.

At the time, though, it seemed like bad news piled on top of more bad news, and they needed a big performance to hold off what appeared to be a tailspin. Boddicker delivered that big performance— a 2–0, five-hit shutout win over Seattle. It was indicative of the value of Boddicker during that 1983 season. "Mike Boddicker was really the savior of our starting rotation that year," Altobelli said. "He won the big games for us. He was always the starter after we lost."

Boddicker's performance propelled the Orioles on to a six-game winning streak. Dennis Martinez gave up five runs in 6⅔ innings in the first game of a three-game series against Oakland, but his teammates managed to score seven on home runs by Murray and Ken Singleton in a 7–6 victory. Ramirez won the second game 3–1, as the rookie came through with his best performance of the season, allowing just one run through eight innings. Murray belted another home run, a two-run blast in the bottom of the eighth, to get Ramirez the win. Tim Stoddard came in for the ninth inning to earn the save. In the next game, Davis held the Athletics to two runs through six innings, and Stewart blanked them for three innings of relief in a 6–2 win for a sweep of Oakland. McGregor kept the streak going, to no one's surprise, because he faced the Angels, a team he owned, and came away with a complete-game 5–1 win. Boddicker, who started the streak, earned the final win of the run, another complete game, saving the beleaguered bullpen in a 10–4 beating of Anaheim. He was supported by Murray's third straight game with a home run and triples by Murray, Dempsey, and Mike Young.

That was the season for Baltimore so far—a run of winning and then a run of losing. But what was so particularly unusual for the Orioles that year was all of the drama off the field, and another ugly episode was about to take place. Reports hit the papers that Dauer and Stewart had testified before a federal grand jury hearing evidence against two alleged cocaine dealers. *The Evening Sun* reported that neither player was the target of the federal probe. This was around the time of the drug scandals that rocked the game, particularly in Pittsburgh, where a probe revealed that a number of players had been involved in drug use. "This is more controversy than I've ever seen around here," Ray Miller told reporters.

Despite the winning streak, Baltimore, now with a record of 48–36, was still in second place. The run ended when Dennis Martinez continued his dismal pitching, giving up five runs in 4⅓ innings pitched in an 8–5 loss to the Angels in the third game of the series. But then, despite all of the controversy and the roster problems—Tippy Martinez, Mike Flanagan, and Palmer, remember, were all still on the disabled list, as was Dan Ford—they started another winning stretch, thanks to Ramirez. The rookie pitcher tossed a complete-game four-hitter in an 11–1 win in the final game of the series. "He pitched some awesome games for us when we needed it," Miller said.

The Orioles headed west for a 10-game road trip, and Davis started it off with a 9–4 win over Seattle at the Kingdome, followed by an 8–1 win the next day by McGregor. Ford came off the disabled list for the final game of the series against Seattle. Altobelli called Ford into his office and said, "Dan, we're going to get you some at-bats to get your bat going, so we're going to lead you off today." Ford responded by turning in one of those games that certainly fall under the category of Orioles magic. He had not played in four weeks, and he swung the bat just three times in the game. But all three were home runs—big blasts—in a 4–2 victory over the Mariners, which put Baltimore back in first place in a tie with Toronto.

"I was ready to play," Ford said. "There was some talk that I wasn't ready to come back and I wouldn't do that good. So I said, 'OK, I'll show you I'm ready. Let's get this thing going again.' And we did."

That was one of the signs that made 1983 appear to be a season of destiny for Baltimore. "Dan Ford is out for about a month, and in his first game back he hits three home runs," Singleton said. "We're all thinking, 'This is not this easy. A guy comes off the disabled list and hits three home runs in his first game back.'"

It sure seemed that way. The Orioles, with Boddicker, Stewart, and Stoddard on the mound, won their fourth straight, and had sole possession of first place, with a 52–37 record. But then they suffered two straight losses to Oakland—9–7 and 4–3. In the first game, Baltimore, because of its depleted starting rotation, was forced to start Mirabella, and he lasted just 2⅔ innings while allowing three runs on four hits and three walks. Baltimore wound up using five pitchers in that game. With the score tied at 7–7, Oakland scored two runs in the bottom of the eighth off relievers Dan Morogiello and Stoddard. Ramirez suffered his first major league defeat in the second game. The second defeat dropped Baltimore back into second place, with three teams—the Orioles, Yankees, and Tigers—bunched closely behind the first-place Blue Jays. But again, they came back to win the next two over the Athletics—Storm Davis winning 7–3, behind home runs by Murray and Cal Ripken, and McGregor nailing a 4–3 win, a vintage gutsy performance. Oakland mustered 10 hits but just three runs in the complete-game victory. Given the uncertainty of the bullpen—the use it had been through recently, plus the absence of its anchor, Tippy Martinez—

complete games were extremely valuable, and this one put Baltimore, with a 54–39 record, back in first place.

The Orioles went south to Anaheim for the final three games of the road trip and lost the first one 5–2, as Tommy John outpitched Boddicker. Now the AL East was a dead heat, with the Orioles, Tigers, Blue Jays, and Yankees all tied for first place. But Baltimore rebounded to win the next game, 5–4, in an interesting turn of events. Altobelli had finally seen enough of Dennis Martinez in the rotation—even given how the rotation had been decimated by injuries—and put him in the bullpen. So what happens? He comes in to relieve Mirabella after three innings and pitches six innings of one-run ball to get the victory, thanks to another Murray home run that broke a fifth-inning 3–3 tie. Then Ramirez gave them 5⅓ innings of good-enough pitching, allowing three runs, to get another win. He and Stewart, who finished the game in relief, had a pretty good cushion to work with—a 10–4 margin of victory. Ripken contributed the most to that margin, with three RBIs in a four-hit game. One day Murray, the next day Ripken. The two men were the heart of the order.

Ripken would eventually prove to be much more than that. He would wind up being the heart of the franchise until he retired after the 2001 season. He became a baseball icon, on par with the likes of Joe DiMaggio, and captured the attention of an entire nation in 1995 when he broke Lou Gehrig's 2,130 consecutive-games record. It came on the heels of the worst labor dispute in the history of professional sports, a players strike that had resulted in the cancellation of the 1994 playoffs and World Series. Ripken's inspiring record run has been widely credited with rejuvenating interest in baseball. Through much of his career, Ripken was the face of the franchise, particularly during the difficult losing years that plagued the club in the mid- to late eighties as well as the franchise's up-and-down years in the nineties.

In this championship season—just Ripken's second full season—he emerged as a star but was not *the* franchise star just yet. Murray was already a three-time All-Star, and Singleton was also a well-known player and one of the team leaders. Then, of course, there was Palmer, a future Hall of Famer. This was also not a team that rode on the shoulders of its star players, even though Ripken would go on to have an outstanding season—27 home runs, 102 RBIs, league highs in hits (211) and runs (121), and a .318 average. He would beat out Murray for the 1983 AL Most Valuable Player award. This, again, was a team whose single contributors, such as an Allan Ramirez, called up for some spot starts, were perhaps just as important as its stars. Ripken, though, stood out for another reason. He was Orioles family.

There is no way to overestimate the impact of the Ripken family on the Baltimore Orioles. While Cal Ripken Jr. was the family member who was best known—one of the most revered and recognized figures in all of baseball—his father, Cal Ripken Sr., had as much influence on the success of the Orioles franchise as any other person in the history of the club. His influence, though, took place behind the scenes, in such places as Aberdeen, South Dakota, Elmira, New York, Asheville, North Carolina, and other small towns where future Orioles greats came through the minor league system and learned the Oriole Way from the elder Ripken. "We always talked about the Oriole Way," Ray Miller said. "Cal Ripken Sr. was the one who indoctrinated every one of us who came in."

He taught generations about the right way to play the game, from Jim Palmer to Eddie Murray to Chris Hoiles. From the time he first began as a minor league Orioles manager in 1961 until his last year as a Baltimore coach in 1993, he had an impact on the careers of several generations of ballplayers. "I learned work ethic from Cal Ripken Sr.," Palmer said. "That was one of the things that Senior taught us. Work ethic was one of the variables in baseball you could control. Paying attention on the bench was one of the variables you could control. Passion was one of the variables you could control. Rooting for your teammates was one of the variables you could control. All of these were integral parts of what I learned in A ball from Cal Sr. Those were all instilled. You are taught certain things and then they are enforced, sort of like a tradition, and it all started with Cal Sr."

Eddie Murray also credits Cal Sr. with setting the tone for the Oriole Way. "Cal Sr. was a good man," Murray said. "You saw what it was like to have someone care 100 percent about kids. This man would be out there early in the morning, fixing the field. Somehow he would fit in a sandwich, and then you would see him coming off the field at 10:00 or

11:00 at night. That is dedication. That is caring about somebody. When you think about Cal Sr., that is what you think about."

Senior, who won 964 games as a minor league manager, was eventually brought up as a coach with the major league club in 1976 as a key member of Earl Weaver's staff. Even though he was passed over by owner Edward Bennett Williams to manage the club when Weaver retired after the 1982 season, he did finally get a chance to manage the Orioles when Weaver resigned after coming back for his second stint. However, he was fired six games into the 1988 season, while the club was 0–6; he wound up with an overall major league managing record of 68–101. Many observers believe he had not been given a fair shot at managing. Frank Robinson, who replaced Ripken Sr., would go on to lose the next 15 games in that infamous 0–21 start in 1988. Ripken Sr. remained with the Orioles as a coach until he was let go after the 1993 season. Six years later, at the age of 63, he died of lung cancer.

There are two memorials in the Orioles dugout at Camden Yards. One is the No. 4 on a plaque on the entrance from the dugout down to the tunnel to the clubhouse. It reads, "Earl Weaver. Manager, 1968–1982 and 1985–1986. Hall of Fame induction, August 3, 1996."

A second plaque hangs on the wall of the dugout, above where the players sit. It has a photo image of Cal Ripken Sr., and it reads, "Cal Ripken, Sr., 1935–1999. Dedicated to a lifelong Oriole of 36 years and one of the game's greatest teachers, coaches, managers and devoted mentors to countless young Orioles. Senior dedicated his life to baseball and passed on his respect for the game to everyone he coached. He preached 'perfect practice makes perfect' and stressed the importance of being prepared, learning the 'right way,' and playing to the best of one's abilities every inning of every game. We will always remember his devotion to the Orioles, his love of the game and his many lessons."

This was the baseball atmosphere that Cal Ripken Jr. grew up in— accompanying his father to minor league ballparks as a young boy and growing up surrounded by some of the greatest players in the game, with one of the greatest teachers being his father. Cal Jr. became a baseball star at Aberdeen High School in Aberdeen, Maryland, and was selected by Baltimore in the second round of the 1978 draft. In high school, he was as good a pitcher as he was a shortstop—perhaps even better—and those within the Orioles organization debated over how he would be developed. Weaver, who was a big fan of the young Ripken, insisted that he should come up as a shortstop, despite his size. At that time, 6'4" shortstops were very rare.

Ripken moved through the minor league system quickly, starting in Bluefield in 1978 and emerging with Double-A Charlotte in 1980 as a power hitter, with 25 home runs. He followed that up with 23 home runs in 114 games with Triple-A Rochester the following year. While he was in Charlotte, Ripken began to see most of his playing time at third base, where he was being groomed by the organization. Mark Belanger was nearing the end of his career with Baltimore, and another young shortstop prospect, Bob Bonner, who had been picked in the third round in the 1978 draft, was considered the heir to the position. Ripken was called up to Baltimore in August 1981, played 23 games, and made the major league roster coming out of spring training in 1982. Ripken won American League Rookie of the Year honors with 28 home runs, 93 RBIs, and a .264 average. He began the season at third base, but switched to shortstop on July 1—one month after he began a consecutive-games streak that would not stop until September 20, 1998—2,632 games later. Ripken retired after the 2001 season with the greatest power numbers ever seen by a shortstop, plus an impressive fielding resume that paved the way for future big men with power, such as Alex Rodriguez, to play the position as well. He finished his career with 431 home runs, 1,695 RBIs, and 3,184 hits—one of six players in the history of the game who had 3,000 hits and 400 home runs.

While Ripken was growing up, the Orioles were the crown jewel organization in baseball, having won or competed for first place for a stretch that began in 1966 and continued through his first full year in 1982, when it came down to the last game of the season against the Brewers to decide the AL East. And then there was 1983, when he played on a winning World Series champion team in just his second year. He figured that this would be the way his career would continue, because that was the history of the Orioles. But 1983 would be the last time Ripken would make it to the World Series. He came close on the 1996 and 1997 teams, when, with Davey Johnson as manager, the Orioles reached the ALCS two straight years, but little did Ripken know that 1983 would be the end of Baltimore's championship run.

Because of that, the future Hall of Famer has a special appreciation for that 1983 squad. "Having gone through a World Series championship and then having never won another championship through my whole career, the rest of the 20 years you appreciate how difficult it is," he said.

He said he had no indication that 1983 would be the last of a great run, and he didn't get the feeling that this group of Orioles sensed the end was near. "There is a special set of circumstances which you have to be part of a good team," Ripken said. "Then things have to play out and build as the year goes on. Just because you are a good team doesn't mean it carries over to the next year. I don't think there was a sense of urgency by some of the players, thinking this was their last chance. I never got that feeling. I got the feeling that we knew we were good. We liked each other and we felt there was good talent and good chemistry on the team. We felt we were capable of taking it a little bit further."

They took it further after Ripken's four-hit game by coming back home and beating Texas 8–6, with Murray getting the big hit—a bases-loaded single in the bottom of the eighth inning. Texas had taken a 6–5 lead in the top of the inning on a wild pitch, but Murray came through with the game-winning hit. He drove in three runs and had 19 runs batted in in his last 20 games, and Ripken continued his hot hitting with three hits, scoring three runs. Stewart got the win in relief for Baltimore, which had now won 15 of their last 19 games and remained in first place with a record of 57–40. The Orioles would go on to sweep the Rangers, winning 7–4 in another comeback effort, with McGregor getting his 13th win of the season and 5th in a row, and getting a 6–0 shutout from Boddicker, with another home run by Murray—his 21st of the season—in the series finale. Boddicker faced just thirty batters, only three over the minimum, and allowed just four hits. With a record of 7–5, he got his third shutout of the season, tying him with the Yankees' Ron Guidry for the league lead. He also had a remarkable record at Memorial Stadium—6–0 with a 1.69 ERA in seven starts.

It was a short homestand, and the Orioles left for Cleveland with a five-game winning streak and a 59–40 record. Before that, though, they would make a brief trip to Cooperstown to play in the Hall of Fame exhibition game as part of the ceremonies to commemorate the induction of Orioles great Brooks Robinson. It was the first visit to the Hall of

Fame for Murray, who would be elected 20 years later, and his memory of that trip illustrates how oblivious he was to such honors when he was playing—and how important his relationships with his teammates were to him. "The only time I went to the Hall of Fame was when we played a game up there," Murray said, recalling the exhibition game against St. Louis, which Baltimore won 2–0. "I led off, Cal hit second, we both got base hits, and we were in the gym playing basketball against each other the rest of the afternoon. That is how our friendship was."

Baltimore fans were paying attention, though, and a crowd of more than twelve thousand showed up in Cooperstown to pay tribute to Robinson. Baltimore mayor William Donald Schaefer attended the event, as did Orioles cheerleader Wild Bill Hagy, who led the crowd in his familiar Orioles cheers. "I must be the luckiest man in the world," Robinson told the crowd. "I keep asking, 'How could any one man be so fortunate?' It's more than any one human being could ask for. . . . One of my blessings was to play in Baltimore. I share this day with my adopted hometown, which supported Brooks Robinson on good and bad days. Baltimore, thank you. I love you all."

The club made the trip from Cooperstown to Cleveland, and just like that they lost two straight to the Indians. Dennis Martinez pitched well, allowing three runs, one earned, over six innings, but they lost 3–1 to Bert Blyleven. Murray didn't belt a home run, but he did crack a double, one of just six hits for Baltimore. Ramirez didn't last long in the second game, leaving after 3⅔ innings and after being reached for three runs on five hits and three walks as the Orioles lost 4–3. But the Orioles found their offense in the final two games of the series. Davis earned his 10th win against four losses in an 8–2 beating of the Indians, as Murray continued to lead the way with a home run and a double, and they finished the series with a split by getting a 4–3 victory. Scott McGregor's record was now 14–4, and, with Palmer and Flanagan both out, the left-hander had stepped up to assume the role as leader of the staff at a time when the team needed him the most. With youngsters such as Boddicker, Davis, and Ramirez, it was important to have a veteran set the tone. McGregor did that and more.

McGregor was a gift to the Orioles from the New York Yankees, coming to Baltimore in the deal that set the stage for the great run from

Joe Altobelli was not the first choice to replace the legendary Earl Weaver as manager at the start of the 1983 season—at least not for most of the players. But his more laid-back approach turned out to be exactly what the veteran ballclub needed. Photo courtesy of Bettmann/Corbis.

In just his second full season—his first at shortstop—Cal Ripken established himself as a team leader, batted .318 with 27 home runs and 102 RBIs, and was voted the 1983 American League Most Valuable Player. Photo courtesy of AP/Wide World Photos.

Switch-hitting slugger Eddie Murray, shown here hitting his second home run in Game 5 of the World Series, put up career numbers in 1983 with 33 home runs, 111 RBIs, and a .306 average. Photo courtesy of AP/Wide World Photos.

Baltimore's role players collectively contributed as much to the 1983 championship as did the stars. Here Benny Ayala is congratulated after scoring what would prove to be the game-winning run in Game 3 of the World Series. Photo courtesy of AP/Wide World Photos.

After finally getting a legitimate chance with the big-league club in 1983, 25-year-old rookie Mike Boddicker responded by going 16–8 with a 3.95 ERA, including an ALCS-record 14-strikeout shutout against the White Sox. Photo courtesy of AP/Wide World Photos.

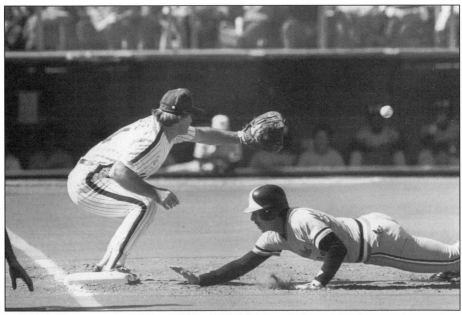

Todd Cruz, shown diving back to first base ahead of Pete Rose's tag in Game 4 of the World Series, turned out to be a key midseason acquisition from Seattle. Photo courtesy of AP/Wide World Photos.

John Lowenstein, shown here homering in Game 2 against the Phillies, teamed with Gary Roenicke to form one of the more successful platoons in recent history. Together in 1983 the pair combined to hit 34 home runs and drive in 124 runs. Photo courtesy of AP/Wide World Photos.

After his disappointing first season in Baltimore, it seemed as if Dan Ford (left) could do no wrong in 1983. Photo courtesy of *The Baltimore Sun*.

With Mike Flanagan fighting injuries and Jim Palmer nearing the end of his career, left-hander Scott McGregor—an 18-game winner in 1983—stepped into the number one starter's role.
Photo courtesy of AP/Wide World Photos.

Jim Palmer struggled with injuries the entire 1983 season and posted just five wins against four losses, but his role in tutoring the staff was invaluable. He did pick up this World Series win in a rare appearance out of the bullpen. Photo courtesy of AP/Wide World Photos.

Eddie Murray broke out of his postseason slump in a big way against Charles Hudson and the Phillies in Game 5, belting two home runs to pace the World Series–clinching victory. Photo courtesy of AP/Wide World Photos.

A liability with the bat for most of his 24-year career, Rick Dempsey broke through in the 1983 World Series, hitting .385 with two home runs to earn Most Valuable Player honors. Photo courtesy of AP/Wide World Photos.

1979 to 1983. He was the Yankees' first-round selection in the 1972 draft and moved through the Yankees system until he came to Baltimore in the June 15, 1976, trade that sent McGregor, Dempsey, Tippy Martinez, Rudy May, and Dave Pagan to Baltimore in exchange for pitchers Doyle Alexander, Ken Holtzman, and Grant Jackson and catcher Elrod Hendricks. McGregor started out with Triple-A Rochester but was a September call-up to Baltimore that year, and he made the team coming out of spring training in 1977. He pitched out of the bullpen for most of that season, going 3–5 with a 4.42 ERA in 29 appearances, with only 5 of them starts. He broke out to become a consistent winning starter in 1978, with a record of 15–13 with a 3.32 ERA. After a 13–6 record during the 1979 pennant-winning season, McGregor had his career year, posting a 20–8 record with a 3.32 ERA, in 1980. Like most pitchers, he struggled with some arm problems throughout his career, particularly in 1982 when he had a 14–12 record but an uncharacteristic 4.42 ERA. He went 2–5 in his last 13 starts with a 6.83 ERA, plagued by weakness in his left shoulder. But he bounced back in 1983 to lead the young staff to the World Series championship, posting a record of 18–7 with a 3.18 ERA while pitching a career-high 260 innings. His career would start heading on the downhill side after 1983, until he retired in 1988 with a career mark of 138–108.

If Palmer was the voice of the Orioles pitching staff, and Flanagan was the heart, McGregor represented the steady nerves. "Scotty had an inner confidence about himself when he walked out on the mound," Dempsey said. "It didn't matter if he was up or down in the game. He had the same tempo all the time. It was amazing he could go up there and throw some of the pitches that he would throw in certain situations. He had that magical speed. It wasn't very hard or very soft, and the hitter had to provide his own power to drive the ball through the infield. He would get the ball to move enough to throw the hitter off balance. Scott had pinpoint control."

McGregor credited the system—the Oriole Way—for giving those young pitchers that year a framework with which to succeed. "There was a way of doing business, a proper way," he said. "It was simply doing fundamentals right, doing things right, practicing right, and not beating yourself.

"We had a lot of guys that came through for us that year."

Still, it was McGregor's excellence that helped the Orioles get through their pitching injuries and still be a first-place team. He believes that 1983 was his best season. "I won 18 games that year, but I thought I pitched better that year than I did the year I won 20 games, in 1980," he said. "It just didn't work out to 20 wins that year."

Things seemed to be working out for the Orioles in early August. They were in first place with a record of 61–42 and coming back home to play another series against the White Sox. It was Brooks Robinson Night at Memorial Stadium, with a crowd of about forty thousand on hand. Though the game was delayed by rain, the Orioles came back in the bottom of the ninth inning to score three runs and beat Chicago 5–4. With two outs and nobody on base, Ripken singled. Then Murray singled. John Lowenstein singled, driving in Ripken. Singleton singled, scoring Murray. And Dauer got the game-winning single off reliever Dick Tidrow to score pinch-runner John Shelby. It was a great night for the Orioles, and good things appeared to be ahead. Flanagan was coming off the disabled list and scheduled to make his first start in three months in the series finale against the White Sox. Palmer was scheduled to make a rehabilitation start in Hagerstown the day after. What could go wrong?

Nearly everything.

7 | A Savior from East Palatka

The White Sox and the Orioles were on the road to a destined meeting at the end of the 1983 season. When the White Sox came to Baltimore, they were on an eight-game losing streak at Memorial Stadium—then lost their ninth straight on Brooks Robinson Night in Baltimore. And it looked as if they would lose their 10th straight in Baltimore, even though Chicago led by a 6–0 margin after five innings. The Sox knocked Dennis Martinez out of the box after 4⅔ innings, and the pitcher left the game hearing boos from the hometown fans. But the Orioles came back to score three in the bottom of the sixth, thanks to a two-run home run by Gary Roenicke and an RBI hit by Dan Ford, who went 3-for-4 that night. And Ken Singleton made it a 6–4 game with an RBI single in the bottom of the eighth. But after suffering through a blown lead the day before, this time the White Sox bullpen would hold the lead and get the 6–4 win, breaking their Memorial Stadium jinx. Eddie Murray, who had strained his knee on Friday night, did not play. He had played in 204 consecutive games before sitting this one out. Cal Ripken was at 223 straight and counting.

Chicago's win, though, seemed to cast a new spell, and this one was hanging over the Orioles when everything should have been falling into place for them. Mike Flanagan made his first start since May 18—against the very team that he suffered his knee injury against. Fans stood and cheered as the left-hander made his way from the bullpen to the dugout after his pregame workout. "The fan reaction made me feel good," Flanagan said after the game. "It got me pumped up more than I might have been at that moment. I was just trying to stay relaxed and to remember what I did before to make me 6–0."

What he did do was give up four runs in 4⅔ innings, as Flanagan wound up losing his first game of the season 4–3. Meanwhile, up in Hagerstown, Jim Palmer deemed his rehabilitation start for the minor league Suns a success. He gave up two runs on seven hits and said he pitched pain-free. It was a boon for the Suns, who normally drew about 1,000 fans a game but had a crowd of about 6,100 on hand to watch Palmer pitch—along with about 34 reporters and photographers, from *Sports Illustrated* to *The New York Times* and ABC-TV. "My arm felt a lot better than I thought it would," Palmer told reporters. "I was surprised it felt as good as it did. I just hope it feels that well the next time. Today I just tried to throw the ball over."

The Indians arrived next in Baltimore, and the Orioles lost their third straight, 9–4. Storm Davis was blasted for eight runs in just 2⅔ innings, and Dennis Martinez—banished to the bullpen after Flanagan returned to the rotation—gave up the ninth run in relief. Murray sat out again, and it was clear the Orioles missed their big bat and leader on the field. He had been on a tear, batting .483 (14-for-29) over eight games before he was hurt. The loss gave Baltimore a record of 62–45, and though they remained in first place, it was by a slim margin—a half-game lead over the Tigers. They managed to hang onto that lead despite losing their next two games, by identical scores of 4–3, with Scott McGregor and Mike Boddicker taking the losses, for a three-game sweep by the Indians. All three Cleveland pitchers—Rick Sutcliffe, Neal Heaton, and Lary Sorensen—had complete-game victories. The only good news for the Orioles was the return of reliever Tippy Martinez from the disabled list.

The Orioles appeared to be in a potentially devastating free fall at the worst time—about to head to Chicago for a four-game series with the White Sox again. And even with Murray back in the lineup, the Orioles couldn't stop the losing streak, dropping their sixth straight, a 9–3 thumping, with Floyd Bannister getting the victory for Chicago. Allan Ramirez, who had come through for the club when he had first come up earlier in the season, now lost his third straight game, as he was slammed for six runs on four hits and five walks in just 2⅓ innings pitched. Murray went 0-for-4, striking out three times. And the Orioles dropped from first place to third in the AL East, falling behind the Tigers and the Yankees. The only positive that came out of the loss was that Lenn Sakata broke a career 0-for-66 drought against White Sox pitching, singling to center in the top of the seventh inning.

The feud between the White Sox and the Orioles was exacerbated because Chicago manager Tony LaRussa believed the Orioles were showing the White Sox up because some players on the bench had their hats turned around and were cheering for Sakata to break his 0-for-66 slump when he got his hit. Altobelli was angry that LaRussa would accuse him of trying to show anyone up, and he told a Chicago writer, "You tell Tony that I'm mad at him for thinking I would show him up. We got a guy on our club who had never gotten a hit off the White Sox, and some of the guys on the bench were doing things like turning their hats around to try to break the jinx. We're rooting for a guy to get a hit, and he thinks I'm showing him up. I've never walked into a clubhouse and ridiculed another manager, and he's done it to me twice. It's crazy. I don't understand it, and to tell you the truth, I don't want to."

The season seemed to be spinning out of control now. The Orioles dropped their seventh in a row, this one a tough 2–1 defeat to Chicago pitcher La Marr Hoyt, who would conjure up nightmares for Orioles hitters. It was a particularly deflating loss, since Flanagan, in the second start of his comeback, pitched well, not allowing an earned run through six innings (Chicago's two runs came as a result of errors by Ripken and Todd Cruz). Hoyt, on his way to a Cy Young season, won his 15th, striking out nine in the process. Orioles hitters were batting .207 during this seven-game losing streak and had 31 strikeouts in their last three games. The tension was taking its toll in the dugout, as Altobelli was tossed out of the game in the eighth inning for arguing a called third strike on Jim Dwyer. The Orioles were now in fourth place, though they were just one game out of first in the bunched-up AL East. It equaled the longest losing streak of the season for Baltimore. "Those seven-game losing streaks were rough," Ray Miller recalled.

The only sliver of good news came from Hagerstown, where Palmer had another successful outing, pitching eight innings, allowing three earned runs—each on solo home runs—and six hits. He said he threw even better than he did in his first start. "I was pleased with the command of my pitches," he told reporters.

But the Orioles needed a pitcher the next day for the third game of the series against Chicago, and it couldn't be Palmer. They had made yet another call to Rochester for an unproven starter to bail them out—under the most desperate of times, a seven-game losing streak, and under the most difficult conditions, facing the AL West–leading White Sox. Bill Swaggerty, with a 9–5 record at Rochester, got the call, and another improbable hero would save the 1983 season for the Orioles.

There may be no better single figure to illustrate the beauty of the 1983 team than Swaggerty. He was considered a decent prospect but not necessarily one of the franchise's future pitching stars. He grew up in East Palatka, Florida, just west of St. Augustine, and had been a high school pitching star—the first player from East Palatka to make the major leagues. He went on to play ball at Stetson University before signing with the Orioles. He moved through the system slowly, from Bluefield to Charlotte and then to Rochester—the limbo for young Orioles pitchers, who, like Boddicker, toiled while waiting for a slim chance to break into the standout Baltimore pitching staff.

Swaggerty, who was 26 at the time, was scheduled to pitch in the Triple-A All-Star Game when he was called into manager Lance Nichols' office. "He said, 'I got good news and bad news,'" Swaggerty said. "The bad news was that I wouldn't be able to play in the All-Star Game. The good news was that it was because I was going to join the Orioles in Chicago. It was a wonderful tradeoff."

"When I got the call, I was so excited I couldn't stand it," Swaggerty said. "Ever since I was five years old, it was my dream to play in the big leagues. Now I was about to realize a dream come true. I wasn't nervous until the next day. It was exciting to just make the trip to Chicago, put on the uniform, and just be in Comiskey Park and watch it that night."

Swaggerty had called his father, Herman Swaggerty, with the good news as soon as he learned of the call-up. "My dad was a huge influence on me and baseball growing up," he said. "He never played, but he watched it on television faithfully and knew how to teach the game. He taught me how to pitch from the time I was in Little League. He would tell me to watch this guy or that guy." One of the guys that Herman Swaggerty told his son Bill to watch was Jim Palmer.

He still recalls the excitement of being in an Orioles uniform in Comiskey Park as he sat on the bench charting Flanagan's pitches the day before he would start. "I had never been to the big leagues before," Swaggerty said. "I went to big-league camp in 1982, when I made the 40-man roster, so I had a little contact with these guys before, not that we had a lot of interaction. It was so eye-opening to feel the tension and electricity that night for a regular-season major league baseball game, as opposed to a spring-training game where everyone is relaxed and loose. The only tension in those games is for the guys who are on the bubble. It was very cool. I had been picturing what it would be like my entire life, and to sit there and soak it in was a thrill, even if I had never gotten a chance to pitch."

Swaggerty would get a chance to pitch, though—a big chance. On Saturday, August 13, little-known Bill Swaggerty was scheduled to start against veteran left-hander Jerry Koosman, who was going for his 200th career victory. He woke up early that day and went over to a mall on Michigan Avenue to have lunch and walk around. "I was sort of walking around in a daze because I don't think I had ever seen a mall that big or nice," he said. "There was marble everywhere. They don't have that kind of stuff in East Palatka." As he walked around, Swaggerty kept saying to himself, "Keep the ball down. Keep the ball down. Rick Dempsey is my catcher. He knows the hitters. Just try to hit the mitt."

He arrived at Comiskey Park at about 3:30 P.M. He was still muttering to himself, "Keep the ball down, throw strikes." His locker was next to a familiar face—Boddicker, his former Rochester teammate. "He was like the only guy I felt like I really knew," Swaggerty said. "I played with Cal, but I wanted to talk to a pitcher. He was telling me this guy is a fastball hitter, this guy is a curveball hitter, this guy you don't want to get behind in the count so make sure you try to get the first pitch over for a strike. He was giving me these tips."

Boddicker wasn't the only one. This veteran club was a team of coaches in some ways. McGregor and Flanagan also stopped by Swaggerty's locker to talk to him.

"Relax, you've got the best team in the American League behind you," Flanagan said.

Swaggerty walked out to the visiting bullpen at Comiskey Park with bullpen coach Elrod Hendricks. "Rook, if they didn't think you could win, you wouldn't be here," Hendricks said.

Ray Miller came out and, after watching him throw, told him the same thing. "If we didn't think you could win, we wouldn't have called you," Miller said. "We would have called somebody else. The main thing I want you to do is enjoy the moment. Have fun. We'll win."

Swaggerty was relaxed until he walked back from the bullpen to the dugout. The Chicago papers had published stories about the rookie pitcher who the White Sox hitters were going to feast on, and the fans were on Swaggerty. "I looked up and saw about thirty-five thousand people, and I started hearing the razzing about being a rookie," he said. "The crowd was giving it to me pretty good."

The Orioles went down in order in the top of the first, and Swaggerty took the mound in the bottom of the inning. The first hitter he faced was Rudy Law, who grounded to second for the first out of the inning. Scott Fletcher reached on an error. Harold Baines popped up to second, but Swaggerty walked Greg Luzinski and Tom Paciorek to load the bases. He was in trouble until Cal Ripken came in to talk to him.

Ripken was only in his second full season, but he had already taken command as a leader on the field. He was a well-versed student of the game, growing up with one of its greatest teachers as his father, and knew pitching very well, having been a star high school hurler himself. He would serve as a coach on the field throughout his career, and many times pitchers would look to him, even to call what pitches to throw for certain hitters.

Ripken went over to Swaggerty and said, "You've got to call your game."

"I looked at him like he had two heads," Swaggerty said. "I'm thinking, 'I got Rick Dempsey behind the plate. I'm throwing what Rick Dempsey calls. Who am I to shake off Rick Dempsey?'"

Miller came out of the dugout and joined the rest of the infielders at the mound for a conference. "You're nibbling," Miller said. "You've got good players behind you. You've got to throw strikes."

After everyone left the mound, Ripken came back again after Swaggerty went 2–0 on Greg Walker. "You've got to throw what got you here," he said.

"Then it clicked for me," Swaggerty said. "Dempsey had never caught me before. He was calling pitches that one of the other guys might throw in those situations, and he really didn't know what I had. That's when I realized what Cal was saying. So I shook Dempsey off a couple of times then. He was calling 2–0 breaking balls, which is great if you could get them over on the corners, but I needed to try to get ahead. I threw a 2–0 fastball that he [Walker] fouled off. Dempsey called for a curveball and I shook him off again. I threw a 2–1 fastball. So I got the count even, 2–2." With the bases loaded and two outs, Walker hit a fly ball to left to end the inning, with no runs scored.

"Dempsey didn't know me yet," Swaggerty said. "After he catches me for a few innings and sees what my ball can do, then he can set the hitters up with my stuff. It wasn't anything against Rick or anything. That was the turning point in the game for me. After that we were pretty much in sync."

Swaggerty gave up a run in the second and another one in the fourth, but holding the Chicago hitters to two runs through six innings was good enough to put the Orioles in a position to win.

"I felt good and strong after six innings, and thought I would get a chance to pitch in the seventh," Swaggerty said. "But Ray said, 'You've pitched too good to let an accident happen. We're going to turn it over to Sammy.'"

Stewart and Tippy Martinez pitched shutout relief for the last three innings. Ripken broke the game open with a two-run home run in the top of the eighth inning, and Baltimore won 5–2.

Swaggerty didn't get the win, but his impact went far beyond the six quality innings he pitched. He stopped the Orioles' seven-game losing streak and may have saved the season. After Bill Swaggerty took the mound on August 13, the roller-coaster ride was over. The Baltimore Orioles went 34–10 in their final 44 games, running away with the AL East.

"That was a big game Bill Swaggerty pitched for us," Altobelli said. "He held them down in the innings he gave us, and that is big for a young guy coming up to pitch from Triple-A."

Swaggerty was sent back down to Rochester after Palmer came off the disabled list later that month, then came back up with the September call-ups. Overall, he pitched well for the Orioles in his limited role, with a 1–1 record and a 2.91 ERA. He wasn't on the postseason roster, but he dressed for the ALCS against Chicago in case a pitcher got hurt. Altobelli asked Philadelphia manager Paul Owens if Swaggerty could dress and sit in the dugout for the World Series, but Owens refused to allow it. "I was in the clubhouse for the games," Swaggerty said. "But it was still a huge thrill to be around the Series. As exciting as it was during the regular season, it was 10 times that in the playoffs and World Series."

It wasn't as exciting for Swaggerty in 1984. He started the season in Rochester and got off to a 5–0 start, but after he was called up, he was used sporadically. He wound up spending the rest of his time with the Orioles going up and down between Rochester and Baltimore until he became a minor league free agent in 1987. He signed with the Kansas City Royals, but wound up with their Triple-A team in Omaha. Swaggerty called it quits the next year. He thinks if he hadn't been stuck behind such a quality pitching staff in the Orioles organization, he might have had more of a chance at a longer major league career. "But I wouldn't have traded my time with the Orioles for anything," he said. "The chance to be part of a world championship team and get a World Series ring meant so much more to me than maybe pitching an extra couple of years someplace else."

Things started falling the Orioles' way, so to speak, after that. The next day, the White Sox were beating them 1–0 in the bottom of the fifth. With a runner on first, Carlton Fisk lined a shot into the left-field seats that appeared to be a two-run home run. Third-base umpire Greg Kosc called it a home run. But Altobelli and the Orioles argued that a fan had reached down and caught the ball and brought it into the stands. The umpiring crew met on the field, then reversed the call, deciding that Fisk would stay at second with a double and Law would go back to third. Chicago manager Tony LaRussa went ballistic, then was tossed out of the game for pulling third base out of the ground and throwing it. At first he refused to leave the dugout until Altobelli came back out and complained to crew chief Jim Evans, who ordered LaRussa to leave the game.

McGregor, on the mound for Baltimore, intentionally walked the next hitter, Paciorek, loading the bases. Luzinski hit a pop foul for the second out, and Ron Kittle struck out to end the inning, with no runners crossing the plate.

Baltimore tied the game at 1–1 in the top of the sixth on a double by Ripken, a passed ball, and a sacrifice fly by Murray. Then Joe Nolan delivered the game-winning RBI single in the top of the ninth off White Sox starter Richard Dotson, who walked five but allowed just three hits in taking the complete-game loss. McGregor allowed eight hits and also walked five, but what happened the day before with the remarkable performance by Tippy Martinez put the Orioles on the sort of run where your starting pitcher can give up eight hits and walk five batters and still give up only one run. Tim Stoddard came in and retired the side in the bottom of the ninth for the save.

The victory gave Baltimore a 64–49 record and put them back into first place in the AL East. It also fueled the rivalry between the Orioles and the White Sox. After the game, LaRussa blasted the Orioles for appealing Fisk's home run. "All the Orioles do is cry and moan over every call, and pretty soon the calls don't go against them," he told reporters. "That gives them a good edge. They just moan, moan, moan, and the umpires get tired of listening to them . . . and that was a chicken thing they did about me being in the dugout. I can't believe they would think I would make that much of a difference in the game. I guess I should take it as some kind of compliment."

The feud continued in the Baltimore clubhouse. "What am I, an American Legion manager and he's a major league manager?" Altobelli responded to writers after the game. "Why can't I have the same priorities he does? Why can't I be a major league manager, too? What am I supposed to do, sit there and let them call a double a home run, and be a nice guy?"

The Orioles left Chicago before things got any uglier and headed for Arlington, Texas, and the good times continued to roll. Boddicker held the Rangers to three runs through six innings, good enough for a 6–4 victory, Baltimore's third win in a row. They lost to the Rangers the next day in a tough 2–0 defeat for Ramirez. But Baltimore would not lose too many more close games. Flanagan started the final game of the series against Texas, and he hung tough, allowing 10 hits but just two runs through nine innings, just enough for the Orioles to cling to a 2–2 tie until Mr. Clutch of 1983, Dan Ford, delivered the game-winning RBI double in the tenth. Ripken, who had his third four-hit game of the season, followed with another RBI double for an insurance run, and

Tim Stoddard came in to close out the 4–2 victory, his third save in four days. Most notably, it was Flanagan's first win since May 11, giving him a 7–2 record, though it was a painful one. After the game, Flanagan's left foot was bleeding because of the hard mound at Arlington Stadium. The Orioles now had a 66–50 mark. However, even though they had won four of their last five games, they found themselves in second place behind the Milwaukee Brewers, who had swept a doubleheader from the Red Sox. It was one of the few days during the stretch run in which the Orioles did not occupy first place in the AL East.

They returned home to Baltimore for an 11-game homestand, starting with a four-game series against the Royals, beginning with a twi-night doubleheader. The first game was another signal that the Orioles were gaining more confidence and momentum. They were losing 3–0 when they scored two runs in the eighth inning and three more in the bottom of the ninth on RBI singles by John Shelby, Singleton, and Sakata, putting the Orioles on top 5–4 and back into first place with a 67–50 mark. In the second game, Boddicker shut Kansas City down. He allowed just three hits over seven innings, and Tippy Martinez got the save, his 13th of the season, for their fourth straight victory.

The streak ended when Palmer, the former Orioles ace—the pitcher who had been the stopper on losing streaks earlier in his career, not winning streaks—was beaten by the Kansas City hitters in an 8–3 loss. Even in defeat, though, the club saw positive signs. It was the first time Palmer pitched for the major league club since he went on the disabled list for the second time seven weeks earlier, and he threw for six innings without discomfort, giving up four runs. Stewart surrendered the rest of the damage with four runs in the bottom of the ninth. But after the game, pitching coach Ray Miller declared he liked what he saw. "He had good command of his pitches," Miller said. "Maybe his location wasn't as sharp as it could have been. He was spotting the ball maybe a little too much inside. But I was happy he was throwing free and loose."

The loss left the Orioles in a tie with Milwaukee for first place, and they faced Toronto next. The Blue Jays won the first game at Memorial Stadium by a score of 9–3, as Flanagan got lit up for seven runs in three innings. The Orioles, with their second straight loss, slipped to second place with a record of 69–52.

But the next day, there was The Game.

The Baltimore Orioles did win an exciting league championship series against the Chicago White Sox in 1983. They did go on to win the World Series against the Philadelphia Phillies. But on August 24, 1983, they won one of the most talked-about games in the history of the organization, often simply referred to as "the Tippy game." There were 25,882 fans at Memorial Stadium that night, but as time has gone on, that number has expanded to perhaps two hundred and fifty thousand with all the people who have said they were there to witness the historic contest.

Baltimore was on its way to losing its third straight game as Toronto was leading 3–1 going into the bottom of the ninth inning. Blue Jays starter Jim Clancy had held the Orioles to two hits through eight innings—a third-inning double to Cruz and a two-out single to Singleton in the fourth inning. They had scored their only run on a sacrifice fly by Al Bumbry in the bottom of the third. The Orioles had a chance to break the game open in the seventh inning when they loaded the bases, but they failed to get even one run across the plate. After John Lowenstein grounded out to start the inning, Clancy walked Singleton, Rich Dauer, and Dwyer, who was pinch-hitting for Cruz. Altobelli called catcher Joe Nolan in from the bullpen to pinch hit for Dempsey with one out. But Nolan hit a pop foul to first, and Bumbry hit a ground ball back to Clancy to end the inning.

Orioles starter Scott McGregor had thrown a strong game through nine innings. Two of the runs that Toronto had scored came on sacrifice flies by Garth Iorg and Buck Martinez. The third was an unearned run in the fifth when Cruz, who had been the Orioles' defensive anchor, committed his second error of the game and his third in two nights when he bobbled a ground ball by Cliff Johnson and threw the ball late to first, allowing Lloyd Moseby to score from third.

In the bottom of the ninth, the Orioles were down to their final out. Singleton and Sakata had reached on singles when Benny Ayala, now pinch hitting for Nolan, singled, bringing Shelby, who was pinch running for Singleton, across the plate. Bumbry then hit a ball that bounced off Iorg's glove at third and into left field, scoring Sakata with the tying run.

Now, Altobelli had put himself in a corner for an extra-inning game. He had pinch hit for Cruz, Dauer, and now Nolan, and he was out of players.

So the Orioles opened the tenth inning with Roenicke at third base, John Lowenstein at second, and Sakata behind the plate. Roenicke had never played third base before in the major leagues. Lowenstein hadn't seen any time at second base in eight years. The last time Sakata had caught in a game was in Little League.

It appeared that all the Orioles bought when they tied the game in the bottom of the ninth was another inning before they would lose. Stoddard came in to pitch the top of the tenth, and just like that, on the first pitch to Cliff Johnson, the Blue Jays went ahead 4–3 when Johnson sent the ball over the center-field wall for a home run. Barry Bonnell singled to center, and then the game entered the Twilight Zone.

This is what the Orioles expected to happen: "It was Sakata's first time catching, and he had to catch a guy [Tippy] who had the best curveball in the game at the time," bullpen coach Elrod Hendricks said. "He bounced it quite a bit, and when the guys got on base, we just figured they would come around and score."

Instead, a series of events that only Rod Serling could have predicted followed.

Tippy threw to first and picked off Bonnell.

Tippy walked Dave Collins.

Tippy picked off Collins.

Willie Upshaw hit an infield single off Lowenstein's glove.

Tippy picked off Upshaw.

Three of the strangest outs you would ever want to see. A second baseman behind the plate catching. One outfielder at third base. Another one playing second base. And a pitcher who was hardly known for a good pickoff move picking off not just one runner, but the entire side.

"I had played second base for several years," Lowenstein said. "But I was using an outfielder's glove. I was hoping they wouldn't hit me the ball. I remember the fear in Lenny Sakata's eyes. I thought, 'Lenny, don't even worry about doing anything except catching the ball. Let Tippy do the work.' And he did do the work.

"Tippy didn't want to throw the ball to the plate—'Why take that kind of chance?' he thought. He walks off the mound, looks at third and sees Roenicke, looks at second and sees me. It was strange to see your own pitcher looking at you like you were the enemy."

Was it destiny? Absolutely.

If you need any more proof, look at the bottom of the tenth inning.

Ripken led off the inning with a home run off Toronto reliever Joey McLaughlin to tie the game at 4–4.

Murray walked and moved to second on a ground ball by Lowenstein.

Shelby was intentionally walked.

Toronto brought in Randy Moffitt, who struck out Roenicke for the second out.

Up came the out-of-place catcher who had hit just 16 home runs over his seven-year major league career. Sakata sent a pitch into the left-field seats for a three-run home run.

Orioles win 7–4.

Oh, yes, it was Cal Ripken's birthday as well.

"That was one of those games that you look back on and smile and laugh about it, and feel privileged that you played in it, because those sorts of things just don't happen," Ripken said. "When you come out and win, it is that much better."

It was a game that has resonated through the years, one that both the Orioles and the Blue Jays still talk about.

"I ran into Jimy Williams, the manager of the Astros, several years ago in Atlanta," Roenicke said. "I was scouting, and he brought up the game against Tippy in Toronto. You know they are going to be running. And he winds up picking off all three. How does that happen? Three guys get picked off when you have a guy who never plays catcher back there, and then he winds up with the game-winning home run.

"When you win, you have to have games like that, games that you think you're not going to win."

"That is one of the most famous games in Oriole history," Singleton said. "I'll be with Tippy at a golf tournament or someplace, and someone will always bring up about picking off the three guys, and Tippy will answer, 'I didn't recognize the catcher.'

"I was DHing, and thinking there was no way we were going to get out of this," Singleton said. "But we were finding ways every single game. Nobody knew where anybody was playing. Tippy did the right thing, putting them on and picking them off. If they hit it anywhere, we were in trouble."

Altobelli said the win reverberated throughout the season for the team. "The atmosphere in the clubhouse after that was remarkable," he said. "It was electric, like a World Series. The big guns on the team were glad to see one of the other guys step up like that off the bench and do something like that, catch, when he hasn't caught all year, and then hit the game-winning home run.

"It might have been the game that propelled us for the rest of the year. When things like that happen and you win, you start thinking, 'If we can win with this team on the field, we ought to be able to win them all.'"

It's often the subtleties that win a baseball game, and with all of the craziness that was going on, it was a little-noticed move by Murray at first that did the trick. "Eddie did a good job of anticipating," Hendricks said. "These guys knew Tippy didn't have a good move, and they would be off and running on Sakata anyway, first chance he got. I remember seeing Eddie pointing to his chest, which was the signal for the left-hander to throw over there. Eddie had it perfectly timed, and Tippy threw the ball over. It was the element of surprise in all three cases. Nobody could believe it. How dumb could they be? These guys didn't need to get any kind of big jump because Tippy had a high leg kick and Sakata wasn't a catcher, so what was the big rush?"

Ray Miller also said Murray was the one who set the stage for three of the more remarkable outs in Orioles history. "Eddie should have gotten credit for that," Miller said. "In those days we didn't have signs to throw over. We just let the players take care of it. Tippy got the first runner on, looked over at Eddie, and Eddie always put his glove in front of his face, and he put his hand inside his glove and wiggled his index finger, like throw over here. After the game, they asked Tippy why he kept throwing over to first, and he said that he looked around and Eddie was the only guy that he recognized so he kept throwing to him.

"Eddie was the one telling him to throw over there. Eddie was laughing because the Toronto first-base coach was telling the runners, 'Sakata can't throw; get off there. Sakata can't throw; get off there.' The batter would get to first, the coach would come over and say, 'Get a good lead and wait until he throws, because Sakata can't throw.' By the third guy, the coach was saying, 'Now don't get off base, we don't need another guy to get picked off.' So the guy took a short lead and still didn't get back to first in time."

Murray acknowledged that he did give Tippy a signal to come to first. "They got a little overanxious and were ready to run on Lenny," he said. "They didn't really pay attention to Tippy, who was not known for picking people off. Sometimes I would give him a signal to throw the ball home, but what I was actually doing with my off hand was to tell him to throw the ball to me. They might have fell for it. At times that was what I used to do at first base."

That is one of the more remarkable things about this turn of events for the Orioles—Tippy Martinez was the last guy on the staff they would have thought would pick off one runner, let alone three. "Tippy had a horrible move, the worst pickoff move on earth," McGregor said. "I think Lenny behind the plate distracted the runners. When we do FanFests and autographs shows, that is all people seem to ask Tippy about, and we laugh about it. It was like he never saved any games or did anything else."

It wasn't a consensus that Tippy had a bad pickoff move, though. Dempsey thought otherwise. "Tippy had a good move," he said. "He did a lot of little things very good back then. He had a nice little head fake where he looked like he was coming home and he would go to first base. One time he faked me out bad. In Cleveland, Brett Butler was on first. Tippy picked his leg up and he was throwing a curveball, or I called a curveball, and he picked his leg up like he was absolutely going to first base. The runner stopped and started to dive back. But Tippy knew he was coming home with the ball and had no intention of going to first base. I came out from behind home plate, took my mask off, and was ready to go up toward first base to back up the play when all of a sudden that front leg wheeled around and started to come back home. I couldn't get back behind home plate and get my mask on at the same time, and I fell down. The ball went over my head and the runner from third base scored. I felt like the biggest idiot in the world, but he faked me out."

This is the way Tippy Martinez remembers the game: "We were fighting Toronto in the division race, going back and forth. We got into a jackpot because of using pinch-hitters. I looked around and didn't recognize a lot of people out there. Eddie Murray was about the only guy I recognized.

When I went into the game, we were losing by a run. There was a man on base, and I picked off the first guy and didn't think much of it. The next guy walked, and I made a couple of dummy moves to first. We used to have a thing called the 'Little Field' in spring training. We practiced moves to bases every day. I remember Ray Miller working with me on my pickoff move. I took that to heart, and for some reason it really jelled at the right time and the right moment. On my second pickoff, I made a good move, because the guy was not that far off first.

"With two guys picked off now, Bobby Cox, the Blue Jays manager, hollered at his first-base coach, 'I don't want anybody leading off; if anything, stay on the bag.' Cox was pissed off. He was throwing things around the dugout and kicking the water cooler. Upshaw got a hit off Lowenstein's glove. Upshaw couldn't have been more than a step off first, and that lightbulb turned on, and I got him. I'm sure they were trying to steal off Sakata, who was so anxious to try to throw somebody out. He wasn't playing very much, and Rick Dempsey wasn't playing very well, so he is figuring, 'This is my chance to shine.' I said, 'Not at my expense, you're not.'

"Sakata said to me, 'Throw me a curveball.' I said, 'You won't even touch it if I throw a curveball.' I had to throw all fastballs because there was no way he was going to catch my breaking ball. I was working the fastball in and out, away from the hitters. When I picked off Upshaw, everyone went wild. That was a big turning point for us in the rest of the season. You get that feeling when something like that happens that you can't lose. Just stay close, and something will happen. That was our attitude, even if somebody was throwing a no-hitter or something like that against us. Just stay close, and something will happen."

They couldn't believe what they were seeing in the dugout. "I still smile when I think about that game with Tippy," Storm Davis said. "That was so awesome. I was wondering how would we get out of this one. After that, Tippy got back to the bench and said, 'I had it planned the whole time.' When he picked the first guy off, I thought to myself, 'Wow, that's kind of cool.' He did it the second time, and I thought that was outrageous. But I figured there was no way he could pick off the third guy. And he did, and it was unbelievable. When he picked the first guy off, nobody said anything much in the dugout. Then when he picked the second guy off, we were all laughing about it. And then the third guy, it was wild. Those little things like that go into a team's psyche, and they wind up thinking, 'This is our year. We're not going to lose.' That was one of those nights."

It was appropriate that Tippy Martinez would be at the center of one of the biggest games of that championship season. He had become the club's most consistent reliever ever since coming over in that big 1976 trade with the Yankees. He would lead the team in saves six times over his 10 years in Baltimore, and, at a time when saves were not as easy to come by, and when the Orioles did not rely on one particular closer, he'd save at least 10 games a year, each year from 1980 to 1984. The Orioles leaned heavily on the reliever in 1983, and he produced (despite his stint on the disabled list for his appendectomy), with a career year—a 9–3 record with 21 saves and a 2.35 ERA. He would finish his career in 1988 with the Twins, retiring with a career mark of 55–42 with 115 saves and a 3.45 ERA.

"That was one of my best years," Tippy Martinez said. "They used to call me the run-maker. Earl, he would go on hunches and visions, and then he pins things on people. Sometimes when I would come in, the club would start scoring runs. And sometimes he would put me in just to get the club going. And sometimes it worked."

But it never worked for Weaver like it worked for Altobelli on that August day at Memorial Stadium.

"That was a period of time when we started thinking that we couldn't lose," Hendricks said. "You couldn't wait to get to the ballpark because you wanted to see what would happen the next day. It was one of those years where everything fell into place."

8 | The Stretch Run

Tippy Martinez didn't just pick off three Toronto runners on that August day in Memorial Stadium. He picked off the rest of the American League East.

Tippy won the next day as well, a 2–1 victory over the Blue Jays that came in the bottom of the tenth inning on another game-winning hit by Dan Ford—the win that put them on top of the AL East for good. Then they greeted the Twins with a 9–0 shutout win by Mike Boddicker, with three RBIs by Todd Cruz and three more by the Al Bumbry–John Shelby combo for their third straight win.

Jim Palmer won the fourth straight while looking like the Palmer of old, allowing just one run with three hits and one walk over seven innings for a 5–3 victory. Mike Flanagan completed the sweep over Minnesota with an 11–4 win, their fifth straight victory, improving their record to 74–52.

The Orioles took off for a seven-game road trip. They slapped the Royals around again in two straight—a Scott McGregor 9–2 win and a Storm Davis 12–4 victory for their sixth and seventh straight wins and a 2½ game lead over Milwaukee in the AL East. John Lowenstein was on a tear, with a single, two doubles, and a triple. The offense exploded for 32 runs in three games, but the Orioles didn't need all that offense to win. The pitching was just as outstanding. In fact, for the last eight games of August, Baltimore pitching did not give up a total of more than four runs in any single game.

"We've been getting some great pitching, and now the hitting is starting to come around," Cal Ripken told reporters after the game. "If you have that combination going, you're going to be in pretty good shape."

125

They had the right combination, but little did they know that there was one more piece of the championship puzzle missing. It arrived after the two victories in Kansas City, in a package from St. Louis. Tito Landrum became an Oriole on the last day of August, completing the deal that had sent Floyd "Sugar Bear" Rayford to the Cardinals on June 14. Landrum was with the Cardinals' Triple-A team in Louisville at the time, where he was batting .292 with 18 home runs, 77 RBIs, and 12 triples. Over four major league seasons with the Cardinals, Landrum had appeared in 201 games and batted .260.

This was another little story that makes the tale of the 1983 Orioles so unique. They made a back-door deal to "borrow" Landrum from the Cardinals—a secret agreement that would have both players switch back to their respective teams when the season ended.

"We dealt him for Floyd Rayford," said Larry Lucchino, "but the understanding that [general manager] Hank Peters had with them, a loose one, is that they would both be returned after the season. When they both got returned a month after the season, Roland Hemond [general manager of the Chicago White Sox, the Orioles' opponent in the ALCS] squealed to high heaven."

Allan Ramirez was the victim of the move, sent back down to Triple-A Rochester with a 4–4 record and a 3.56 ERA in 10 games. He would soon be back when the rosters expanded on September 1. His stay—and major league career—would be brief but valuable to this championship season. "I was a little upset, but I probably would have done the same thing in their case," Ramirez said. "I got sent down a day or two before September 1, and then a few days later got called back up with the September call-ups.

"The following season in spring training I hurt my shoulder. I figured I had a great shot to make the team. About the seventh day, I felt something pull on my shoulder. It got progressively worse. I got sent down to Triple-A to try to work through it, but it never panned out. After that season, they discovered I had torn my rotator cuff. I had surgery right after the season and tried to come back in 1985. I felt great the first month or so, with no pain. But it got progressively worse again, and finally I said I had enough and went home. This might have been in June of 1985. I had started in Hagerstown and went to Charlotte. John

Hart [the future Cleveland Indians general manager] was the manager. I said I had enough. I wanted to go home. I didn't want to try to pitch anymore. It got to the point where I couldn't even lift my arm. It was my right shoulder. It was a lot of pain."

Ramirez is now a medical equipment salesman back in his hometown of Victoria, Texas. He looks back at his time with that Orioles team with fondness. "I was so appreciative of the way they treated me," Ramirez said. "They played as a team, and they treated you as a teammate in the clubhouse. It was a great group of ballplayers. They would lose a couple of games and say, 'No big deal, we'll come back.' That really impressed me about that team."

While the offense had opened up at this stage of the season, they didn't need much in the way of hitting when they played two games in Toronto. Boddicker won his 12th game, holding the Blue Jays to two runs over seven innings, while Baltimore hitters backed him with ten runs. They got three more RBIs by Cruz on a three-run home run in the first inning, part of a seven-inning barrage by Baltimore hitters, and two more by Eddie Murray with a double and a triple. It was their eighth straight win and their fifteenth in 18 games. Lowenstein singled in his first two at-bats to give him seven straight hits, dating back to the game before against Kansas City. And Toronto manager Bobby Cox, who had his fill of the Orioles by now, was tossed from this game in the fourth inning for arguing balls and strikes.

The Orioles were determined to put the hammer down on the rest of the division. They didn't want the season to go down to the final game, as it did in 1982. "The lesson we learned from the season before when we went to the last game of the season really pushed us," Ripken said. "We were so hot in August and into early September. Earl used to say there is no momentum in baseball because there is a new pitcher out there each and every day. But there is certainly a building of confidence that takes place like when you win games like we did on August 24. You have people playing different positions, and we won. It relieves any kind of tension. You build on your confidence as a team. You think, 'If we can win a game like this, what can't we do?' That is the confidence and energy that kept moving forward as we went on."

What made the Orioles' 1983 stretch run so impressive was that they were not coming from behind to win. They had been in or around first place for the entire season. The team had developed the chemistry of a finisher.

"We always finished strong," Rich Dauer said. "Terry Crowley would say that if we were within five games in September, you could start printing the playoff tickets. Pitching takes over; pitching and defense wins that late in the season. We would go on a roll. We always thought we would win every game because of the guys we had taking the mound. Our guys would always give us seven innings, and going nine was a common thing for our starting pitchers."

Just like an Oriole Way, it was an Oriole attitude. "We always said to ourselves every year that if we can get to the All-Star break without being more than five games behind whoever was in first place, that the season would be ours," Rick Dempsey said. "It was a mental toughness that we had about the second half of the season."

Losing a game here and there didn't seem to matter, either. After winning eight straight, the Orioles lost to Toronto 5–3. Palmer got the loss, even though he did not pitch that poorly, giving up four runs through seven innings. He just didn't pitch well against Jesse Barfield, giving up a triple and a home run, as Barfield drove in two runs and scored two.

But they got back on the winning track the next day in Minnesota in an inspiring performance by Flanagan—no runs over 8⅓ innings. He needed to be that effective, because this was one time the Orioles would not deliver a host of runs. They would score just one against Twins starter Frank Viola, on a fourth-inning solo home run by Ken Singleton. It was the first 1–0 game in the history of the Metrodome, which had opened the year before, and also Flanagan's 14th straight win over Minnesota (the Twins had not beaten Flanagan since May 29, 1977).

The Orioles saved their runs for McGregor the next day, scoring 13 in a complete-game shutout of the Twins. Baltimore had 18 hits to break a club record. Ripken had five of them, including two doubles and two home runs. They were his 22nd and 23rd of the season, breaking Ron Hansen's club record for Orioles shortstops, and his two doubles were his 37th and 38th of the year, which tied Brooks Robinson's season mark. His 13 total bases tied the club record. (Ironically, the day before, in their 1–0 victory over the Twins, Ripken had an 11-game hitting streak stopped.) Singleton had his second straight game with a home run, this one a grand slam, and Dauer went 4-for-5 with a home run as well.

They completed the visiting sweep of Minnesota with a 9–6 victory behind Davis the next day. It was their third win in a row, which kept them in control in the AL East with an 80–53 record. Landrum delivered dividends with a home run, and Tippy Martinez recorded his 14th save of the season.

They came back to Baltimore to begin the final four weeks of the season with a brief three-game home series against the Red Sox. Boston, behind a young left-hander named Bobby Ojeda, shut out the Orioles 2–0. But it was wins, not losses, that were coming in bunches for the Orioles at this point of the season, and they met that loss with an 8–1 win the next day. The crowd of 19,710 at Memorial Stadium enjoyed a satisfying victory, particularly because Palmer was on the mound. He held Boston to one run on eight hits over 7⅓ innings.

Palmer, who had clammed up to the media after so many questions were raised about his numerous trips to the disabled list that year, broke his silence and spoke to reporters after the game. "All of a sudden, in the last two weeks, the zip is back," he said. "I feel I can pitch again."

The zip, it turned out, would not last. But still, among the wins in this final stretch of the season for the Orioles, this was one to savor. Led by home runs by Murray and Dempsey, the Orioles had 12 hits. Jim Dwyer robbed Chico Walker of a home run by leaping over the right-field wall. And Cruz made a sparkling play by barehanding a shot by Gary Allenson and throwing to second to get a force play. Pitching, hitting, fielding, it was all there. Baltimore was now 81–54 and had a four-game lead in the AL East. Palmer, who was known to vent his frustrations if he was backed by poor play, was elated. He made up for his media blackout by holding court on a number of issues after the game.

"I've made good progress as far as my velocity goes," he said. "That's good. But it's a matter of being patient. Sometimes I want to feel better than I do. But I've got to realize that past history shows it takes time, just like it does in spring training. People want instant answers. So do I, but that's just not possible. I hope I can pitch consistently for the rest of the year.

"It all comes back to age. When you're 37 and don't do it, your career is over. When you're 27 and you don't do it, you've had a bad year. I still think I can pitch. I wasn't sure six weeks ago when I couldn't lift my arm. But I've been encouraged ever since. I don't have the great velocity, but I can still throw in the 88- to 91-mile-per-hour range. I know how to pitch. The key to being successful for me is just getting out there.

"It's a pleasure to pitch for this ballclub. Our club is playing as well as it can play. I hope it continues. But we're not safe at all, and we're aware of that. I shouldn't even say 'we' because I just got back. They have played extremely well to be in the position we're in now. But anyone who looks at the 1982 season can see what can happen. We could go into a seven-game losing streak. It's happened twice already. I don't expect it. But the race could change drastically."

He took another opportunity to talk about the contrast between Joe Altobelli and Earl Weaver. "Joe had brought tranquility, and I think a lot of guys like it," Palmer said. "I think he's done a great job. Joe is a low-key guy, but he's tough when he has to be. If he was Earl, he would be blowing his horn for Manager of the Year. So would everybody else. But that's not Joe's way."

So why the imposed silence for a man who clearly likes to talk? "I like to talk, but I don't like to be misquoted," Palmer told reporters. "They take things out of context and make me look like a jerk. I make myself look like a jerk enough without help."

He was no jerk, though. Jim Palmer was a valuable member of that 1983 team, beyond the numbers that he had when he took the mound.

Flanagan beat the Red Sox 5–2 to win the series for Baltimore the next day, and his story continued to be a remarkable part of the 1983 success. Despite missing so much time, he now had an outstanding 10–3 record. He helped the Orioles keep the good feeling they had about themselves as they left Memorial Stadium for a key eight-game road trip to New York and Boston.

They lost to the Yankees in the first game of the series, as Ron Guidry defeated McGregor 5–3. But the offense and the bullpen kept the loss from becoming a losing streak, continuing the tone this team had set for the final weeks of the season the next day in a twi-night doubleheader against the Yankees. Davis got the start in the first game, and he left after five innings with his team behind 2–0. But Sammy Stewart came in from the bullpen and kept the team in the game until the offense could score single runs in the sixth and seventh innings to tie the game. Baltimore then exploded for six runs in the top of the ninth inning, thanks largely to a grand slam by Lowenstein off ace reliever Goose Gossage, for an 8–4 win. Boddicker got his 13th victory of the season in the nightcap, allowing just one run over seven innings, and Tippy Martinez closed it out for his 16th save in a 3–1 win. The sweep extended Baltimore's division lead to 5½ games.

Since it was the Yankees, it was particularly sweet to finish the four-game series by winning the finale. They prevailed 5–3 before a Sunday afternoon crowd of 45,649 at Yankee Stadium behind Flanagan's 11th season victory. It was the Orioles' third straight—all over the Yankees within a 24-hour period. Cruz, who had been struggling at the plate of late, hit a two-run double off Dave Righetti. But all anyone wanted to talk about after the game—besides the joy of beating the Yankees so thoroughly—was the play of Shelby, who had three assists in the game, including throwing out two Yankee runners at home plate. The first one came right at the start, in the bottom of the first inning. Willie Randolph led off with a double, and Ken Griffey Sr. followed with a single to center. As Randolph headed for home, Shelby overthrew the cutoff man and hit Dempsey, who was up the line from home plate and tagged Randolph as he went by for the first out. The second one wasn't as close. As Griffey tried to score in the bottom of the fourth, Shelby unleashed a bullet to the plate and easily nailed him. "The fans were pretty mad there after that," Shelby recalled.

The Orioles, with an 85–55 record, headed for Boston for four games against the Red Sox. Both of these series, against the Yankees and the Red Sox, were key moments in the 1983 season. They could have either put two of their division rivals away or let them back in the race. The Orioles put them away. After the opening game was rained out, Baltimore played—and won—their second doubleheader in four days, sweeping Boston by scores of 7–4 and 7–1. The first win in the twi-night doubleheader came in the twelfth inning, when Dwyer, with the bases loaded and two outs, drove a ball to left-center field off Boston reliever Bob Stanley. It bounced off left fielder Jim Rice's glove as he hit the wall for a three-run double. Stewart, the fourth Orioles pitcher in the game, pitched 2⅔ innings of shutout relief to get the win.

In the second game, Bill Swaggerty finally got his first major league win, pitching 5⅔ innings of relief and allowing one run. He was given more than enough run support courtesy of Gary Roenicke, who hit an eighth-inning grand slam. It was five in a row and counting, and the good fortune continued. Dennis Martinez, who had not started since August 6 and had not pitched for nearly a month, shut out Boston hitters for six innings before Stewart came in and pitched the last three innings for a 5–0 victory. The offense was supplied by doubles from Ford, Murray, and Lenn Sakata, and another home run by Roenicke, this one a two-run shot off John Tudor. The grousing that you heard from Dennis Martinez earlier in the year was now replaced by gratitude for just getting a chance to pitch. The Orioles were winning without him, and it had been made clear to him that he was not bigger than the team. "I will help any way I can," he said after the game. "Bullpen or starting, it does not matter." It was now six straight and nineteen of the last twenty-two for the Orioles, who kept their first-place lead by 5½ games with an 88–55 mark, despite the fact that the Tigers had also won six straight. Detroit's season-ending run of 1983 would be a precursor to the Tigers' 1984 championship season, but it was not to be in 1983. There was only one team of destiny in the American League, and it was firmly in first place in the AL East.

The winning streak stopped with a 7–1 loss to Boston in the final game of the series. Bruce Hurst held the Orioles to one run over 7 innings, while Davis got tagged for five runs in 4⅓ innings pitched. Davis, Swaggerty, and Dan Morogiello gave up a total of 15 hits to the Red Sox.

The Orioles returned to Baltimore for a quick four-game home series against Milwaukee. They handed out a measure of poetic justice by sweeping the Brewers—their rivals who had beaten them out for the AL East title on the last day of the 1982 season. Boddicker pitched a complete game in an 8–1 victory. The Orioles lineup played with five Brewers pitchers, totaling 17 hits including five doubles—two by Ripken and one each by Bumbry, Dwyer, and Dauer—and a triple by Shelby. By now the crowds were flocking to Memorial Stadium, and 41,137 people were there the next day to see Flanagan win his fifth straight, 5–4. The victory gave the Orioles a record of 90–56—the 17th time in the last 23 years that the club reached 90 wins or more. Baltimore now led the division by seven games, and the countdown had begun.

In the third game, the Orioles' crowd of 35,804 pushed the season total to 1,811,520, breaking the record of 1,797,438 set in 1980. This was during the time when the main sports enthusiasm in Baltimore was changing from football to baseball. Despite the continuous excellence of the franchise starting in 1966, the Orioles were always second fiddle in Baltimore to the Colts. They set a franchise record that 1966 season by drawing 1.2 million people to Memorial Stadium, but they didn't exceed that mark until their pennant-winning season of 1979, when they drew 1.6 million fans. That was when the shift began, and the Orioles started drawing much larger numbers. The Colts, under the ownership of Robert Irsay, had turned into a disaster on and off the field, and in 1983 they would play their last season in Baltimore. Also, under the ownership of Edward Bennett Williams, the Orioles began to heavily market themselves to Washington, D.C., which had been without a team since the Senators moved to Arlington, Texas, after the 1971 season and became the Rangers.

On this night, the record-setting crowd would get a treat—a hometown boy making good, though it didn't begin that way. Palmer's zip was zapped by seven Milwaukee runs in the top of the first inning. But after that, the bullpen—Morogiello, Tim Stoddard, and Tippy Martinez—held the Brewers to two runs. Baltimore came back to score one in the fourth inning, two in the seventh, and then six in the eighth, thanks to a Murray grand slam, allowing the Orioles to take a 9–7 lead. Milwaukee would come back to tie it in the top of the ninth. With one out in the last of the ninth, Glenn Gulliver, playing third base on this day, singled and moved to second on a walk to Sakata. John Stefero, a catcher from Odenton, Maryland, and a graduate of Mount St. Joseph High School in Baltimore, was playing in just his fifth major league game. But he made it a memorable one, sending a 2–1 pitch from Pete Ladd just beyond the glove of first baseman Cecil Cooper, sending Gulliver home with the winning run in a 10–9 victory. It was another small piece playing a big role in the championship puzzle.

Stefero did not have much of a major league career, but he made the most of his cup of coffee in Baltimore that season. The very next day he did it again, this time in the bottom of the eleventh inning with an RBI single to cap off a comeback in an 8–7 win. The victory gave Baltimore a 92–56 record and a 7½ game lead over Detroit, with 14 games left to play. The loss, fittingly, eliminated the Brewers from the division race.

"I always dreamed of playing in the big leagues, but I didn't think it would be with the Orioles," Stefero told reporters after the game.

The kid from Odenton was a baseball star growing up in the Baltimore metro area, lettering four times in baseball at Mount St. Joseph and graduating in 1977. The 5'8", 185-pound Stefero, who was born in Sumter, South Carolina, played at Motlow Community College in Tullahoma, Tennessee, in 1978 and was named all-conference, playing primarily as a third baseman. He played semipro ball in Baltimore in 1977 and 1978, and he played on the Baltimore team that faced the Korean National College All-Stars at Memorial Stadium on June 25, 1979. Stefero homered in that game and was signed as a free agent the next day by scout Dick Bowie.

Stefero moved through the minor league system, from Bluefield to Miami to Hagerstown, where he had a breakout year, with 25 home runs, 82 RBIs, and a .287 average in 1981. He followed that in Charlotte with 17 home runs and 60 RBIs, but he would never show that production in the major leagues—save for two memorable September days in 1983.

The final hurdle lay ahead for the Orioles—a four-game series against the second-place Tigers in Detroit, and it didn't start out well. The Tigers pounded the Orioles 14–1. It could have been worse, but the game was called on account of rain after the Orioles batted in the fifth inning. Whatever Dennis Martinez had found in his previous start, he had lost again, lasting just one-third of an inning and giving up seven runs. Among the month of brilliance by this club, this was a pathetic moment. Dennis Martinez, who had been a solid major league starting pitcher on the verge of becoming an ace hurler, lasted less than an inning. And who came in for the mop-up work? Palmer, who also gave up seven runs in 4⅔ innings of relief.

The next day was made for the Orioles—a doubleheader. Baltimore swept Detroit 6–0 and 7–3, with Boddicker getting his league-leading fifth shutout in the first game, improving his record to 15–7. In the second game, after trailing 3–1 in the top of the ninth, Lowenstein hit his second grand slam in 10 days in a six-run Baltimore inning. Stewart, pitching relief in a game that Swaggerty had started, got the win. The Orioles lost the series finale the next day 5–4 in 10 innings—a game that Flanagan started and Stewart, the victor the day before, took the loss for, even though Murray had belted two home runs. But by splitting the series, the Tigers were unable to gain any ground on Baltimore.

The final chapter of this division race would end in an appropriate setting. The Orioles took a short trip from Detroit to face the Brewers at County Stadium in Milwaukee. McGregor won his 18th game, and the Orioles won for the 10th time against the Brewers in 11 games, 4–2, thanks to back-to-back doubles by Dauer and Dempsey and a single by Bumbry in a three-run second inning.

Then came a 5–2 loss—Dennis Martinez's 16th defeat of the year. But this team took losses like insults during these final weeks, and they never suffered two insults in a row. The Orioles came back to beat Milwaukee the next day 5–1, with Davis pitching six innings of one-run ball to get his 13th win and Tippy Martinez finishing for his 19th save. Dwyer and Joe Nolan led the way with home runs. And, by the way, the win on Sunday, September 25, clinched the AL East title for the Baltimore Orioles, who were now 96–59.

McGregor led the team in a short prayer after the game, and then the beer flowed and the cigar smoke filled the room. Since Tippy Martinez had picked off those three Toronto runners, Baltimore had gone 27–7.

"I'm relieved it's over," Altobelli told reporters while soaked in champagne and beer. "It's exciting to do what you set out to do. We've done that. When we went to spring training, we wanted to win our division. It's a good feeling, but there's another season coming up and it's the shortest season around."

It was fitting that Nolan and Dwyer delivered the hits to clinch the division. Two role players, they were the type of guys who defined the character of this 1983 team. Dwyer was the outfielder/pinch-hitter who was picked instead of Terry Crowley for the roster at the end of spring training. Nolan, the backup lefty-hitting catcher, had been acquired in a trade with the Cincinnati Reds in March 1982.

"It seemed like every day, somebody was there to pick us up," Ripken said after the game.

They flew back to Baltimore after the game, and waiting for them at Baltimore-Washington International Airport was a crowd of five thousand fans, including their unofficial mascot, cab driver Wild Bill Hagy. He led the crowd in an "O-R-I-O-L-E-S" cheer as players and officials stood on the back of a truck used for a makeshift stage. "This is a big day for the Orioles, and better things are coming," Altobelli told the crowd. "We're off tomorrow, and we're going to celebrate. And then we're going to continue the magic." As they left, Dan Ford told one reporter, "Baltimore is the best city in the world. I love this town and all the people."

What a difference a year makes.

The rest of the season was hardly magic, but it mattered little, as Altobelli concentrated on resting players, getting them healthy, and having his team ready to play the team they had seemed destined to face in the ALCS all year, the AL West champion Chicago White Sox. Baltimore lost three in a row to the second-place Tigers by scores of 9–2, 9–5, and 9–4, and then lost in the opening game of the final series of the season at home against the Yankees, 6–4. Despite clinching the division, no one wants to finish the season losing their last seven games, and the team needed a win to at least stop the atmosphere of losing. It was the old veteran, Palmer, who reminded the team that winning is better than losing by beating the Yankees 3–2. He pitched seven innings, allowing just two runs on two hits, and Tippy Martinez got his 20th save. They lost to New York the next day, 5–4 in 12 innings, but finished the regular season on a winning note—a 2–0 shutout. Boddicker, who didn't even come up to the major league club until May, got his 18th win, tying McGregor for the most wins on the staff. Murray homered—his 33rd of the season—and Tippy Martinez helped the Orioles finish at 98–66 by getting his 21st save before a crowd of 41,314.

In that final week of the season, Palmer's winning performance came at the right time. But little did the 44,986 fans at the ballpark that day know that they were watching the great Jim Palmer getting his last major league victory—number 268.

Jim Palmer is a member of the royal family of the Orioles—players and others who have been part of the organization who will forever be revered by the Orioles faithful. Brooks Robinson is a member of that royal family. So is Frank Robinson, as are Cal Ripken and Eddie Murray. In the nonplayer category, there is Earl Weaver and Cal Ripken Sr. There are others, of course, who are close to the hearts of Orioles fans, such as the late Dave McNally, coach Rick Dempsey, and many of the players on the 1983 team. But there is a hierarchy to the Orioles family, and that handful whose numbers have been retired by the organization are a small and elite group.

Palmer is the only member of that royal family who is still a presence in and around the franchise. Both Brooks and Frank Robinson are estranged from the Orioles, driven away by the heavy-handed regime of owner Peter Angelos. Cal Ripken is still connected to some extent—he operates a short-season Class-A minor league club in Aberdeen, Maryland, that is an Orioles affiliate—but he has a distant relationship at best with the people who run the team now. Ripken's father has passed away, and Weaver will make an occasional appearance at Camden Yards for certain events. Murray left the Orioles coaching staff after the 2001 season to take a job as the hitting coach with the Cleveland Indians (though he is featured on the cover of the 2003 Orioles media guide because of his election to the National Baseball Hall of Fame).

Palmer, though, remains. He is in his 11th season as an analyst for Orioles televised games. He is often seen on the field before a game, talking baseball with either Orioles players or opposing teams, but mostly he is counseling young pitchers. He is cooperative with the media, which often seeks his advice on baseball issues, and is pleasant in his interactions with fans.

Because he is here, and has been here for so long, there is a tendency to take his contributions to the organization for granted. Those contributions went far beyond his Hall of Fame numbers—268 wins, 152 losses, eight 20-win seasons, a career 2.86 ERA, three Cy Young Awards, and four Gold Gloves.

Palmer had a tremendous influence on the Orioles pitching during the club's championship years, both as a leader on the mound and an instructor away from it. It is more than coincidence that the span of the club's success—from 1966 to 1983—is pretty much the same as Palmer's major league career. He was the only one, out of all of the great Orioles players, to have been part of every one of the club's American League pennant and World Series championship teams.

The 6'3", 195-pound right-hander grew up in Arizona, where he had been an all-state player at Scottsdale High School in football, basketball, and baseball. He was signed as a free agent in 1963, at the age of 18, by Jim Russo and Jim Wilson. He spent just one season in Aberdeen with Cal Ripken Sr. and the minor league club there, compiling a record of 11–3 with a 2.51 ERA. He was promoted to the major league team at the age of 19 in 1965, posting a 5–4 record, primarily in a relief role (ironically, it was the same record he finished with in 1983). Palmer led the staff in wins with 15 during their 1966 championship season, and he became the youngest pitcher, at the age of 20 years, 11 months, to toss a complete-game World Series shutout, defeating Sandy Koufax and the Los Angeles Dodgers during Baltimore's upset four-game sweep of the Dodgers. He went through a series of arm and back problems for the next several years. But after surgery in 1968, with a 16–4 record, he established himself as one of the team's aces on their standout 1969 staff, which included Dave McNally and Mike Cuellar. Palmer would win 20 games in each of the next four seasons (83–38), including the 1971 season, in which the staff featured a record four 20-game winners—Palmer, McNally, Cuellar, and Pat Dobson.

Palmer, along with Tom Seaver and Steve Carlton, would go on to become one of the dominant pitchers of his era, and was elected to the National Baseball Hall of Fame in his first year of eligibility in 1990. Palmer also became a national celebrity for his underwear commercials and his work as a television analyst for ABC Sports. He was good-looking—nicknamed "Cakes"—and well spoken, but he was also considered eccentric for his complaints about injuries and, of course, his well-publicized, longtime, theatrical feud with Weaver. All of this over-shadowed Palmer's immense contributions to the many years of winning Orioles teams—including the 1983 team, though he had only five wins that year.

"It all began with Jim Palmer," Dempsey said. "He was a very unique teammate and a very unique pitcher. He knew the game of baseball. He knew the hitters, their strengths and weaknesses, and never forgot a pitch that he threw, even 10 years before. He categorized hitters, which is how I learned how to call games, from catching great pitchers like Jim Palmer. I studied Jim, how he changed speeds on hitters, why he pitched certain guys up and in, down and away. I learned about hitters and what they look for and what they tried to do in certain situations.

"Palmer helped guys think their ways through their careers. Jim never tried to superimpose himself on those guys. Storm Davis tried to be like Jim Palmer, but he couldn't quite cut the mustard, but later on became a good pitcher on his own. They [McGregor, Flanagan, Boddicker, and Davis] all became sort of mental clones of Jim Palmer, and then they took off on their own. They were all thinking pitchers. Jim taught them how to think to make adjustments for themselves. He was a good influence on them."

He offered his help to both the veterans and the young kids who came up. "Jim Palmer was a big help," Ramirez said. "Jim came by my locker and sat down and told me what each hitter liked and didn't like before I went out there and pitched."

But it was McGregor and Flanagan who were his prize pupils. "Jim was great," McGregor said. "He could drive you nuts. He would talk all day long and say controversial things. But he taught us how to pitch. He taught us the game. He remembers probably all of my games, probably better than I do. He was there for us when we came up and taught us the philosophy of pitching. He was a great example of how to play the position, how to field it and pitch. At the same time, he was moving around outfielders and would stare at you if you made an error behind him. But that's Jimmy. He couldn't help himself. But to win 20 games eight out of nine years—that was impressive. I know how hard it is; I did it almost twice. He was so consistent and in control.

"He and Flanny and I pitched every game together, watching each other, talking about each pitch, telling each other if we were doing something wrong. We were in Detroit once, and Jimmy was on the disabled list. Flanny was pitching and gave up a home run to somebody. After the game we would go back to our rooms and talk about the game. When we got back to the room, the phone rings, and it's Palmer, chewing Flanny out."

Palmer said he was simply offering the same helping hand that he got when he was a young pitcher, passing on the game from one generation to another. "I learned to do that [help] from Robin Roberts [who pitched for the Orioles at the end of his career]," Palmer said. "For whatever the reason, Robin Roberts was willing to share with me, and I wanted to learn. My nickname used to be 'Brash' because I asked so many questions. I used to ask everyone—Charley Lau, Dick Hall, Harvey Haddix, John Orsino, Sherm Lollar, who was a terrific catcher and was our bullpen coach. They had a tremendous wealth of knowledge, and they were willing to share it with me, even though ultimately I guess I would wind up taking one of their jobs. But once those values are instilled, the organization's values are instilled. That's how you operate.

"You had different generations passing their knowledge on to the next generation, and that's the way I was taught. It wasn't that I was a great guy. I understood it was a process that would be good for everyone. You understood it was a team effort. You don't win Cy Young Awards unless you have great people behind you, or a catcher who communicates, or other pitchers who support you when you come back to the bench.

"It was almost like I had sons when I had Scotty and Flanny and Storm Davis and Boddicker and all those guys. Even though they respected me, they treated me as a peer, even though I was much older. And if they saw something, they would say something to me and we talked about it. It was like maybe a professor when you have a relationship as a student where you respect the teacher, but the student is interactive with them. It is not like a professor who acts like he knows everything and is immune from learning anything else. The great thing about baseball, and I find this every day I go to the ballpark, as a player or a broadcaster, there is not one day if you look around that you won't learn something or see another way of looking at or doing something. That is what is so great about the game. Anyone who thinks what they know is the be-all and end-all, they are mistaken. I learned that and was able to share that, and it was very satisfying."

With Palmer's help, though, came baggage and idiosyncrasies, particularly for management. His battles with Weaver have been well documented, and he was just as tough for Altobelli as well—particularly in a year in which he was on and off the disabled list and won just five games. "It was a difficult year for him," Altobelli said. "I know Jim quite well. He means well. I told him that I couldn't do the same thing that Earl did with him. I didn't want to fight with him, and when I hear something negative coming out of your mouth, you're coming out of the game. He could pitch four or five scoreless innings for you, pitch no-hit ball, and come in and say that his arm is stiff. What happens is you send him out there for the next inning and he gets crushed. He tells the press, 'I told Altobelli that my arm was stiffening up,' and they would all come running to me. Pitchers are different. He was getting up there in age, and had thrown a lot of pitches, and he had been hurt a few times. Palmer was a good influence on a pitching staff, though. He loved to run, and he never cut his workday short. He led on the field."

As the pitching coach, Ray Miller was front and center for some of those tensions with Palmer and Weaver and then Altobelli. "Palmer was very tough for Altobelli to handle," Miller said. "Weaver and Palmer had this love-hate relationship, and Weaver would embarrass him in front of the club. Joe couldn't do that. That was a tough situation.

"Jimmy was tough, even when he was at his best, to deal with. Every game in around the second inning he would come over to me and say, 'I'm not feeling real good. Don't tell anyone.' I would panic, and if I said something to Weaver, he would go nuts. 'I don't want to hear that shit. Don't tell me that,' he would say to me. I would tell Joe, and he was like me. You have a five-time 20-game winner here, and you don't want to hurt him if he is not feeling good. I remember the first year I was with Weaver—he did that 'Don't tell anybody' about five or six times in a row, and then he got knocked out in the sixth start. After the game, he would say, 'I don't know why I was in there.' I got up the next morning and read the paper, and he had said, 'I told Miller. I didn't know why he didn't tell anybody.' I was ready to kill him. I got to the ballpark early and Weaver was there before me. He called me in his office and told me to keep my mouth shut. He said, 'I know you are pissed off, and I know you do a good job, but we need this guy, so don't make a big deal of it. Just take it.' Jimmy was just a very hypersensitive individual—a great talent who always had the negative fear in the back of his mind, and had to express it to get rid of it."

Even though he wasn't the Palmer of old in 1983, and couldn't express his talent as he once had, his teammates still admired what he did and listened to what he said.

"Cakes was as much the captain of the team as anyone," Lowenstein said. "If Altobelli steered the ship, Cakes was the rudder. He was like a pitching coach. He was not only a friend of his teammates, he was a coach. And if you didn't take time to listen to what he had to say, you were a fool. He had a lot to offer. Not only did he know a lot about pitching, he knew a lot about hitting. If you're a good pitcher, you had better know something about hitting. Cakes did, and still does."

Palmer loved baseball, and he didn't want it to end. But it did in 1984, although he had a failed comeback effort during the spring of 1989. "When I first got to the Orioles, I thought he was the best pitcher in the league," Singleton said. "But by 1983, it was more difficult for him to win. You had to use the bullpen more."

Tippy Martinez was one of those who were called on often in the final years Palmer pitched. "I am the last guy who saved his last winning game," he said. "I kid him whenever I see him about it, that he better be nice to me because I saved his last winning game. He had been a dominant pitcher, and now he no longer was. But he was so smart. When he really didn't have much of a fastball, he would get behind in the count 2–0 and the hitter was looking for the mediocre fastball down the middle so he could jack it. . . . So often that year, when he got behind in the count, he would throw a change-up with the ball going away from the hitter, and the guy would hit a weak ground ball. He would pitch that way until about the fifth inning and then get out. He was amazing. I applaud how he pitched that year. He did everything he could to win, and he did it with intelligence. He knew the game so well. We learned a lot from him."

They learned a lot from him, and all of his teammates were proud to have played with him—fiercely proud. "In his comeback years later, he got hammered by the Red Sox, and Al Bumbry was a coach with the Red Sox then," Singleton said. "The players in the dugout were all laughing at Palmer, and Bumbry just looked at them and said, 'Ten years ago, you guys wouldn't have even got close to him.'"

Throughout that 1983 season, Palmer felt he still had something to offer that team. "I could still help them in 1983," he said. "I had been there and had the experience and could help them. That ballclub in 1983 was a reflection of what the Orioles were all about."

They were all about winning. They had been ever since Jim Palmer put on an Orioles uniform. Now they were about to see if they had one more championship effort left in the marriage between a great pitcher and a proud franchise.

9 | Bad Blood

When the Baltimore Orioles looked at the Chicago White Sox in 1983, it was as if they were looking in a mirror. They were both teams that won with great pitching and timely hitting from a whole host of players. They were one-two in offensive categories in the American League—the White Sox scored 800 runs over the season, while the Orioles scored 799. Chicago had 1,439 hits, Baltimore 1,492. The White Sox clubbed 157 home runs, the Orioles 168. The White Sox had a team batting average of .262, while the Orioles squad batted .269. The one offensive area where the teams were vastly different was stolen bases—Chicago had 165 steals compared to just 61 for Baltimore.

As for pitching, the Orioles and White Sox were second and third in the league, with Baltimore's staff posting a 3.63 ERA and Chicago's a 3.67.

And the mirror showed in the standings as well. The Orioles won 98 games during the 1983 regular season. The White Sox won 99. But they had a much easier time of it in their division, winning the AL West by 20 games, compared to the 6-game lead the Orioles finished with in the AL East.

Even in the stands, the numbers were close. At Memorial Stadium, the Orioles drew 2,042,971. At old Comiskey Park, the White Sox had 2,132,821 come through the turnstiles.

On offense, Chicago—a team tagged with the "Winning Ugly" nickname because of its scrappy victories—was led by one of the franchise's greatest and most popular players and, ironically, one of the greatest players ever born in the state of Maryland. Harold Baines was born and raised in St. Michael's, on the state's Eastern Shore. The legend is that he was discovered by White Sox owner Bill Veeck, who had a home on the Chesapeake Bay, during a Little League game when Baines was 12 years old. Six years later, the White Sox made Baines, a high school All-American, the first choice in the 1977 draft. Three years later, Baines was playing with the major league club. He quickly became a fan favorite at Comiskey for his hustling, no-nonsense style and his clutch hitting. His breakthrough year came in 1982, when he hit 25 home runs with 105 RBIs and a .271 average. And in 1983, Baines hit 33 doubles, socked 20 home runs, and drove in 99 runs, with a .280 average.

Baines would suffer serious knee injuries in 1986 that would plague him for the rest of his career and limit his play to the designated hitter role. But it remained a long and fruitful career—twenty-two seasons, including parts of seven in Baltimore with the Orioles. Before he stopped playing after the 2001 season, Baines had been named to six All-Star teams and had a career batting average of .289, with 2,866 hits, 488 doubles, 384 home runs, and 1,628 RBIs, which ranks him 22nd all time. After his first 10 seasons in Chicago, he was traded in 1989 to Texas and an owner named George W. Bush for a young outfielder named Sammy Sosa. The White Sox retired his No. 3 even though he was still active as a player.

In 1983, Baines was still playing the outfield. The White Sox DH was a big, big man who had made his mark in his first 11 seasons with the Philadelphia Phillies. Greg Luzinski had been part of the one-two tandem (with Mike Schmidt) that led the Phillies to National League East titles in 1976, 1977, and 1978 and then to the World Series championship in 1980. But because of his ballooning weight and knee problems, he could no longer be counted on as an everyday outfielder. He went to Chicago in 1981 to be the DH—a job that he did very well, particularly in 1983, when he hit 32 home runs and drove in 95 runs.

Another big bat was behind the plate for the White Sox. Carlton Fisk became a star with the Boston Red Sox and forever hit his way into baseball lore when he hit a twelfth-inning walk-off home run in Game 6 of the 1975 World Series against the Cincinnati Reds. He was a New England boy, born and raised in Bellows Fall, Vermont, and was at home in Boston. Or so he thought. The Red Sox ownership alienated Fisk and then paid the consequences. Because of a missed contract deadline by the club, Fisk became a free agent after the 1980 season and signed with the White Sox in the same year that Luzinski did. He would play in Chicago until he retired after the 1993 season. He had his best season there in 1985, when he slugged 37 home runs and drove in 107 runs. He was elected to the Baseball Hall of Fame in 1999, going in as a Red Sox. But he was a big factor in the 1983 success in Chicago, where he matched his previous career high in home runs and batting average, totaling 26 home runs, 86 RBIs, and a .289 average.

The last and biggest run producer in the White Sox lineup was the one who put them over the top in 1983, pushing them from an 87–75 record and a third-place finish in 1982 to their division title in 1983. After coming up to play just 20 games in September 1982, Ron Kittle blasted his way into the 1983 lineup, hitting 35 home runs and driving in 100 runs en route to being named AL Rookie of the Year. Kittle, iron-ically, would also play for Baltimore before the end of his career—a brief stay in 1990 for 22 games, when the man who had drafted him in Chicago, general manager Roland Hemond, was running the Orioles. One year later, Kittle was finished, with 176 home runs and 460 RBIs. He never bested his 1983 rookie season.

The power hitters in the Chicago lineup had one particular player who set the table for them. Outfielder Rudy Law came to the White Sox in 1982 after two seasons with the Los Angeles Dodgers, and in 1983 he led the team in runs scored, with 95, and steals, with 77. These key players were complemented by some good role players, just as the Orioles were. There was Tom Paciorek, Greg Walker, Scott Fletcher, Tony Bernazard, Vance Law, and Jerry Hairston—whose son, Jerry Jr., now plays second base for the Orioles.

But the strength of the White Sox was their pitching—particularly their starting rotation. La Marr Hoyt, a big right-hander, led the way with a 24–10 record and a 3.66 ERA, good enough to win the Cy Young Award. He was 15–2 in the second half of the season, and he walked just thirty-one hitters—four intentionally. It would be Hoyt's career year. Four years later, after his final two seasons with San Diego, Hoyt was out of baseball with a 98–68 record. He suffered from drug abuse and was arrested twice in February 1986, missing part of the season. He came back to go 8–11 in 1986, but he was arrested for the third time that year in October at the Mexican border for possession of illegal drugs. Hoyt was sentenced to 45 days in jail and was suspended by commissioner Peter Ueberroth for one year in 1987, although an arbitrator later reduced Hoyt's suspension to 60 days. Hoyt was invited to try out for the White Sox in 1988 following his 45-day stay in prison, but he was arrested and went to jail again after police discovered marijuana and cocaine in his Columbia, South Carolina, apartment.

The entire White Sox starting rotation, taken over their careers, never approached the greatness that Jim Palmer, Tippy Martinez, Scott McGregor, or Mike Flanagan had achieved over their playing days. But they shone brightly in 1983. Joining Hoyt as a 20-game winner that season was another right-hander, Richard Dotson, who, in the middle of an unremarkable career—111–113 over 12 years—went 22–7 with a 3.22 ERA in 1983. He became, at age 24, the youngest pitcher since 1913 to win 20 games for the White Sox. The year before, Dotson had gone 11–15. The year after, he went 14–15 and developed circulatory problems in his pitching arm.

But, like the Orioles, everything seemed to click for the White Sox in 1983. In four seasons with Seattle, Floyd Bannister had gone 40–50. Upon joining Chicago in 1983, Bannister went 16–10 with a 3.35 ERA. He would match those numbers only one more time in his career, when he went 16–11 for the White Sox in 1987, and he, like Dotson, would finish his time in baseball with a losing record, 134–143. Rounding out the rotation were two left-handers—Britt Burns, who went 10–11 with a 3.58 ERA, and veteran Jerry Koosman, who went 11–7 in a year in which he won his 200th career game.

Where the Orioles appeared to have the edge was in the bullpen. They boasted the outstanding threesome of Tippy Martinez, Sammy Stewart, and Tim Stoddard. The best of the Chicago bullpen that year was converted starter Dennis Lamp, who had 15 saves and a 3.71 ERA. He was followed by Salome Barojas, with 12 saves and a 2.47 ERA, and Dick Tidrow, with 7 saves and a 4.22 ERA.

The heart of the Chicago team, though, was in the dugout. Unlike the Orioles, who seemed to run on autopilot that year with Joe Altobelli at the helm, the White Sox were molded and motivated by their fiery young manager, Tony LaRussa. A former utility infielder with the Athletics, Braves, and Cubs, LaRussa graduated with a law degree from Florida

State in 1978 while he was in his second year managing in the White Sox minor league system. At the age of 34, LaRussa was hired in 1979 to replace Don Kessinger in Chicago. The team turned around under LaRussa, finishing third in 1981 and 1982 before winning the AL West in 1983. Writers clearly thought that LaRussa's effort was greater than Altobelli's, since they named the White Sox skipper Manager of the Year. He would be fired by Chicago in 1986, then go on to Oakland to make his mark as one of the most successful managers of his time, with three AL pennants from 1988 through 1990 and a World Series championship in 1989. He has been managing the St. Louis Cardinals since 1996, and he owned a career record of 1,924–1,712 going into 2003. He will most likely wind up in the Baseball Hall of Fame for his managing career.

LaRussa is also known to have a Hall of Fame temper, and back in 1983 he showed it often. As a result, he wound up in a feud with Altobelli and the Orioles. Their regular-season games that year led to a rivalry, even though they were in different divisions. "The White Sox turned out to be a rivalry for us," Gary Roenicke said. "We had some wild games with them, and Comiskey Park was a tough place to play."

Elrod Hendricks used the same word—*wild*—to describe the games the two teams played against each other. "The White Sox were wild games that year," he said. "I think we developed a rivalry and hatred for each other as the year went on, and I think it had more to do with their staff than their players."

Rich Dauer remembered that Hendricks on one occasion had a problem with LaRussa. "We had a running animosity with the White Sox," Dauer said. "LaRussa was young and cocky. We had some balls thrown at each other throughout the year, and one time Elrod and Tony went at it at home plate, I think when they took the lineup cards up to the plate. I don't know if it was that year or another time."

The animosity between Altobelli and LaRussa went back to the game in which LaRussa accused the Orioles of manipulating the umpires after they called back a Chicago home run in a game the Orioles eventually won. The umpire who ejected LaRussa from that game—Jim Evans— would work the ALCS. Moreover, the Orioles staff believed LaRussa was willing to engage in beanball wars. "Nobody liked LaRussa, and that helped make it worse," Ray Miller said.

The bad blood turned slightly bizarre between LaRussa and Todd Cruz, who had played briefly for LaRussa in Chicago. The papers reported the drama of the two Cruzes, Todd and Julio, who had made such a powerful double-play combination in Seattle and were now playing against each other in the ALCS. Julio had been traded during the season to Chicago. And there were concerns about Todd Cruz's slumping bat going into the postseason.

But when the series began, Todd Cruz and LaRussa had a strange encounter. "Tony LaRussa and I had an incident," Cruz said. "Once he made me bunt for him. He wouldn't let me start at shortstop when I came from the Angels to the White Sox. He wanted me to bunt, and we were winning the game by 5–3. Why bunt the guys over? I ended up doing it, but I let him know I didn't want to. He gave me some crap about that: 'I'm the manager; you do what you're told to do,' and all that. I wanted to swing the bat. If it was a crucial game and we were losing by two runs instead of winning, I could understand that. I thought he did it on purpose.

"In the playoffs, I went in the trainer's room in the White Sox clubhouse after the first practice in Baltimore. I sat on the trainer's table like I always did. Julio was in there, and I was talking to him, and I put my batting glove on the trainer's table, and I walked around talking to them before they went out to take batting practice. Well, somebody stole my glove. I had backup gloves to use, but nobody could find it. I never lost a glove like that. I went into the clubhouse to talk to some guys, and went back to get my glove, and it wasn't there. I went into Tony LaRussa's office and told him, 'Where's my fucking glove?' He played dumb. I can see it to this day, see his face, sitting there at his desk, I could see it in his face. I was mad. I wanted to whip them now."

The Orioles didn't whip anyone in Game 1 of the series in Baltimore, though. Neither did the White Sox, for that matter. Both teams shut each other down, but Hoyt managed to do it just one run better than Scott McGregor in a 2–1 Chicago win before a shocked and wet (there was a 42-minute rain delay) crowd of 51,289, who saw something they had never seen before. In every postseason series the Orioles had been in, they had never lost the opening game. The Orioles cracked just five hits against Hoyt, and they didn't score their lone run until the bottom of the ninth inning, when Dan Ford doubled and pinch-runner Tito Landrum came home on Cal Ripken's single. "He jammed me so bad that it blooped out into center field and we scored a run," Ripken remembered.

But with Ripken, the tying run, on base with two outs, Eddie Murray grounded into a fielder's choice to end the game. It was a tough day for the Orioles' normally clutch first baseman. He went 0-for-4 and committed an error in the sixth inning that allowed the game-winning run to score. And in the seventh inning, McGregor, who had control problems despite allowing just two runs over 6⅔ innings, walking three, tried to throw to first on a pickoff play, only to find Murray charging toward home to defend against a sacrifice bunt. McGregor was called for the balk. It seemed everyone wearing an Orioles uniform was a little shaky that day. Todd Cruz, still steaming over his batting gloves, misplayed a ball hit by Tom Paciorek in the third inning that allowed Rudy Law to score Chicago's first run. Tippy Martinez threw an eighth-inning wild pitch that sailed at least 10 feet over Rick Dempsey's glove.

"We gave them the game," Dempsey told reporters afterward. "Todd had a tough play, but one that could have been made. Eddie's ball was spinning so much he couldn't come up with it."

In a five-game series, winning one game in the opposing team's ballpark was big. The White Sox knew it, and they felt confident they would go on to win the series after the 2–1 victory. "I feel our chances are real good now to win the whole thing," Hoyt said.

But the Orioles' savior for the season still had some salvation left in his arm. Mike Boddicker, the Game 2 starter, expressed his thoughts in a first-person story he wrote for the *Baltimore News American*. "It would have been nice to win the first game, but losing doesn't change anything," he wrote. "Nothing is different. I'll go out against the White Sox and do the best I can. I'll just be pitching to keep the game close to the seventh or eighth inning. My goal is for us to be even, down a run or ahead by a run. Somewhere in that range. If I'm successful at that, I've done my job."

He did a little better than that. Boddicker struck out 14 Chicago hitters on his way to a 4–0 Orioles win—the first complete-game shutout in the ALCS since McGregor beat the Angels 8–0 in 1979. He won this game in front of a crowd of 52,347, who were led by the cheers of Wild Bill Hagy and treated to an inspired National Anthem opening by Chuck Mangione. This time it was the White Sox who were nervous on the field. In the bottom of the second, Roenicke led off against Chicago starter Floyd Bannister with a double to left, and nearly went to third on a poor throw by Ron Kittle. He then scored when Vance Law bobbled a Ken Singleton ground ball and threw the ball way over the head of Paciorek at first base, as Singleton went to second. That would be all the runs they would need, but they scored again when Singleton drove Roenicke home with a double in the fourth inning and when Roenicke crushed a two-run homer in the sixth.

Years later, Boddicker, in Orioles fashion, gave McGregor, the losing pitcher the game before, credit for his win. "All I was looking for in the second game against the White Sox was to throw close to as good as McGregor did in the first game," Boddicker said. "I just followed Mac's game plan. People don't understand what a great pitcher Scott McGregor was. He was amazing."

And McGregor, of course, sees it differently. "Boddicker was so crucial that year," he said. "He came back in Game 2 and struck out 14 guys. He stepped up for us that year time and time again, when we needed it."

There was controversy, though. After the game, Kittle was upset, saying a beer was dumped on him in the sixth inning while he was trying to run after a Ripken double. Earlier in the day, Stewart had been sentenced to 18 months probation for his driving-while-intoxicated conviction.

But the biggest controversy swirled around the little general who was gone from the Orioles dugout but never forgotten. It was reported that Earl Weaver resigned his job as special consultant to owner Edward Bennett Williams even though he had a year to go on his contract. Instead, he signed a deal as a television analyst for ABC for the 1984 All-Star Game and ALCS. Speculation arose that Weaver made the decision because he wanted to make a deal with another club to manage again. The Orioles maintained that any club that wanted to sign Weaver would have to compensate the Orioles. Meanwhile, some speculated that if Altobelli faltered and the Orioles fell short yet again in the postseason, Weaver would return to the Orioles dugout.

And there was one more piece of brewing controversy: Boddicker had hit Paciorek and Luzinski, both with breaking balls, with no apparent intent. But the White Sox didn't see it that way. Some Chicago players pointed out that the Orioles pitchers had hit five batters (although it was actually ten) all year, and now in one game they had hit two. Some insinuated that the Baltimore staff was trying to intimidate the Chicago hitters.

The first two games had been pitching masterpieces. The third game was a circus, a bar brawl, anything but a classic game—at least as far as the White Sox and their starting pitcher, Richard Dotson, were concerned. In the top of the first inning, with one out, Jim Dwyer, starting in place of Ford, hit a double to left, then moved to third on a single by Ripken. Up came Murray, the heart of the order who had been on life support during the postseason—0-for-8 so far in the ALCS and 0-for-29 in postseason play since 1979. No more, though. Murray drove a 2–0 pitch into Comiskey Park's upper deck for a three-run home run. Baltimore made it a 4–0 lead in the top of the second when, with two outs, Rick Dempsey walked and scored on a double by Al Bumbry. Chicago came back to score one in the bottom of the inning off Mike Flanagan when Kittle doubled, moved to third on a ground ball by Baines, and scored on a single by Vance Law.

Two innings later, Kittle was hit by a 3–2 pitch by Flanagan. This feud didn't need much to set things off, and Kittle tried to rush the mound to get at Flanagan. He was held back by home-plate umpire Nick Bremigan as the dugouts and bullpens emptied, but no punches were thrown. Kittle went to first, but he was thrown out on a double-play grounder by Baines, and Vance Law flied out to right for the third out.

In the top of the fifth, Bumbry and Dwyer both grounded out. Ripken was coming up to bat next, and he received a strange reception as he walked to the plate. Fisk had backed up first base on the ground ball by Dwyer, and he walked back to the plate with Ripken, who said to Fisk, "Why did Kittle get so mad? We're not throwing at anybody intentionally."

"You hit five all year and three in the series," Fisk shot back.

Ripken stepped into the box and took ball one, a breaking ball that bounced out of the box. He moved up a little on the plate and was nailed with the next pitch, a fastball, on his backside. It didn't hurt, and at first Ripken said he laughed it off. "Then I replayed the conversation in [the context of] the climate that what was going on, and I realized I was just set up. He hit me on purpose."

So Ripken yelled at Dotson from first base, "If that's all you've got, you shouldn't throw at people."

Murray, who had homered earlier, came up next, and a pitch went just over his head. Murray pointed a finger at Dotson, and LaRussa led the charge out of the dugout. Again, no punches were thrown, but Bremigan gave both sides warnings. Murray wound up walking, and then John Lowenstein exacted revenge with a two-run double, opening up the game with a 6–1 lead. In that inning, some might argue that the entire series turned around.

"Our buddy [LaRussa] got a little frustrated in the third game," Hendricks said. "He hit Cal and threw at Eddie, and I knew right away what he was trying to do. He wanted to get those guys angry enough to get them kicked out."

Altobelli agreed it was clearly an effort by LaRussa to shake his team out of the beating they were being handed. "Flanagan hit Kittle with a curveball, and if you are knocking somebody down, you don't do it with a curveball," he said. "Kittle knew it, and LaRussa knew it. Maybe he was trying to get his team going, which a manager will do. But then Dotson hits Cal and jackknifes Eddie, and after that we just beat the crap out of them. LaRussa will do that."

Dempsey was behind the plate when Flanagan plunked Kittle. "When Flanny hit Kittle, it was a 3–2 count," he said. He added that Flanagan threw a cut fastball, not a curveball like Altobelli said. "Kittle was hanging over the plate. He was a dangerous guy, and you had to keep the ball in on his hands to keep him from hitting the ball out of the ballpark, and Flanny threw a cut fastball on the inside corner, and it broke so much that it went down and in and caught him on the leg. If we wanted to hit the guy, we certainly would not have waited until the count was 3–2 to do it."

Flanagan had good enough control to limit the Chicago lineup to just one run over five innings, and Stewart pitched four innings of shutout relief. Meanwhile, Baltimore scored five more runs, beginning with an RBI single by Todd Cruz off reliever Dick Tidrow in the eighth inning. Against Koosman in the ninth, they scored the final four on a bases-loaded walk to Roenicke, a two-run error by Jerry Hairston, and a sacrifice fly by Dauer for an 11–1 win to take a 2–1 series lead.

"It woke all of us up," Miller said. "LaRussa tried to make like it was intentional. It wasn't like they got hit with fastballs or anything. One was a slider down by the knee and the other was a change-up in the thigh. And who would you want to put on base on that club anyway? They were like us in that sense, too. The next guy could come up and hit a home run."

After the game, LaRussa said Ripken "was not hit intentionally." But he also pointed out that they were not pleased with the two White Sox hitters that took shots from Boddicker in Game 2. "We didn't like it when Bull [Luzinski] got hit by Mike Boddicker, a pitcher with pinpoint control."

On the other side of the clubhouse, Dotson was coming clean. "Yes, I hit Ripken on purpose," he told reporters. "A lot of pitchers hit batters on purpose, but you don't do it to hurt them every time. I didn't try to hurt Ripken. When you go for the head, that's when you are trying to hurt them. The pitch I hit Ripken with was a purpose pitch. There was a message involved. It said, 'We know what you are doing. Now cut it out, or else.'"

Dotson said the order to hit Ripken "came from the bench. It was passed down by the guys to me. You have to stick up for your own guys when they're being hit by opposing pitchers."

Ripken believes the decision to throw at him might have cost Chicago a championship. "When you look back on it, I wonder if LaRussa and the White Sox in general regretted that strategy, because they were still in that game," he said. "If they win that game, it gives them a chance to get La Marr Hoyt back to the mound. That should have been their biggest challenge, to get La Marr two starts in that series."

In order to do that, there would have to be a Game 5 (the LCS were best-of-five back then). To make that happen, the White Sox, with Britt Burns on the mound, would have to win Game 4. The Orioles were desperately counting on leaving Chicago as American League champions after Game 4 and not staying to play a Game 5. They wanted no part of Hoyt again.

"La Marr Hoyt was really tough on us," Altobelli said. "And what made matters worse, we had already checked out of the hotel the day of the fourth game. That was like the kiss of death. We needed to win that game badly."

In the Orioles' minds, if it came to Game 5, they were beaten. "We couldn't beat La Marr Hoyt," Dempsey said. "It came down to a decision on whether or not he [LaRussa] was going to try to get Britt Burns to try to tie the series and then bring in La Marr Hoyt to finish us off in the fifth game. LaRussa gambled that they would tie the series up with Britt Burns and win it with Hoyt."

As the Orioles sat in the visitor's clubhouse, Murray spoke up before they took the field. "I want to see this clubhouse in a shambles after this game," he said—meaning that he wanted to see a celebration. Then they took the field for one of the most tightly played and memorable games in ALCS history, and it would be a stranger—a player on loan—who would be the hero.

Storm Davis started for Baltimore against Burns, and for six innings, he was up to the task, though it was a struggle. He gave up five hits and allowed two walks, and Chicago put runners on base in four of the six innings he pitched. But none of those White Sox runners crossed the plate.

"I hated old Comiskey," Davis said. "It seemed like it was always cold and damp there, even in the middle of summer, and I was cold on that day. But this was one of the days when you get locked in. I was thinking right along with Demper. I bet I didn't shake him off but maybe once or twice all game. I just knew we were going to win. I was probably too young and naive to understand. This was my second year, and I just knew we were going to win. These guys say we are going to win, and I believed them."

But Burns was matching Davis zero for zero, and then some. Over nine innings, Burns had walked five and allowed five hits—but no runs. "Britt Burns was pitching really well," Ripken remembered. "He had the split and great control and kept everyone off. Britt was making his pitches."

His teammates also had chances to win the game for Chicago and send it to a fifth game. But base-running mistakes in the bottom of the seventh cost them. Tippy Martinez came in to relieve Davis with nobody out and Mike Squires, who had singled off Davis, at first. Vance Law singled off Tippy Martinez, putting runners at first and second. Jerry

Dybzinski attempted to move the runners over with a sacrifice bunt, but Dempsey handled it and threw to third to get the lead runner out. Then Julio Cruz singled to left, but Roenicke made a good play on the ball and threw to Todd Cruz at third, holding Vance Law at the base. But as the throw came in, Dybzinski was rounding second and heading for third. Todd Cruz threw to Dauer at second to try to get Dybzinski going back, and then Vance Law broke for home. Dauer gunned the ball to Dempsey, who was blocking the plate and tagged Law for the out. After a shaky Tippy Martinez balked the two remaining runners to second and third, he got Rudy Law for the third out on a fly ball to left.

One inning later, the Orioles made a move with two outs, when Ripken walked, Murray singled to left, and Roenicke was—guess what?—hit by a pitch, a record fifth hit batter for the series. But Burns got Ford on an infield pop-up to close out the inning with the score still 0–0.

Burns was still in the game in the top of the tenth, closing in on a remarkable 150 pitches thrown, when, with one out, Tito Landrum drove a 1–0 Burns fastball into the upper deck in left field for a 1–0 lead. Baltimore would score two more runs off relievers Salome Barojas and Juan Agosto on an RBI single by Roenicke and a sacrifice fly by Benny Ayala. Tippy Martinez got the save, striking out Luzinski and Paciorek to end the game for a 3–0 win, giving the Orioles their sixth American League pennant since 1966 and complying with Murray's orders for a clubhouse wrecking party. "Altobelli came up to me and asked me if I could give him one more inning," Tippy Martinez remembered. "I was exhausted, but I went out one more time."

Altobelli was surprised that the game turned on a home run. "I didn't think anyone was going to hit a home run that day with the way the wind was blowing in from left field so far," he said. "But Tito hit a bullet, a line shot. They had every chance to beat us in that game, but we made some good plays and they made some bad base-running blunders in that game. We threw guys out twice at second base, and once at home plate. We could have easily lost that game 1–0 and then have to face La Marr Hoyt the next game."

Landrum got the start because Ford was suffering from a foot injury. After the game, he seemed taken aback by the whole turn of events. "I'm surprised by the whole thing," he told reporters. "I'm shocked."

He shouldn't have been. For a while in the eighties, it seemed like Tito Landrum was destined to stockpile World Series rings. He got one as a member of the Cardinals in 1982. Now he had gone from Triple-A Louisville this year to a shot at another World Series ring.

"Tito wins the World Series with the Cardinals, and then gets traded for Floyd Rayford and wins the Series with us, then Rayford comes back to us," Boddicker said, recalling the deal in which Rayford returned to the Orioles the following season, with Landrum going back to the Cardinals. "Poor Sugar Bear, he missed out on everything. Tito came out smelling like a rose everywhere he went."

It was just a cup of coffee for Landrum, but he made the most of it. "I looked up one day and there was Tito sitting in the locker room and I wondered, *Who is this guy?*" Lowenstein said.

After Game 4 of the 1983 ALCS, no Orioles fan would ever forget the name of Tito Landrum.

Singleton certainly will never forget. "When Tito hit that home run, I jumped up in the dugout in Chicago and hit my head and nearly knocked myself out," he said. "That was a great playoff game. Rich Dauer made a great play going home, and Dempsey made an equally great play getting the ball out of the dirt to stop the White Sox from scoring. They should show it on ESPN Classic."

No doubt, it was a classic.

Mike Boddicker was named series Most Valuable Player, winning a new truck. "I took Reino's truck," Boddicker remembered. "Gary Roenicke should have been the MVP. I struck out a lot of guys in one game, that's all." Said Dauer: "Guys were joking with Roenicke: 'Hey, Reino, he took your truck.'"

"I was just along for the ride that year," Boddicker said. "I learned from all the other guys that year. I was so fortunate to have those guys around me pitching."

During the postgame celebration in the clubhouse, the players sang the Steam song that had become a needling favorite for opposing sports fans—one that the home crowd at Comiskey Park had adopted during the season: "Na na na na, na na na na, hey hey hey, good-bye." The champagne was spraying all over the place, as players were both elated and relieved to have won such a hard-fought game to close the series out.

"It had the feeling that every moment, every pitch, was big," Ripken said. "There was not a moment to relax. Not that when you play the game of baseball there is a moment when you should relax, but pressures come and go as situations increase, and in that particular game, any single play could have affected the outcome. You knew that a walk or a bunt, everything was accentuated. So as a fielder, you need to focus on every single pitch, and you are going over the plays over and over again.

"There is a certain excitement and charge to being in that kind of a zone," Ripken said. "If you allow yourself to think about the ramifications of making a mistake, then you start to put more pressure on yourself. But by focusing your attention on it so much, you are engaged in the game deeper than you would be otherwise. So on that level it is much more exciting. It is one of those things that after it is over, you realize how exciting it was because you are so exhausted, once you go through the experience. You got so immersed in each and every pitch and each and every part of the game. You had to be on the highest alert. By the time that series was over, you felt drained mentally and physically."

But they also felt like winners, and they were about to return to the stage that had haunted this franchise since 1979—the World Series.

10 | Redemption

The last time the Baltimore Orioles played in the World Series, they wound up losing to a team from Pennsylvania that would haunt them. Now they were back again in the fall classic, facing another Pennsylvania baseball team. This time, though, it wasn't the Pittsburgh Pirates. It was the Keystone State's other major league representative from the other side of the state—the Philadelphia Phillies.

The 1980 Phillies were a strange team. If you look at the roster, you might think it was the best team since the 1927 Yankees, or maybe a version of the Big Red Machine. Four future Hall of Famers—and one who would be in Cooperstown if he had not been banned from the game on gambling accusations—were on that team: Mike Schmidt, Joe Morgan, Tony Perez, Steve Carlton, and the banned Pete Rose.

Rose, Morgan, and Perez were three of the crown jewels of those great Reds teams in the seventies. But the three former Reds stars, who led Cincinnati to World Series wins in 1975 and 1976, were at the end of their careers. Here are the career numbers that made them the best of their time: in 22 seasons, Morgan scored 1,650 runs with 2,517 hits, 449 doubles, 96 triples, 268 home runs, 1,133 RBIs, 689 stolen bases, and a .271 average; in 23 seasons, Perez totaled 2,732 hits, 505 doubles, 79 triples, 379 home runs, 1,652 RBIs, and a .279 average; and Rose, of course, became the all-time hits leader, with 4,256 hits over 24 seasons, with 2,165 runs scored, 746 doubles, 135 triples, 160 home runs, 1,314 RBIs, and a .303 average.

Rose signed with Philadelphia after the 1978 season and 16 years with the Reds. He was signed by the Phillies to bring some fire and spirit to a talented team that kept falling short in the playoffs in the late seventies, unable to get over the hump and reach the World Series. And he did his job, leading Philadelphia to the 1980 World Series championship over the Kansas City Royals.

By 1983, though, Rose, a first baseman with the Phillies, was a 42-year-old relic, hanging on for a chance to break Ty Cobb's all-time hit mark of 4,191. He had a dismal 1983 season, batting a career-low .245 with just 121 hits and no home runs in 151 games.

Morgan, considered perhaps the greatest second baseman ever to play the game, left Cincinnati one year after Rose did, on the same mission that Rose had been on. Morgan was signed by the Houston Astros, the team he began his career with in 1963. And Morgan, batting just .243 but hitting 11 home runs, driving in 49 runs, and stealing 24 bases in 141 games, nearly did it, going up against Rose and the Phillies in a memorable 1980 National League Championship Series. But Philadelphia prevailed over Houston, and then Morgan left to sign with the San Francisco Giants. At the age of 39, he joined his old teammate Rose in Philadelphia for the 1983 season. But while he turned in decent power numbers, he, like Rose, was hardly the same player who had won two Most Valuable Player awards with the Reds. Morgan hit 16 home runs, drove in 59 runs, and still stole 18 bases. But he hit just .230, with 93 hits in 123 games. By the time the 1983 World Series began, Joe Morgan was 40 years old.

The third former Red Machine player was Tony Perez, the Cuban star who had anchored the Reds infield at first base until he left after the 1976 season. It is worthy to note that the Reds' championship run ended after the departure of Perez, who drove in 100 runs six times over 13 seasons with Cincinnati. He spent the next three seasons in Montreal, with his power numbers slipping to 13 home runs and 73 RBIs in 1979. But he bounced back with Boston in the American League in 1980, with 25 home runs and 105 RBIs. It was Perez's last hurrah. In two more seasons with the Red Sox, Perez tallied just nine home runs and 39 RBIs followed by six homers and 31 RBIs. However, his value as a team leader—and another bat off the bench for a National League team—made him attractive to the Phillies, and he was reunited with Rose and Morgan for the 1983 season.

They joined two other all-time greats—one who also was near the end of his career and another who was still among the most feared hitters in baseball. When Steve Carlton retired in 1988, he was one of the best left-handers of modern times, with a record of 329–244, 4,136 strikeouts, and a remarkable ERA of 3.22 over 24 seasons—including his historic 27–10 mark in 1972, when the Phillies had a record of 59–97. And in 1982, Carlton, at the age of 37, still seemed to be a dominant hurler, with a 23–11 record. But he began struggling in 1983, with a 15–16 record, his first losing season since 1973. He bounced back in 1984 with a 13–7 record, but he went through one losing year after another after that, with stints with the San Francisco Giants, Chicago White Sox, Cleveland Indians, and finally the Minnesota Twins before calling it quits.

Mike Schmidt, though, was still every bit at the top of his game in 1983. He amassed 40 home runs, 109 RBIs, and 104 runs scored. When Schmidt retired after the 1989 season—after 18 years, all with the Phillies—he had amassed the greatest offensive numbers of any third baseman in baseball history, with 548 home runs, 1,506 runs scored, and 1,595 RBIs. A three-time National League MVP, Schmidt was also a stand-out fielder, with 9 straight Gold Gloves from 1976 to 1984, and 10 overall. He had the kind of bat that could carry a team, and he did carry the 1983 Phillies offense. They were ninth in the league in batting, with a team average of .249, and third in the league in runs scored, with 696. They finished first in the NL East with a 90–72 record—eight fewer wins than the Orioles had compiled. Gary Matthews led the regulars in batting, with a .258 average, and Schmidt led in 14 other categories. As a team, the Phillies hit just 125 home runs, fifth best in the league, and Schmidt had nearly a third of that amount. Morgan, with 16 home runs, was second on the team. To offer some perspective, the Orioles scored 799 runs, hit 168 home runs, and batted .269 during the regular season.

The manager of this club was Paul Owens, who had skipped the Phillies briefly for 80 games in 1972 and went to the front office. He was called upon to take over the club 85 games into the 1983 season when the team was struggling and manager Pat Corrales was fired.

While Carlton had a losing record, other Phillies pitchers excelled. John Denny, who posted a 19–6 mark with a 2.37 ERA, won the NL Cy

Young Award in 1983. A host of other starters went in and out of the rotation, including a tall, lanky right-handed rookie named Charles Hudson, who went 8–8 with a 3.35 ERA. And they had a strong bullpen, led by closer Al Holland, who logged 25 saves.

Philadelphia managed to defeat the Los Angeles Dodgers in four games in the National League Championship Series because of strong pitching performances and clutch hitting. The veteran Carlton still had enough to come up big in Los Angeles in Game 1, as he and Holland combined for a 1–0 shutout. The lone Philadelphia run came from a solo home run by Schmidt. Los Angeles came back in Game 2 at Dodger Stadium to win 4–1, defeating Denny. But back home at Veterans Stadium, the rookie Hudson pitched a complete-game win in Game 3, holding the Dodgers to two runs in the fourth inning, while Matthews hit his second home run in two games to lead Philadelphia to a 7–2 victory. And Carlton closed it out by matching Hudson with a 7–2 win in the fourth and deciding game before the hometown fans—a huge crowd of 64,494—as Holland notched his second save of the series. Holland allowed no runs and just one hit in three innings of relief in the NLCS, and he would be a pivotal figure in the World Series—though not the way he would have hoped.

The Phillies may have been the "Wheeze Kids," but there was the perception that the old warriors such as Rose, Morgan, and Perez could rally one more championship run in a short Series. With two wins in the NLCS, Carlton looked like the Carlton of old. Moreover, Schmidt was considered a more dangerous hitter than anyone in the Orioles lineup.

"The Phillies had Pete Rose and Joe Morgan and Mike Schmidt and those names they had on the bench over there," Rick Dempsey said. "They were icons, gods of baseball."

Still, Baltimore felt confident going into the Series. As far as the Orioles were concerned, they had just beaten a better team than the Phillies in the ALCS. "I thought the White Sox were better than the Phillies," Ken Singleton said. "They had better starting pitching. They were a younger team. Philadelphia had the name players, future Hall of Fame players, but they were past their prime." It would be a difficult Series for Singleton to be part of. Under the designated hitter rules in baseball at the time, no DH was used in the Series because it was an odd year—an advantage for the Phillies.

Wherever they were at this stage in their careers, it was good enough to beat the Baltimore Orioles in Game 1 at Memorial Stadium. With a steady rain falling, Earl Weaver in the announcing booth as an ABC-TV analyst, President Ronald Reagan watching along with Baltimore owner Edward Bennett Williams, and over fifty-two thousand fans in the stands, the Orioles wasted a four-hit performance by Scott McGregor and were shut down by Denny in a 2–1 loss. All the runs were scored on solo home runs—one by Morgan, one of the old Reds, in the sixth; a tiebreaking shot by center fielder Garry Maddox in the eighth; and one by Baltimore's Jim Dwyer, who hit a solo shot in the bottom of the first to give the Orioles a 1–0 lead, becoming the 18th player in World Series history to hit a home run in his first at-bat.

It was a near carbon copy of the opening game of the ALCS for McGregor, who had been stacked up against another Cy Young winner in that one, La Marr Hoyt, and lost by the same 2–1 score. "I pitched good, but that is the way it goes," he remembered. "It worked out for us both times, though."

The Orioles had a chance to tie it in the bottom of the eighth when, with two outs, Al Bumbry hit a double to right field. But Owens brought in Holland, and he got Dan Ford, pinch-hitting for Dwyer, to fly out to left to end the inning. Holland retired Cal Ripken in the bottom of the ninth on a pop-up to short. Then he struck out Eddie Murray for the second out. And when he got Gary Roenicke out on a fly ball to left to end the game, Holland jumped up, held one finger high in the air, and yelled for everyone near to hear, "That's one!"

He might as well have set the bench in the Orioles dugout on fire.

Nearly the entire team stood in the dugout glaring at Holland when he made his gesture.

"Holland really didn't have great stuff," Tippy Martinez said. "He could have easily gotten hurt that night, but he got away with it. Then he came off that mound, holding up his finger, gesturing this is the first, really animated. Our dugout looked at him and watched him and said, 'This is not going to happen. You've got to be kidding me.' It kind of woke us up, and we let loose."

McGregor didn't appreciate the gesture and thought Holland was foolish to rub it in their faces. "In those days you didn't showboat," he said. "Our guys were pretty proud, and able to rise to another level. We had the ability to rise up over the years, and respond like, OK that is one, but we will get the next four. It did fire guys up."

The Phillies piled it on in the locker room after the game. Rose was joking about how he planned to take a vacation to Hawaii after they won the Series, and Matthews said the Series would not return to Baltimore. "I kid Gary Matthews about it when I see him," Singleton said. "I tell him, 'You were right, it did not come back to Baltimore.'"

Singleton yelled as they headed up the tunnel back to the clubhouse, "That's the only one they're going to get."

Storm Davis remembers the anger sweeping through the team that night. "Our clubhouse was buzzing about it," Davis said. "It really turned the heat up. When I heard Singleton, I remember thinking, if he thinks that way, then, yeah, we are going to win this."

This was a time when there was still a strong rivalry between the American and National leagues—before the days of interleague play and the manufactured incentives created by the commissioner to stimulate interest in the All-Star Game. "It was that National League–American League mentality that still existed then," Elrod Hendricks said. "In other words, you guys are the junior circuit and what are you doing on the field with us? He put on a little show for us. I remember our guys couldn't wait to face him again."

It was strange, because the World Series was unfolding just as the ALCS had. Mike Boddicker, the Game 2 starter, put the final touches on his savior season by holding the Phillies to just three hits in a 4–1 win at Memorial Stadium. He extended his zero earned-run streak in the post-season to 18 innings and became the first rookie to pitch a three-hitter in the Series since Dickie Kerr did it in 1919.

The lone run the Phillies scored came on an error by Murray in the fourth inning when Morgan singled, stole second, and went to third when Murray dropped a throw from Ripken on a ground ball by Schmidt. Morgan scored on a sacrifice fly by Joe Lefebvre for a 1–0 lead. Then the Orioles broke the game open in the bottom of the fifth inning with a solo home run by John Lowenstein and then a successful run by the "Three Stooges."

Baltimore's lineup consisted of such quality hitters as Ripken, Murray, Roenicke, Bumbry, and Lowenstein. But it also included a group of hitters who sometimes, collectively, were just as dangerous—the bottom of the lineup, which included Rich Dauer, who was "Moe," Rick Dempsey, who was "Larry," and Todd Cruz, who was "Curly."

After Lowenstein homered off Hudson, Dauer singled and Cruz reached first on a bunt safely. With runners on first and second and nobody out, Joe Altobelli played a hunch. Instead of having Dempsey bunt to move the runners over into scoring position, he let his catcher swing away, and Dempsey responded with a double down the right-field line, scoring Dauer. Boddicker came up and, to everyone's surprise, including his own, hit a sacrifice fly, scoring Cruz for a 3–1 lead. "I was just trying to make contact," Boddicker said.

Baltimore added another run in the seventh on an RBI single by Ripken. But all the talk after the game was about the Three Stooges. "We had nicknames for everybody," Dauer said. "Singleton was good about putting nicknames on everyone. We took up the name, the Three Stooges, and went with it."

Singleton said it was a compliment to the group. "It wasn't negative," Singleton said. "Toward the end of the year, Altobelli had me batting sixth, and he said to me, 'You know you had a good year with the guys hitting behind you.' I said in the dugout, 'I had a pretty good year with you Three Stooges hitting behind me.' At first they didn't like it, but then they started getting a little notoriety from it, and by the World Series they loved it. They were fighting over who was going to be who."

Dauer was one of them, for sure, and he was a typical Oriole, in the sense that his game was fundamentals more than talent. He was a first-round pick by Baltimore in the 1974 draft, and after three minor league seasons, he came up as part of the Orioles' 1977 class of youngsters. He put up decent offensive numbers. Over 10 seasons—all with Baltimore, until he retired after the 1985 season—Dauer batted .257. He was money in the bank on the field, setting a major league record in 1978 by playing in 86 straight errorless games at second and handling 425 chances without an error.

"Rich Dauer was a key player," Ray Miller recalled. "If you grade his ability, he wasn't a good runner. He did have a strong arm. He wasn't a great hitter, but he had key hits and made great plays. He was always in the right place at the right time. He would turn the double play and get knocked into smithereens."

Boddicker also remembered Dauer as a role model for fundamentals. "Dauer was exceptional at all the little things—moving runners over and all the fundamentals," he said.

Then there was Dempsey, the feisty, colorful catcher who captured the imagination of Orioles fans with his hard-nosed style of play and also with his humorous antics. He was particularly well known for his big-bellied Babe Ruth rain-delay show, when he stuffed his jersey and did a home run trot around the bases, and slid into home, usually skidding along the water in the process. It was called "Baseball Soliloquy in Pantomime."

John Rickard Dempsey was born in Fayetteville, Tennessee, and raised in Encino, California, the son of parents who had been in vaudeville. Selected by the Minnesota Twins in the 12th round of the 1967 draft, he spent six years in the Twins system, with brief stints with the major league club, before being traded to the New York Yankees for outfielder Danny Walton in October 1972. He played 43 games for the Yankees in 1974 and 71 the year after that. He actually batted .262 in those 71 games—a respectable average. But his future was not in New York. It would be in Baltimore. He was traded to the Orioles on June 15, 1976, in the historic 10-player deal that sent McGregor, Tippy Martinez, Rudy May, and Dave Pagan to Baltimore in exchange for pitchers Ken Holtzman, Doyle Alexander, Grant Jackson, and Jimmy Freeman, and catcher Elrod Hendricks. He caught 91 games for the Orioles in 1977 and then established himself as the starting catcher the following year.

Dempsey learned to become a good catcher by handling so many good pitchers in Baltimore, but he was considered, for the most part, a liability with the bat. Until the 1983 season, Dempsey had a career batting average of .241, with just 38 home runs and 233 RBIs in 928 major league games, and he batted just .231 with four home runs and

32 RBIs in 128 games that year. Then came the fifth inning of Game 2 of the 1983 World Series, a moment that Dempsey says changed his life.

"At that time I had become more of a pull hitter than I ever had in my entire career," Dempsey said. "Earl had me up on top of home plate, pulling everything down the left-field line. He said, 'I don't care what you do; just hit a few home runs. I don't care what you hit; I got enough guys to hit.'

"Charlie Hudson pitched me almost the same way at every at-bat. He threw a pitch on the outside corner, and I doubled down the right-field line, hitting the wall. It gave us the lead in the game, and it was like a two-thousand-pound weight came off my back. I had finally done something significant for the club with a bat in my hand. From that point on, if you look at my career from that game on, I was a fairly productive hitter for the rest of my career. Mentally, it was a breakthrough for me. I had gotten over the hump. I wasn't afraid anymore to make an out. I knew what I could do and use the whole field together. I don't know why it happened like that, but it did."

After that, the World Series belonged to Rick Dempsey. He would bat .385 for the Series with five hits—four doubles—in 13 at-bats, and wound up being named the Most Valuable Player.

"They couldn't get me out in the Series after that," he said. "I hit everything hard. I really can't begin to tell you how relaxing that one hit was and what it did for me mentally. I finally got a brief chance at what it felt like to be Cal Ripken or Eddie Murray or Ken Singleton. There would be another at-bat tomorrow, so don't worry about making a mistake."

His power numbers would improve for the next three years, with 36 home runs and 115 RBIs, but when he retired after 24 seasons in 1992, Dempsey had a career batting average of .233 with 96 home runs and 471 RBIs in 1,766 games. While Dempsey's hitting was certainly valuable in the World Series, it wasn't his primary value to the franchise. In a clubhouse with a businesslike approach to the game, Dempsey was the voice of passion.

"Dempster was our captain, our sparkplug," McGregor said. "He was constantly doing stupid things. He would get all fired up—that was the way he was. He would come out in July and say, 'Come on, guys, this is a big game.' He would act like it was the biggest game of the year. We looked at him like, 'What are you talking about?'

"He would come out to the mound and ask, 'What do you want to throw?' You would say a curveball, and he would go back and put the sign down for a fastball. You would look at him, and he would smack himself in the side of the head and remember curveball. This was our leader. But he was the best defensive catcher in the game at the time. He would block anything, and throw people out. That made it easier for us, particularly in a tight situation. You wouldn't be afraid to throw a curveball down for fear it would get away because you knew he would block it. He was a fierce competitor, and he drove himself and got the most out of his ability."

Some players, like Dauer, fed off Dempsey's fiery attitude. "The best thing that ever happened to me was lockering next to him for nine years," Dauer said. "His tenacity and his desire to compete . . . I felt I had the same type, and he made it grow. He had me so fired up by game time. If we lost, he had me thinking there was something we could have done better, and now we are going to get better because of what we learned by losing."

Roenicke said Dempsey's spirit was his biggest contribution to those great Orioles teams. "You need a guy like Dempsey who loved baseball and would give his heart and soul to the game, putting everything into it and wanting to win so bad," he said. "I think it kind of rubbed off on us."

But while Dempsey was emerging as the star of the Series, a bat that the Orioles had counted on was struggling. Murray had just four hits in 26 at-bats in the 1979 Series against Pittsburgh for a .154 average. He cracked one hit in Game 1 in the 1983 Series, but went hitless in four at-bats against Hudson in Game 2.

The Series went to Philadelphia for Game 3, and it took a strange turn when Owens benched Rose, who had just one hit in eight at-bats. "I was looking across the field into the Phillies dugout, and I was thinking we had a victory," Lowenstein recalled. "I saw that Pete Rose wasn't going to play that day. He was sitting in the dugout. Pete Rose, he's not playing. I think we're going to win this game."

It didn't start out that way. Carlton was starting again, going up against Mike Flanagan, and the Phillies—just as they had in the first game—did their damage with solo home runs. They got one by Matthews to lead off the bottom of the second and another by Morgan to start the third inning, and Philadelphia led 2–0. The Orioles had a chance to come back and even break the game open in the top of the fourth inning, when they loaded the bases with nobody out. But Carlton got Murray to pop up and Roenicke to hit into an inning-ending double play. After pitching the bottom of the fourth, Flanagan was gone, pinch hit for by Ken Singleton in the top of the fifth. With the game still on the line, the Orioles turned to a special reliever in the bottom of the fifth inning—Jim Palmer.

Palmer was left out of the starting rotation in the postseason, and he wasn't happy about it—though he didn't lose his sense of humor. The answering machine at his home had this message: "I'm not home now, but if you'll leave your name and number, I'll get back to you. If it's really important, you can call Memorial Stadium and ask for extension 75." That was the bullpen phone at the ballpark.

"I get to watch the World Series from 350 feet away," Palmer recalled.

Altobelli called extension 75 and told Hendricks to get Palmer up. Then he called him to send him into the game. And Jim Palmer, on the day before he turned 38 years old, pitched two scoreless innings and wound up getting the win. Ford hit a solo home run to cut Philadelphia's lead to 2–1 in the sixth inning. Then, in the top of the seventh, with Palmer still the pitcher of record, Dempsey hit a two-out double to left-center field. Altobelli sent his pinch-hitter extraordinaire, Benny Ayala, to bat for Palmer. Carlton threw a wild pitch that allowed Dempsey to reach third, and then Ayala drove a 3–2 pitch past Schmidt at third, tying the game at 2–2. John Shelby moved Ayala over to second with a single, and then Ford hit a grounder to short that appeared to get the Phillies out of the inning. But the ball went off Ivan DeJesus' glove and into left field, allowing Ayala to score the go-ahead run. The bullpen took over from there. Stewart turned in a terrific performance, retiring six consecutive hitters in the seventh and eighth innings. Tippy Martinez closed out the win for Palmer, who became the first pitcher to appear in the World Series in three different decades.

Ayala's hit was the key blow. Pinch-hitting was his contribution to the Orioles on the field, and his unique and humorous eccentricities were his contributions to the team off the field. Born in Yauco, Puerto Rico, in 1951, Ayala made a big impression the first time he stepped up to the plate as a major leaguer, homering for the New York Mets in 1974. He bounced up and down between the minor leagues and the Mets, and then the St. Louis Cardinals, before being traded to the Orioles for outfielder Mike Dimmel in January 1979. It was in Baltimore where Ayala, under Weaver, found his home as a pinch-hitter. From 1979 until 1984 with the Orioles, he hit 33 home runs and drove in 120 runs in 692 at-bats. He played one more year, in 1985, with the Cleveland Indians, and then left the game, rarely to be heard from again.

"Benny would sit down in the corner of that dugout with a bat in his hand, and not say a word for two weeks," Lowenstein said. "Earl would say, 'Benny, get up there and hit me a home run,' or Joe would say the same thing, and Benny would go up to the plate. He would go up there and give them enormous hacks, and usually do something with the ball. You could rely on him coming off the bench to get his shots. He could put the ball in the seats."

He was the guy that everyone looked to when things were a little tight, to loosen things up. "Everyone waited to hear what Benny had to say," Roenicke said. "He was like a Buddha or something. He was a great pinch-hitter. We asked him what his philosophy of hitting was, and he said, 'I look for something white and coming.'"

Hendricks still laughs when he remembers Benny Ayala. "Benny and Dan Ford would sit together on the bus, and it was fun to listen to them talk," Hendricks said. "They had their own lingo. You would laugh so hard the tears would roll down your face."

The Benny lingo was called "water talk"—Ayala's fractured philosophy. "Benny was one of the funniest guys I ever played with," Singleton said. "He saw the world different from everyone else, and would say things like, 'You can lead a horse to water, but you can't make him talk.' Water talk. He and Dempsey had an argument on a bus, whether it was easier to go across the ocean in a rowboat or walk across the desert without water on foot. It was on the bus from the ballpark in Toronto to the airport. I pretended I was sleeping, because they were asking everyone's opinion.

"He was very rarely put into the outfield. Defensively, he wasn't that good, but he could hit, and he could hit lefties. One day they put him in left field, and he threw two guys out at home plate. Benny came back to the dugout, held his glove up, and said to everyone, 'Look at my glove. It is turning to gold.' It cracked everyone up. Earl used to tell him that he was too good for his own good, because he would hit against the lefty, knock him out of the game, and then put Lowenstein in. Benny would buy a new car every year in Baltimore and have it shipped to Puerto Rico, and then sell it every year, like his own used-car lot. He was a fun teammate."

He was also a clutch teammate, and he helped put the Orioles up 2–1 in the Series. They would face the pitcher who beat them in the Series opener, John Denny, in Game 4. The Orioles went with Storm Davis. The Phillies led 3–2 going into the top of the sixth, and then Baltimore had one of those innings that illustrated the makeup of this championship squad. With one out, Lowenstein singled to center and Dauer followed with a double to left. Cruz was scheduled to bat, but Altobelli sent up Joe Nolan to pinch hit. With runners on second and third, Nolan was walked intentionally, loading the bases and setting up the double play. Altobelli then sent up Singleton, a switch-hitter, to bat for Dempsey, and Denny walked Singleton to score Lowenstein and tie the game at 3–3. Paul Owens brought in reliever Willie Hernandez, and Altobelli used his third straight pinch-hitter, Shelby, another switch-hitter, to bat for Davis. Shelby drove a pitch all the way to the left-field wall, where Matthews caught it, scoring Dauer for a 4–3 lead. The Baltimore manager was on a roll, and he put Ford in to pinch hit for Bumbry, but Ford struck out against reliever Ron Reed to end the inning.

The Orioles would score one more run in the top of the seventh, as Dauer drove in Dwyer with what would turn out to be the winning run—his third RBI of the game. The Phillies scored one in the bottom of the ninth off Tippy Martinez, who followed Sammy Stewart and closed it out for a 5–4 victory for Davis, who had given up three runs on six hits over five innings pitched. "I didn't really pitch that well, but I was fortunate enough to hang in there long enough to get the win," Davis said. "Then Sammy and those guys come in and do a great job. It kind of summed up our whole year." Owens also used four pinch-hitters during the game—for a total of eight on both sides, a World Series record—before a record crowd of 66,947 at the Vet.

Baltimore now led 3–1 in the Series, with Game 5 remaining in Philadelphia, and it was the heaviest 3–1 lead a team might have ever had hanging over them. First, there was Murray's continued slump. He was 2-for-16 through the first four games, and for a player as conscientious as Murray was, to watch as his teammates carried the load was difficult. He was the heart of the order, the cleanup hitter, and the one that others looked to when the pressure was on. And even though the Orioles led 3–1 in the Series, the pressure was on. Baltimore would be playing two teams in Game 5—the 1983 Phillies and the ghosts of the 1979 Pittsburgh Pirates.

"When we had the Phillies down three to one, not one person in the clubhouse said anything about winning it or it was over," Dauer said. "It was like another win, and another day would be coming. It was like night and day between the Series in 1979 and 1983, yet they were the same guys."

The night before the game, Murray and his family went out to dinner, and Ripken—who idolized Murray and credited him for teaching him how to carry himself as a major league ballplayer—went with them. "It was a big group, and we all sat around in a big group," Ripken said. "We all sat around and laughed and had a good time. We were letting off some steam, and I knew the next game that Eddie was going to do something."

It was a quiet visitor's clubhouse before the game. "Nobody wanted to look at each other much before that game," Dempsey said. "We wanted to finish them off. We were not going to give them the chance to get the momentum to come back against us. We knew they were capable of doing it, maybe even more than the Pirates in 1979."

Not this time. Eddie Murray, who failed to come through with the big hits in 1979, and Scott McGregor, who lost Game 7 against the Pirates in 1979, wouldn't let that happen.

McGregor was again facing Hudson, the rookie pitcher who made him look bad in Game 2. Murray got his revenge early in the top of the second inning by sending a fastball over the fence in right field to give Baltimore a 1–0 lead. Dempsey followed in the top of the third with another solo home run. Ripken walked to lead off the fourth inning. Before he went out to hit, Murray turned to pitching coach Ray Miller in the dugout. "Hey, Rabbit, slider," Murray said, predicting what he would see from Hudson when he went up to the plate. Murray blasted the first pitch—a slider—so far that it hit the scoreboard in right-center field, actually hitting Murray's name on the board.

"Eddie studied pitchers as well as anyone I've ever seen," Hendricks said. "The only one I had seen before who came close was Frank [Robinson]. Eddie would study pitchers closely. If a pitcher got Eddie out and he got back to the dugout, he would sit there and think about the pattern of the pitcher, and sometimes he would figure out the pitcher's patterns before the pitcher would realize what he was doing himself. That was what made him so great. He knew the pitchers better than they knew themselves. He loved hitting with guys on base. They don't just happen by accident. He was probably the greatest clutch hitter I've ever seen. He studied the game. He knew the game."

What was always evident about Murray in the 21 seasons he wore a major league uniform was that he respected the game, perhaps more than anyone in his generation. He grew up in a baseball family in Los Angeles, with four brothers who also played the game. His older brother Charles hit 37 home runs and drove in 119 runs in the California League while in the Houston organization in 1964.

Murray was selected by the Orioles in the third round of the 1973 draft, and, after four seasons in the minor leagues, became part of that 1977 class of prospects that wound up changing the Orioles roster. He made a big impact right away, hitting 27 home runs, driving in 88 runs, and batting .283 while playing a solid first base.

He would play for the Orioles until 1988, when he was traded in December to the Los Angeles Dodgers in a deal that brought young shortstop Juan Bell to Baltimore. It may have been the lowest point of the Baltimore franchise. The Orioles posted losing records in 1986 and 1987, and they lost their first 21 games in that unforgettable 1988 season. Murray had become the target of the wrath of fans and owner Edward Bennett Williams. Murray also fell out of favor with the local media, and it resulted in some bitter feelings that forced the club to trade Murray, a seven-time All-Star who had just hit 28 home runs. This was the time that Murray's difficult reputation was solidified. He became very distrustful of the media and rarely granted interviews in the latter part of his career.

But this public image was the exact opposite of the reputation Murray had inside the clubhouses of the teams he played for. He was considered a great teammate, a leader who was willing to take young players under his wing and show them how to handle the life of a major league baseball player. When he finally stopped playing after 21 seasons, Murray had Hall of Fame numbers—504 home runs, 3,255 hits, 1,917 RBIs, and a .287 average. He was one of just three players in baseball history to have more than 500 home runs and 3,000 hits. But his legend inside the game was that of a respected teammate and clutch performer.

"Eddie was probably the greatest all-time hitter in a clutch situation that will ever play the game," Dauer said. "If there was a guy that you needed something from, whether it was a three-run home run or a single, this was the guy you wanted there. He even won games for us just by being out there on deck. He was that much of a quality player. He was very humble. On a personal level and as a human being to people who are inside his inner circle, there is not a better guy."

Singleton—who played with a lot of great players—said Murray was better than all of them. "Eddie was the best player I ever played with," he said. "He was the best clutch hitter. He was a great teammate, too, and he was totally misrepresented at times by the press, which is unfortunate, because I think both sides missed out. He is a funny guy to get along with, but he was by far the best. Rip was good, but Eddie was the best."

Boddicker gave the all-time testimonial to Murray, though. "If my life depended on a run being driven in, Eddie Murray would be the only guy I would want up at the plate," Boddicker said. "He was the best clutch hitter I've ever seen. It wouldn't have to be a home run, but he would bring that run home when you needed it."

Murray said his whole way of playing was to be part of a team, and he tried to make others around him feel the same way. "I was vocal when I needed to be, but if you do that too much, sometimes they are not liable to hear what you are saying," he said. "Then you have to lead by example. Anyone who knew me knows there was a passion when I took the field. It was about team, trying to get people slacking off a little bit to step up. I left it on the field out there, and I'm proud of that."

Murray would return to the Orioles in 1996 in a midseason trade and help lead the club to the wild-card and the ALCS for the first time since

1983. After 55 games with Anaheim and the Dodgers in 1997, he retired. He came back to coach with Baltimore for four seasons before taking a job in Cleveland as the hitting coach in 2002. In 2003, he was elected to the National Baseball Hall of Fame—for performances just like the one he delivered in Game 5 in Philadelphia in 1983.

Murray broke out of his postseason slump in style, with two home runs and three RBIs, and McGregor was vindicated for 1979, holding the Phillies to five hits and no runs over nine full innings. A record-setting crowd of 67,064 saw Gary Matthews' prediction come true—the Series didn't return to Baltimore. But the Orioles did, as victors and the toast of Maryland.

After the game, the locker room was a madhouse, filled with a celebration and a feeling of relief that, finally, they had a World Series championship to show for their efforts with the Orioles. President Reagan, who was on hand to watch the Orioles lose the opening game of the Series, placed a call to the Baltimore clubhouse and spoke to Dempsey—the unlikely Series Most Valuable Player with a .385 average and five extra-base hits. "Mr. President," Dempsey said, "you go tell those Russians that we're having a good time over here playing baseball."

Ripken and Murray finished first and second in the AL Most Valuable Player voting, but this was a team consisting of many valuable players. It was a pure Orioles Way performance—clutch hitting by not just the big bats, but the little ones as well, and outstanding pitching. The Orioles moundsmen held Philadelphia hitters to a .195 batting average. In the ALCS and World Series combined, Baltimore pitchers gave up just 10 earned runs in eight games—a 1.10 ERA.

"We won the one-run ballgames and we got the excellent pitching," Altobelli said after the game. "That's what did it for us."

It was a particularly gratifying Series for Altobelli, who used the Orioles' bench deftly and outmanaged his rival, Owens, in the other dugout. One of the keys was the way Baltimore pitchers handcuffed Schmidt, who had just one hit in 20 at-bats in the Series, a broken-bat hit off Storm Davis. "Our advance scouts had told us everybody was scared to death to throw Mike Schmidt a fastball," pitching coach Ray Miller said. "They walk him, and he does most of his damage on sliders and hanging breaking balls. So we did nothing but throw high, hard fastballs, even Scott McGregor, all fastballs, all above the belt. Dempsey would hold his glove up high. He kept swinging through the ball, and then he started pressing. I don't think we threw him a strike. Everything was high and he kept swinging and missing."

Back in Baltimore, about thirty thousand fans gathered around Memorial Stadium to welcome the triumphant team home, with horns honking and noisemakers banging well past midnight. As the team bus made its way down Interstate 95, fans hung banners on the overpass bridges, like the one just over the Susquehanna River that read "Havre De Grace Loves The Orioles." When the bus arrived at the stadium, Wild Bill Hagy led the raucous crowd in cheers. The next day, more than one hundred thousand fans filled the downtown streets of the city for a parade to honor the World Series champions. Dempsey was among the players who spoke to the cheering crowd at City Hall. "You helped us all the way," he said.

Looking back now, 20 years later, a player who has always been very careful in choosing his words chose these words to describe the magic of 1983. "That season was as good as it gets, and unfortunately we only got to do it once," Murray said. "At that time, the Mark Madsen dancing [Los Angeles Lakers reserve basketball player Mark Madsen drew attention due to his awkward dancing at a Lakers world championship celebration in Los Angeles] wasn't out, but you did feel like dancing because you don't get to do that very often. There are a lot of great players who have not had the opportunity to experience that at all."

Epilogue

There have been better Orioles teams than the 1983 World Series squad. The team that won three straight pennants from 1969 to 1971, with Frank and Brooks Robinson, was certainly more talented. But there are two particularly special teams in Orioles history— the 1966 team, the one that upset the defending champion Los Angeles Dodgers in four straight games, and the 1983 club that beat the Phillies in five games.

Why? Because those teams marked the beginning and the end of one of the greatest eras any baseball team outside of New York has ever experienced. The 1966 team was the first Orioles club to win a world championship since the old St. Louis Browns moved to Baltimore in 1954, and 1983 has turned out to be the last time the Orioles have won a world championship—though no Oriole or Orioles fan realized that back in 1983.

Cal Ripken has often said that he just assumed that he would be playing his career on championship Orioles squads—just as he had seen growing up and just like the one that just missed the playoffs in the final game of the 1982 season and then won it all in 1983. But it didn't turn out that way. Game 5 against Philadelphia would be the last World Series game for Ripken, who went on to play for 18 more years before retiring after the 2001 season.

It would never be the same again, and it would get as bad as it was once good for the Baltimore Orioles organization just five years later. After the team's 0–21 start in 1988, they finished with a record of 54–107—equaling the lowest win total in the history of the Baltimore franchise, which won just 54 games in its first season in 1954.

"Nobody knew it was the end in 1983," Ken Singleton said.

Mike Boddicker, who had such a remarkable season, certainly had no idea. "I figured it would be like it always seemed to have been for the Orioles, fighting for the pennant or getting to the World Series, year after year, because of what had been going on there for so long."

Another young pitcher, Storm Davis, also thought he was on the ground floor of a career full of postseason appearances. "For me personally, what a way to start a career off," Davis said. "I said to myself, we have to do this every year, not knowing how hard it would be to do that. I thought that was the way it would be the rest of my career. But it was a little different the next year, and by the time I was traded [in 1986], it was gone."

The collapse didn't come in one fell swoop. It was piecemeal, over several seasons. The 1984 season was over before it began, when the Detroit Tigers, who finished strong in 1983, got off to a mind-boggling start the following year, with 35 wins in their first 40 games. The pennant race was over by the middle of May.

"We thought coming back in 1984 that we would win it again," Rich Dauer said. "But the Tigers got off to that great start and all of a sudden, instead of going out there and playing like we were in 1983, we were chasing and chasing right out of the box, and we always got off to bad starts in April. In order to try to change that, we tried to do different things to change. Before, we didn't do that. We just stayed the course and the ship would right itself. When you get so far back, you have to do things differently, like pinch hit earlier or take guys out earlier. You have to go get them, but the Tigers never stopped."

Gary Roenicke thought the seeds for the fall were planted in 1982. "We started to make changes then, and I think that did something to change the team," he said. "It began to change the chemistry that we had. It wasn't that the people they brought in weren't good people. But some people's roles had changed. It changed some of that togetherness that we had. In 1983, Joe didn't do a lot. Cal Sr. and Ray Miller were like managers to us. In 1984, Joe would take me out of the game if a right-hander came in, and then they would lose my glove defensively late in the game. Things like that. It was starting to be a different team. It's hard to sit back and not do anything when you win. They were trying to improve the team, but it didn't work out."

Three longtime Orioles—Singleton, Al Bumbry, and Jim Palmer—were released in 1984, and the team finished with an 85–77 record, good for fifth place in the AL East, 19 games behind the Tigers. It was their worst full-season record in 17 years. "I leave in May," Palmer said. "Then Ken Singleton is gone. Bumbry is gone. All of a sudden, some of the mainstays were gone. You don't know how free agents are going to fit in. The Orioles got away from doing some of the things they used to do."

Others began to leave after that, either in trades or simply let go, and were replaced not by young players from the farm system, but by free agents that were not part of the Oriole Way—guys such as Lee Lacy and Alan Wiggins. The farm system had gone dry. "A lot of it had to do with the minor leagues," Boddicker said. "You have to have people ready to come up and fill in and pick up the slack, and it stopped happening."

After the disastrous 1988 season and the trade of Eddie Murray after the campaign, the fall was complete.

"It seemed like after the World Series, we made different trades, and key players were gone and coming to the end of their careers," John Shelby said. "It was a different atmosphere."

Altobelli didn't even last two more years; he was fired by Edward Bennett Williams in the 1985 season, even though the team had a 29–26 record. He was replaced by the Orioles legend that Williams was infatuated with and whose presence haunted Altobelli the entire time he was in the Baltimore dugout—Earl Weaver.

"I was fired through the grapevine, which I didn't like at all," Altobelli recalled. "We were in Detroit the week before. I went to the ballpark, and I couldn't get ahold of Hank [Peters]. He was in a meeting with Edward Bennett Williams in Washington. When I went to the ballpark that Saturday night, we had more television and media there from Baltimore than the Tigers had, and they wanted to ask me questions about my job. I said I haven't talked to Hank and I don't know anything. Sunday came around. That night, Dauer was going real tough, hitting line drives to outfielders and infielders, and I remember telling him when he was coming in after lining out, 'I don't know who is going worse, you or I.' It so happened I was, I guess.

"After the Sunday game, we went back to Baltimore, and then I was told they wanted me to meet with Hank Peters at 3:00 P.M. on a Monday.

I knew what was happening. I got to the ballpark at 9:00 A.M. and emptied out my locker and stuff. It was all out of there by 9:30 A.M. I knew what was happening. I took it out, then I went to lunch, and then I went back to the ballpark for the meeting. They told me, I said my good-byes, and that was it. I went in and wished Earl well, said my good-byes to the players, and that was it. I went home.

"Williams did most of his talking through Hank. I don't think we ever had harsh words. We were never in a drag-out argument. Edward Bennett Williams didn't know anything about baseball. He would sit there and watch the game, and when someone would hit a pop-up to short center, he would think it was going over the fence. It was his money and his ballclub, though. I don't know what triggered it, but somebody was talking to Williams."

That somebody might have been Weaver, Altobelli's replacement. "I don't know who was talking to Williams," Altobelli said.

Weaver's second act was not nearly as successful as his first, and he left after posting a 73–89 record in 1986. The losing continued, in 1987 under Cal Ripken Sr. (67–95) and in 1988 under Ripken Sr. and Frank Robinson. Then came the wonderful brief interlude of winning again in 1989, when a team patched together from young players and castoffs managed to win 87 games and finish just behind the division champion Toronto Blue Jays, with the AL East title decided on the last weekend of the season. Then came two more losing seasons, as Robinson was fired and replaced by Johnny Oates in 1991.

Williams passed away in 1988, and his estate sold the franchise to a little-known New York financier named Eli Jacobs. Unlike Williams, Jacobs shunned the spotlight, although he also was unwilling to spend money on the roster. But he benefited from the political will of Williams, who forced Maryland state officials to build a new ballpark that opened as Oriole Park at Camden Yards in 1992. That changed not just the Orioles, but all of baseball, as teams began following the Camden Yards blueprint of building a downtown, retro-style ballpark that featured sellout crowds. Jacobs had to sell the franchise in bankruptcy court in 1993, and a lawyer named Peter Angelos purchased it at an auction in New York in the fall. He was willing to put money into the team, and he brought in free agents such as Rafael Palmeiro and

Roberto Alomar. He also hired Pat Gillick as general manager and former Baltimore second baseman Davey Johnson as manager, and the two combined to lead the Orioles to two straight ALCS appearances in 1996 and 1997. But Johnson quit after a dispute with Angelos after the 1997 season, and Gillick left after his contract expired in 1998. Since winning the AL East in 1997, the Orioles have made one bad decision after another under the Angelos regime, with six straight losing seasons and a record of 432–534 over that period. They are the exact opposite of everything the 1983 Orioles stood for.

"That is why it is so hard to watch now," said Singleton, now a broadcaster for the New York Yankees. "It has been a long time."

Whatever the Orioles do, though, it cannot erase the pride of what this franchise once accomplished, culminating in 1983. "It was not just our year," Scott McGregor said. "It was our era. When I came up in 1976, from then until 1984 we were always in the pennant race, always right there. We were so used to winning. That whole team from the sixties to the early eighties, we didn't lose a whole lot. It was a real great era for baseball in Baltimore."

Appendix I
The 1983 Baltimore Orioles Roster

#	Pitcher	Height	Weight	Throws	Bats	Date of Birth
52	Mike Boddicker	5'11"	172	right	right	8-23-1957
34	Storm Davis	6'4"	207	right	right	12-26-1961
46	Mike Flanagan	6'0"	195	left	left	12-16-1951
30	Dennis Martinez	6'1"	185	right	right	5-14-1955
23	Tippy Martinez	5'10"	180	left	left	5-31-1950
16	Scott McGregor	6'1"	190	left	both	1-18-1954
39	Paul Mirabella	6'2"	196	left	left	3-20-1954
21	Dan Morogiello	6'1"	200	left	left	3-26-1955
22	Jim Palmer	6'3"	196	right	right	10-15-1945
36	Allan Ramirez	5'10"	180	right	right	5-01-1957
53	Sammy Stewart	6'3"	208	right	right	10-28-1954
49	Tim Stoddard	6'7"	250	right	right	1-24-1953
32	Bill Swaggerty	6'2"	186	right	right	12-05-1956
51	Don Welchel	6'4"	205	right	right	2-03-1957

#	Catcher	Height	Weight	Throws	Bats	Date of Birth
24	Rick Dempsey	6'0"	190	right	right	9-13-1949
18	Dave Huppert	6'1"	190	right	right	4-17-1957
17	Joe Nolan	6'0"	190	right	left	5-12-1951
9	John Stefero	5'8"	185	right	left	9-22-1959

#	Infielder	Height	Weight	Throws	Bats	Date of Birth
2	Bobby Bonner	6'0"	185	right	right	8-12-1956
10	Todd Cruz	6'0"	175	right	right	11-23-1955
44	Rich Dauer	6'0"	180	right	right	7-27-1952
11	Glenn Gulliver	5'11"	175	right	left	10-15-1954
3	Leo Hernandez	5'11"	170	right	right	11-06-1959
33	Eddie Murray	6'2"	200	right	both	2-24-1956
8	Cal Ripken Jr.	6'4"	225	right	right	8-24-1960
6	Aurelio Rodriguez	5'10"	180	right	right	12-28-1947
12	Lenn Sakata	5'9"	160	right	right	6-08-1954

#	Outfielder	Height	Weight	Throws	Bats	Date of Birth
27	Benny Ayala	6'1"	185	right	right	2-07-1951
1	Al Bumbry	5'8"	175	right	left	4-21-1947
28	Jim Dwyer	5'10"	175	left	left	1-03-1950
15	Dan Ford	6'1"	185	right	right	5-19-1952
39	Tito Landrum	5'11"	175	right	right	10-25-1954
38	John Lowenstein	6'0"	175	right	left	1-27-1947
35	Gary Roenicke	6'3"	205	right	right	12-05-1954
37	John Shelby	6'1"	175	right	both	2-23-1958
43	Mike Young	6'2"	195	right	both	3-20-1960

#	Designated Hitter	Height	Weight	Throws	Bats	Date of Birth
29	Ken Singleton	6'4"	213	right	both	6-10-1947

Appendix II
1983 Regular-Season Game Summaries

Game summaries read as follows:

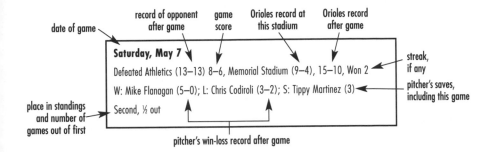

date of game

record of opponent after game

game score

Orioles record at this stadium

Orioles record after game

Saturday, May 7

Defeated Athletics (13–13) 8–6, Memorial Stadium (9–4), 15–10, Won 2

W: Mike Flanagan (5–0); L: Chris Codiroli (3–2); S: Tippy Martinez (3)

Second, ½ out

streak, if any

pitcher's saves, including this game

place in standings and number of games out of first

pitcher's win-loss record after game

Monday, April 4
Lost to Royals (1–0) 7–2, Memorial Stadium (0–1), 0–1
W: Larry Gura (1–0); L: Dennis Martinez (0–1)
Third, 1 out

Wednesday, April 6
Defeated Royals (1–1) 11–1, Memorial Stadium (1–1), 1–1
W: Mike Flanagan (1–0); L: Dennis Leonard (0–1)
Third, 1 out

Saturday, April 9
Lost to Indians (3–1) 8–4, Cleveland Stadium (0–1), 1–2
W: Rick Sutcliffe (2–0); L: Sammy Stewart (0–1); S: Dan Spillner (2)
Fourth, 1½ out

Sunday, April 10
Defeated Indians (3–2) 13–2, Cleveland Stadium (1–1), 2–2
W: Dennis Martinez (1–1); L: Lary Sorensen (0–1)
Second, ½ out

Tuesday, April 12
Defeated White Sox (2–4) 10–8, Comiskey Park (1–0), 3–2, Won 2
W: Sammy Stewart (1–1); L: Dennis Lamp (1–1)
First

Thursday, April 14
Lost to White Sox (3–4) 12–11, Comiskey Park (1–1), 3–3
W: Salome Barojas (1–0); L: Don Welchel (0–1); S: Kevin Hickey (2)
Second, ½ out

Saturday, April 16
Defeated Indians (4–4) 2–0, Memorial Stadium (2–1), 4–3
W: Jim Palmer (1–0); L: Lary Sorensen (0–2); S: Tippy Martinez (1)
Second, ½ out

Lost to Indians (5–4) 7–4, Memorial Stadium (2–2), 4–4
W: Neal Heaton (1–0); L: Dennis Martinez (1–2); S: Dan Spillner (4)
Second, ½ out

Sunday, April 17
Defeated Indians (5–5) 6–1, Memorial Stadium (3–2), 5–4
W: Mike Flanagan (2–0); L: Bert Blyleven (0–3)
First

Monday, April 18
Defeated Indians (5–6) 4–1, Memorial Stadium (4–2), 6–4, Won 2
W: Scott McGregor (1–0); L: Len Barker (2–1)
First

Tuesday, April 19
Defeated Rangers (7–5) 4–2, Memorial Stadium (5–2), 7–4, Won 3
W: Sammy Stewart (2–1); L: Charlie Hough (1–1)
First

Wednesday, April 20
Lost to Rangers (8–5) 11–2, Memorial Stadium (5–3), 7–5
W: Mike Smithson (2–0); L: Dennis Martinez (1–3)
First

Thursday, April 21
Defeated Rangers (8–6) 3–2, Memorial Stadium (6–3), 8–5
W: Tim Stoddard (1–0); L: Odell Jones (1–1)
First

Friday, April 22
Lost to Angels (10–6) 6–5, Anaheim Stadium (0–1), 8–6
W: Luis Sanchez (1–0); L: Don Welchel (0–2)
First

Saturday, April 23
Defeated Angels (10–7) 3–1, Anaheim Stadium (1–1), 9–6
W: Scott McGregor (2–0); L: Tommy John (2–1)
First

Sunday, April 24
Lost to Angels (11–7) 7–3, Anaheim Stadium (1–2), 9–7
W: Mike Witt (1–3); L: Dennis Martinez (1–4)
First

Tuesday, April 26
Lost to Athletics (10–8) 4–3, Oakland–Alameda Coliseum (0–1), 9–8, Lost 2
W: Chris Codiroli (2–1); L: Jim Palmer (1–1); S: Tom Burgmeier (2)
Third, ½ out

Wednesday, April 27
Defeated Athletics (10–9) 6–0, Oakland–Alameda Coliseum (1–1), 10–8
W: Mike Flanagan (3–0); L: Bill Krueger (2–2); S: Sammy Stewart (1)
Second, ½ out

Friday, April 29
Defeated Mariners (7–16) 9–1, Kingdome (1–0), 11–8, Won 2
W: Scott McGregor (3–0); L: Jim Beattie (0–1)
First

Saturday, April 30
Lost to Mariners (8–16) 6–2, Kingdome (1–1), 11–9
W: Bob Stoddard (2–3); L: Dennis Martinez (1–5); S: Ed Vande Berg (1)
First

Sunday, May 1
Defeated Mariners (8–17) 8–2, Kingdome (2–1), 12–9
W: Storm Davis (1–0); L: Gaylord Perry (2–3); S: Tippy Martinez (2)
First

Tuesday, May 3
Defeated Angels (13–10) 4–2, Memorial Stadium (7–3), 13–9, Won 2
W: Mike Flanagan (4–0); L: Geoff Zahn (3–2)
First

Wednesday, May 4
Lost to Angels (14–10) 16–8, Memorial Stadium (7–4), 13–10
W: Luis Sanchez (2–1); L: Scott McGregor (3–1)
Second, ½ out

Friday, May 6
Defeated Athletics (13–12) 9–2, Memorial Stadium (8–4), 14–10
W: Dennis Martinez (2–5); L: Mike Norris (3–2)
Second, ½ out

Saturday, May 7
Defeated Athletics (13–13) 8–6, Memorial Stadium (9–4), 15–10, Won 2
W: Mike Flanagan (5–0); L: Chris Codiroli (3–2); S: Tippy Martinez (3)
Second, ½ out

Sunday, May 8
Lost to Athletics (14–13) 1–0, Memorial Stadium (9–5), 15–11
W: Bill Krueger (3–3); L: Tippy Martinez (0–1); S: Dave Beard (4)
Second, ½ out

Monday, May 9
Lost to Mariners (11–20) 6–4, Memorial Stadium (9–6), 15–12, Lost 2
W: Jim Beattie (2–1); L: Scott McGregor (3–2); S: Bill Caudill (6)
Second, 1½ out

Tuesday, May 10
Defeated Mariners (11–21) 13–2, Memorial Stadium (10–6), 16–12
W: Dennis Martinez (3–5); L: Edwin Nunez (0–4)
Second, ½ out

Wednesday, May 11
Defeated Mariners (11–22) 1–0, Memorial Stadium (11–6), 17–12, Won 2
W: Mike Flanagan (6–0); L: Gaylord Perry (2–4)
First

Friday, May 13
Defeated Rangers (16–14) 8–1, Arlington Stadium (1–0), 18–12, Won 3
W: Storm Davis (2–0); L: Charlie Hough (2–3)
First

Saturday, May 14
Defeated Rangers (16–15) 14–11, Arlington Stadium (2–0), 19–12, Won 4
W: Tippy Martinez (1–1); L: Dave Tobik (0–1); S: Tim Stoddard (1)
First

Sunday, May 15
Lost to Rangers (17–15) 2–1, Arlington Stadium (2–1), 19–13
W: Danny Darwin (2–3); L: Dennis Martinez (3–6); S: Odell Jones (5)
First

Tuesday, May 17
Defeated White Sox (13–18) 7–2, Memorial Stadium (12–6), 20–13
W: Tim Stoddard (2–0); L: La Marr Hoyt (2–6)
First

Defeated White Sox (13–19) 5–0, Memorial Stadium (13–6), 21–13, Won 2
W: Mike Boddicker (1–0); L: Dennis Lamp (3–3)
First

Wednesday, May 18
Defeated White Sox (13–20) 1–0, Memorial Stadium (14–6), 22–13, Won 3
W: Tippy Martinez (2–1); L: Richard Dotson (4–4)
First

Chicago's Rich Dotson pitches a one-hitter against the Orioles, yet loses 1–0. Baltimore's lone hit is Dan Ford's eighth-inning home run.

Thursday, May 19
Defeated Blue Jays (18–16) 2–1, Exhibition Stadium (1–0), 23–13, Won 4
W: Scott McGregor (4–2); L: Mike Morgan (0–3); S: Tippy Martinez (4)
First

Friday, May 20
Lost to Blue Jays (19–16) 7–5, Exhibition Stadium (1–1), 23–14
W: Jim Gott (1–3); L: Dennis Martinez (3–7); S: Joey McLaughlin (2)
First

Saturday, May 21
Lost to Blue Jays (20–16) 6–0, Exhibition Stadium (1–2), 23–15, Lost 2
W: Dave Stieb (8–2); L: Sammy Stewart (2–2)
First

Sunday, May 22
Lost to Blue Jays (21–16) 5–0, Exhibition Stadium (1–3), 23–16, Lost 3
W: Jim Clancy (4–2); L: Mike Boddicker (1–1)
First

Monday, May 23
Lost to Twins (19–23) 12–4, Memorial Stadium (14–7), 23–17, Lost 4
W: Frank Viola (2–2); L: Storm Davis (2–1)
Second, 1 out

Tuesday, May 24
Lost to Twins (20–23) 6–1, Memorial Stadium (14–8), 23–18, Lost 5
W: Bobby Castillo (2–3); L: Scott McGregor (4–3)
Third, 1 out

Wednesday, May 25
Lost to Twins (21–23) 7–4, Memorial Stadium (14–9), 23–19, Lost 6
W: Ken Schrom (3–0); L: Dennis Martinez (3–8); S: Ron Davis (7)
Second, 1 out

Thursday, May 26
Lost to Royals (19–18) 8–2, Royals Stadium (0–1), 23–20, Lost 7
W: Steve Renko (4–3); L: Mike Boddicker (1–2)
Fourth, 2 out

Friday, May 27
Defeated Royals (19–19) 7–4, Royals Stadium (1–1), 24–20
W: Storm Davis (3–1); L: Larry Gura (4–6); S: Tippy Martinez (5)
Third, 2 out

Saturday, May 28
Defeated Royals (19–20) 1–0, Royals Stadium (2–1), 25–20, Won 2
W: Scott McGregor (5–3); L: Mike Armstrong (2–2)
Third, 1 out

Sunday, May 29
Lost to Royals (20–20) 4–0, Royals Stadium (2–2), 25–21
W: Paul Splittorff (2–1); L: Dennis Martinez (3–9); S: Dan Quisenberry (11)
Second, 1 out

Monday, May 30
Defeated Twins (21–28) 6–1; Hubert H. Humphrey Metrodome (1–0), 26–21
W: Mike Boddicker (2–2); L: Bobby Castillo (2–4)
Third, 1 out

Tuesday, May 31
Lost to Twins (22–28) 10–3, Hubert H. Humphrey Metrodome (1–1), 26–22
W: Ken Schrom (4–0); L: Storm Davis (3–2)
Fourth, 1½ out

Wednesday, June 1
Defeated Twins (22–29) 6–3, Hubert H. Humphrey Metrodome (2–1), 27–22
W: Scott McGregor (6–3); L: Rick Lysander (1–5); S: Tippy Martinez (6)
Third, 1½ out

Friday, June 3
Defeated Blue Jays (27–21) 3–2, Memorial Stadium (15–9), 28–22, Won 2
W: Tippy Martinez (3–1); L: Joey McLaughlin (1–2)
Second, 1 out

Saturday, June 4
Defeated Blue Jays (27–22) 6–4, Memorial Stadium (16–9), 29–22, Won 3
W: Mike Boddicker (3–2); L: Dave Stieb (8–4); S: Sammy Stewart (2)
Second, 1 out

Sunday, June 5
Lost to Blue Jays (28–22) 5–2, Memorial Stadium (16–10), 29–23
W: Jim Clancy (5–4); L: Storm Davis (3–3); S: Joey McLaughlin (5)
Second, 1 out

Monday, June 6
Defeated Blue Jays (28–23) 8–1, Memorial Stadium (17–10), 30–23
W: Scott McGregor (7–3); L: Luis Leal (5–4)
First

Tuesday, June 7
Defeated Brewers (26–25) 6–4, Memorial Stadium (18–10), 31–23, Won 2
W: Dennis Martinez (4–9); L: Mike Caldwell (5–5); S: Tippy Martinez (7)
First

Wednesday, June 8
Defeated Brewers (26–26) 7–3, Memorial Stadium (19–10), 32–23, Won 3
W: Tim Stoddard (3–0); L: Tom Tellmann (3–2)
First

Thursday, June 9
Defeated Brewers (26–27) 10–7, Memorial Stadium (20–10), 33–23, Won 4
W: Mike Boddicker (4–2); L: Jerry Augustine (2–2); S: Tippy Martinez (8)
First

Friday, June 10
Defeated Red Sox (28–27) 3–0, Fenway Park (1–0), 34–23, Won 5
W: Storm Davis (4–3); L: Bruce Hurst (4–5)
First

Saturday, June 11
Defeated Red Sox (28–28) 10–6, Fenway Park (2–0), 35–23, Won 6
W: Scott McGregor (8–3); L: Bob Ojeda (3–2)
First

Sunday, June 12
Lost to Red Sox (29–28) 7–6, Fenway Park (2–1), 35–24
W: Bob Stanley (5–3); L: Tippy Martinez (3–2)
First

Monday, June 13
Defeated Brewers (28–29) 3–2, County Stadium (1–0), 36–24
W: Allan Ramirez (1–0); L: Don Sutton (4–4); S: Tippy Martinez (9)
First

Wednesday, June 15
Defeated Brewers (28–30) 11–8, County Stadium (2–0), 37–24, Won 2
W: Tippy Martinez (4–2); L: Bob Gibson (1–1)
First

Thursday, June 16
Lost to Brewers (29–30) 2–1, County Stadium (2–1), 37–25
W: Jim Slaton (6–2); L: Tim Stoddard (3–1)
First

Friday, June 17
Lost to Red Sox (31–30) 5–3, Memorial Stadium (20–11), 37–26, Lost 2
W: Bob Ojeda (4–2); L: Dennis Martinez (4–10); S: Bob Stanley (13)
First

Saturday, June 18
Lost to Red Sox (32–30) 3–2, Memorial Stadium (20–12), 37–27, Lost 3
W: John Tudor (4–4); L: Tippy Martinez (4–3)
First

Sunday, June 19
Defeated Red Sox (32–31) 6–3, Memorial Stadium (21–12), 38–27
W: Jim Palmer (2–1); L: Mike Brown (5–4)
First

Tuesday, June 21
Defeated Yankees (34–31) 5–2, Memorial Stadium (22–12), 39–27, Won 2
W: Tippy Martinez (5–3); L: Shane Rawley (7–6)
First

Wednesday, June 22
Lost to Yankees (35–31) 5–2, Memorial Stadium (22–13), 39–28
W: Ron Guidry (10–4); L: Scott McGregor (8–4)
First

Friday, June 24
Lost to Tigers (38–30) 9–0, Memorial Stadium (22–14), 39–29, Lost 2
W: Dan Petry (7–5); L: Dennis Martinez (4–11)
First

Saturday, June 25
Lost to Tigers (39–30) 9–3, Memorial Stadium (22–15), 39–30, Lost 3
W: Doug Bair (2–1); L: Jim Palmer (2–2)
First

Sunday, June 26
Defeated Tigers (39–31) 3–1, Memorial Stadium (23–15), 40–30
W: Storm Davis (5–3); L: Jack Morris (8–6); S: Tippy Martinez (10)
First

Baltimore's Storm Davis holds the Tigers hitless for eight innings, then needs help from reliever Tippy Martinez to complete a 3–1 victory. Pinch hitter Rick Leach, who had been in a 3-for-35 slump, breaks up the no-hit bid with his first home run of the year leading off the ninth.

Monday, June 27
Lost to Yankees (37–33) 4–3, Yankee Stadium (0–1), 40–31
W: Rich Gossage (4–2); L: Tim Stoddard (3–2)
Second, ½ out

Wednesday, June 29
Lost to Yankees (38–33) 7–0, Yankee Stadium (0–2), 40–32, Lost 2
W: Dave Righetti (9–3); L: Mike Boddicker (4–3)
Second, 1 out

Thursday, June 30
Lost to Yankees (39–33) 4–3, Yankee Stadium (0–3), 40–33, Lost 3
W: Rich Gossage (5–2); L: Tim Stoddard (3–3)
Second, 2 out

Friday, July 1
Defeated Tigers (40–34) 9–5, Tiger Stadium (1–0), 41–33
W: Storm Davis (6–3); L: Milt Wilcox (7–8)
Second, 1 out

Saturday, July 2
Defeated Tigers (40–35) 7–2, Tiger Stadium (2–0), 42–33, Won 2
W: Scott McGregor (9–4); L: Dan Petry (7–6)
Second, 1 out

Sunday, July 3
Lost to Tigers (41–35) 10–1, Tiger Stadium (2–1), 42–34
W: Juan Berenguer (4–1); L: Mike Boddicker (4–4); S: Doug Bair (3)
Second, 1 out

Friday, July 8
Lost to Mariners (31–51) 3–0, Memorial Stadium (23–16), 42–35, Lost 2
W: Jim Beattie (7–5); L: Storm Davis (6–4)
Second, 2 out

Saturday, July 9
Lost to Mariners (32–51) 3–2, Memorial Stadium (23–17), 42–36, Lost 3
W: Bill Caudill (2–5); L: Sammy Stewart (2–3)
Second, 3 out

Sunday, July 10
Defeated Mariners (32–52) 2–0, Memorial Stadium (24–17), 43–36
W: Mike Boddicker (5–4); L: Matt Young (7–9)
Second, 3 out

Monday, July 11
Defeated Athletics (38–46) 7–6, Memorial Stadium (25–17), 44–36, Won 2
W: Dennis Martinez (5–11); L: Steve Baker (3–3); S: Dan Morogiello (1)
Second, 3 out

Tuesday, July 12
Defeated Athletics (38–47) 3–1, Memorial Stadium (26–17), 45–36, Won 3
W: Allan Ramirez (2–0); L: Gorman Heimueller (0–1); S: Tim Stoddard (2)
Second, 3 out

Wednesday, July 13
Defeated Athletics (38–48) 6–2, Memorial Stadium (27–17), 46–36, Won 4
W: Storm Davis (7–4); L: Tim Conroy (2–2); S: Sammy Stewart (3)
Second, 2 out

Thursday, July 14
Defeated Angels (44–41) 5–1, Memorial Stadium (28–17), 47–36, Won 5
W: Scott McGregor (10–4); L: Ken Forsch (8–6)
Second, 2 out

Friday, July 15
Defeated Angels (44–42) 10–4, Memorial Stadium (29–17), 48–36, Won 6
W: Mike Boddicker (6–4); L: Tommy John (7–6)
Second, 2 out

Saturday, July 16
Lost to Angels (45–42) 8–5, Memorial Stadium (29–18), 48–37
W: Geoff Zahn (6–4); L: Dennis Martinez (5–12); S: Luis Sanchez (5)
Second, 3 out

Sunday, July 17
Defeated Angels (45–43) 11–1, Memorial Stadium (30–18), 49–37
W: Allan Ramirez (3–0); L: Byron McLaughlin (1–2)
Second, 2 out

Monday, July 18
Defeated Mariners (36–56) 9–4, Kingdome (3–1) 50–37, Won 2
W: Storm Davis (8–4); L: Jim Beattie (8–6)
Second, 2 out

Tuesday, July 19
Defeated Mariners (36–57) 8–1, Kingdome (4–1), 51–37, Won 3
W: Scott McGregor (11–4); L: Glenn Abbott (3–2)
Second, 1 out

Wednesday, July 20
Defeated Mariners (36–58) 4–2, Kingdome (5–1), 52–37, Won 4
W: Sammy Stewart (3–3); L: Matt Young (8–10); S: Tim Stoddard (3)
First

Thursday, July 21
Lost to Athletics (42–52) 9–7, Oakland–Alameda Coliseum (1–2), 52–38
W: Dave Beard (3–3); L: Dan Morogiello (0–1); S: Tom Burgmeier (4)
First

Friday, July 22
Lost to Athletics (43–52) 4–3, Oakland–Alameda Coliseum (1–3), 52–39, Lost 2
W: Tom Burgmeier (5–5); L: Allan Ramirez (3–1)
Second, 1 out

Saturday, July 23
Defeated Athletics (43–53) 7–3, Oakland–Alameda Coliseum (2–3), 53–39
W: Storm Davis (9–4); L: Tim Conroy (2–4)
Second, 1 out

Sunday, July 24
Defeated Athletics (43–54) 4–3, Oakland–Alameda Coliseum (3–3), 54–39, Won 2
W: Scott McGregor (12–4); L: Steve McCatty (3–5)
First

Monday, July 25
Lost to Angels (48–49) 5–2, Anaheim Stadium (1–3), 54–40
W: Tommy John (8–7); L: Mike Boddicker (6–5); S: Andy Hassler (3)
First

Tuesday, July 26
Defeated Angels (48–50) 5–4, Anaheim Stadium (2–3), 55–40
W: Dennis Martinez (6–12); L: Geoff Zahn (7–5)
First

Wednesday, July 27
Defeated Angels (48–51) 10–4, Anaheim Stadium (3–3), 56–40, Won 2
W: Allan Ramirez (4–1); L: Mike Witt (4–8); S: Sammy Stewart (4)
First

Friday, July 29
Defeated Rangers (49–51) 8–6, Memorial Stadium (31–18), 57–40, Won 3
W: Sammy Stewart (4–3); L: Dave Schmidt (2–2)
First

Saturday, July 30
Defeated Rangers (49–52) 7–4, Memorial Stadium (32–18), 58–40, Won 4
W: Scott McGregor (13–4); L: Mike Smithson (6–10); S: Tim Stoddard (4)
First

Sunday, July 31
Defeated Rangers (49–53) 6–0, Memorial Stadium (33–18), 59–40, Won 5
W: Mike Boddicker (7–5); L: Frank Tanana (4–4)
First

Tuesday, August 2

Lost to Indians (43–60) 3–1, Cleveland Stadium (1–2), 59–41
W: Bert Blyleven (7–9); L: Dennis Martinez (6–13); S: Bud Anderson (3)
First

Lost to Indians (44–60) 4–3, Cleveland Stadium (1–3), 59–42, Lost 2
W: Tom Brennan (1–1); L: Allan Ramirez (4–2); S: Bud Anderson (4)
First

Wednesday, August 3

Defeated Indians (44–61) 8–2, Cleveland Stadium (2–3), 60–42
W: Storm Davis (10–4); L: Rick Sutcliffe (12–7)
First

Thursday, August 4

Defeated Indians (44–62) 4–3, Cleveland Stadium (3–3), 61–42, Won 2
W: Scott McGregor (14–4); L: Bud Anderson (0–3); S: Tippy Martinez (11)
First

Friday, August 5

Defeated White Sox (56–50) 5–4, Memorial Stadium (34–18), 62–42, Won 3
W: Mike Boddicker (8–5); L: Dennis Lamp (5–7)
First

Saturday, August 6

Lost to White Sox (57–50) 6–4, Memorial Stadium (34–19), 62–43
W: Floyd Bannister (9–9); L: Dennis Martinez (6–14); S: Salome Barojas (10)
First

Sunday, August 7

Lost to White Sox (58–50) 4–3, Memorial Stadium (34–20), 62–44, Lost 2
W: La Marr Hoyt (14–10); L: Mike Flanagan (6–1); S: Dennis Lamp (8)
First

Monday, August 8

Lost to Indians (46–65) 9–4, Memorial Stadium (34–21), 62–45, Lost 3
W: Rick Sutcliffe (13–7); L: Storm Davis (10–5)
First

Tuesday, August 9
Lost to Indians (47–65) 4–3, Memorial Stadium (34–22), 62–46, Lost 4
W: Neal Heaton (6–4); L: Scott McGregor (14–5)
First

Wednesday, August 10
Lost to Indians (48–65) 4–3, Memorial Stadium (34–23), 62–47, Lost 5
W: Lary Sorensen (6–9); L: Mike Boddicker (8–6)
First

Thursday, August 11
Lost to White Sox (61–51) 9–3, Comiskey Park (1–2), 62–48, Lost 6
W: Floyd Bannister (10–9); L: Allan Ramirez (4–3)
Third, 1 out

Friday, August 12
Lost to White Sox (62–51) 2–1, Comiskey Park (1–3), 62–49, Lost 7
W: La Marr Hoyt (15–10); L: Mike Flanagan (6–2)
Third, 1 out

Saturday, August 13
Defeated White Sox (62–52) 5–2, Comiskey Park (2–3), 63–49
W: Sammy Stewart (5–3); L: Jerry Koosman (8–5); S: Tippy Martinez (12)
Second, 1 out

Sunday, August 14
Defeated White Sox (62–53) 2–1, Comiskey Park (3–3), 64–49, Won 2
W: Scott McGregor (15–5); L: Richard Dotson (12–7); S: Tim Stoddard (5)
First

Monday, August 15
Defeated Rangers (56–60) 6–4, Arlington Stadium (3–1), 65–49, Won 3
W: Mike Boddicker (9–6); L: Mike Smithson (7–12); S: Tim Stoddard (6)
First

Tuesday, August 16
Lost to Rangers (57–60) 2–0, Arlington Stadium (3–2), 65–50
W: John Butcher (4–3); L: Allan Ramirez (4–4)
First

Wednesday, August 17

Defeated Rangers (57–61) 4–2, Arlington Stadium (4–2), 66–50
W: Mike Flanagan (7–2); L: Odell Jones (3–5); S: Tim Stoddard (7)
Second, 1½ out

Friday, August 19

Defeated Royals (58–59) 5–4, Memorial Stadium (35–23), 67–50, Won 2
W: Sammy Stewart (6–3); L: Dan Quisenberry (5–2)
First

Defeated Royals (58–60) 3–1, Memorial Stadium (36–23), 68–50, Won 3
W: Tippy Martinez (6–3); L: Eric Rasmussen (1–2)
First

Saturday, August 20

Defeated Royals (58–61) 6–1, Memorial Stadium (37–23), 69–50, Won 4
W: Mike Boddicker (10–6); L: Larry Gura (10–15); S: Tippy Martinez (13)
First

Sunday, August 21

Lost to Royals (59–61) 8–3, Memorial Stadium (37–24), 69–51
W: Bud Black (7–4); L: Jim Palmer (2–3); S: Dan Quisenberry (34)
First

Tuesday, August 23

Lost to Blue Jays (70–55) 9–3, Memorial Stadium (37–25), 69–52, Lost 2
W: Luis Leal (11–10); L: Mike Flanagan (7–3)
Second, 1½ out

Wednesday, August 24

Defeated Blue Jays (70–56) 7–4, Memorial Stadium (38–25), 70–52
W: Tippy Martinez (7–3); L: Joey McLaughlin (7–3)
Second, 1½ out

Thursday, August 25

Defeated Blue Jays (70–57) 2–1, Memorial Stadium (39–25), 71–52, Won 2
W: Tippy Martinez (8–3); L: Roy Lee Jackson (8–2)
Second, 1½ out

Friday, August 26
Defeated Twins (56–73) 9–0, Memorial Stadium (40–25), 72–52, Won 3
W: Mike Boddicker (11–6); L: Ken Schrom (12–5)
First

Saturday, August 27
Defeated Twins (56–74) 5–3, Memorial Stadium (41–25), 73–52, Won 4
W: Jim Palmer (3–3); L: Albert Williams (9–12); S: Tim Stoddard (8)
First

Sunday, August 28
Defeated Twins (56–75) 11–4, Memorial Stadium (42–25), 74–52, Won 5
W: Mike Flanagan (8–3); L: Bobby Castillo (8–12); S: Sammy Stewart (5)
First

Monday, August 29
Defeated Royals (64–65) 9–2, Royals Stadium (3–2), 75–52, Won 6
W: Scott McGregor (16–5); L: Gaylord Perry (6–13)
First

Tuesday, August 30
Defeated Royals (64–66) 12–4, Royals Stadium (4–2), 76–52, Won 7
W: Storm Davis (11–5); L: Eric Rasmussen (2–3)
First

Wednesday, August 31
Defeated Blue Jays (72–62) 10–2, Exhibition Stadium (2–3), 77–52, Won 8
W: Mike Boddicker (12–6); L: Jim Gott (7–12)
First

Thursday, September 1
Lost to Blue Jays (73–62) 5–3, Exhibition Stadium (2–4), 77–53
W: Doyle Alexander (2–8); L: Jim Palmer (3–4)
First

Friday, September 2
Defeated Twins (58–78) 1–0, Hubert H. Humphrey Metrodome (3–1), 78–53
W: Mike Flanagan (9–3); L: Frank Viola (7–12); S: Tim Stoddard (9)
First

Saturday, September 3
Defeated Twins (58–79) 13–0, Hubert H. Humphrey Metrodome (4–1), 79–53, Won 2
W: Scott McGregor (17–5); L: Ken Schrom (12–7)
First

Sunday, September 4
Defeated Twins (58–80) 9–6, Hubert H. Humphrey Metrodome (5–1), 80–53, Won 3
W: Storm Davis (12–5); L: Ron Davis (3–7); S: Tippy Martinez (14)
First

Monday, September 5
Lost to Red Sox (67–71) 2–0, Memorial Stadium (42–26), 80–54
W: Bob Ojeda (8–7); L: Mike Boddicker (12–7); S: Bob Stanley (27)
First

Tuesday, September 6
Defeated Red Sox (67–72) 8–1, Memorial Stadium (43–26), 81–54
W: Jim Palmer (4–4); L: Dennis Eckersley (7–12)
First

Wednesday, September 7
Defeated Red Sox (67–73) 5–2, Memorial Stadium (44–26), 82–54, Won 2
W: Mike Flanagan (10–3); L: "Oil Can" Boyd (4–5); S: Tippy Martinez (15)
First

Friday, September 9
Lost to Yankees (79–60) 5–3, Yankee Stadium (0–4), 82–55
W: Ron Guidry (18–8); L: Scott McGregor (17–6)
First

Saturday, September 10
Defeated Yankees (79–61) 8–4, Yankee Stadium (1–4), 83–55
W: Sammy Stewart (7–3); L: Shane Rawley (14–12)
First

Defeated Yankees (79–62) 3–1, Yankee Stadium (2–4), 84–55, Won 2
W: Mike Boddicker (13–7); L: Rudy May (1–5); S: Tippy Martinez (16)
First

Sunday, September 11
Defeated Yankees (79–63) 5–3, Yankee Stadium (3–4), 85–55, Won 3
W: Mike Flanagan (11–3); L: Dave Righetti (14–7); S: Tippy Martinez (17)
First

Tuesday, September 13
Defeated Red Sox (69–75) 7–4, Fenway Park (3–1), 86–55, Won 4
W: Sammy Stewart (8–3); L: Bob Stanley (8–10)
First

Defeated Red Sox (69–76) 7–1, Fenway Park (4–1), 87–55, Won 5
W: Bill Swaggerty (1–0); L: Al Nipper (0–1)
First

Wednesday, September 14
Defeated Red Sox (69–77) 5–0, Fenway Park (5–1), 88–55, Won 6
W: Dennis Martinez (7–14); L: John Tudor (11–11); S: Sammy Stewart (6)
First

Thursday, September 15
Lost to Red Sox (70–77) 7–1, Fenway Park (5–2), 88–56
W: Bruce Hurst (12–10); L: Storm Davis (12–6)
First

Friday, September 16
Defeated Brewers (79–68) 8–1, Memorial Stadium (45–26), 89–56
W: Mike Boddicker (14–7); L: Tom Candiotti (4–2)
First

Saturday, September 17
Defeated Brewers (79–69) 5–4, Memorial Stadium (46–26), 90–56, Won 2
W: Mike Flanagan (12–3); L: Bob Gibson (2–3); S: Tippy Martinez (18)
First

Sunday, September 18
Defeated Brewers (79–70) 10–9, Memorial Stadium (47–26), 91–56, Won 3
W: Tippy Martinez (9–3); L: Pete Ladd (3–4)
First

Monday, September 19
Defeated Brewers (79–71) 8–7, Memorial Stadium (48–26), 92–56, Won 4
W: Tim Stoddard (4–3); L: Tom Tellmann (9–4)
First

Tuesday, September 20
Lost to Tigers (86–64) 14–1, Tiger Stadium (2–2), 92–57
W: Dan Petry (18–9); L: Dennis Martinez (7–15)
First

Wednesday, September 21
Defeated Tigers (86–65) 6–0, Tiger Stadium (3–2), 93–57
W: Mike Boddicker (15–7); L: Jack Morris (19–12)
First

Defeated Tigers (86–66) 7–3, Tiger Stadium (4–2), 94–57, Won 2
W: Sammy Stewart (9–3); L: Dave Gumpert (0–2)
First

Thursday, September 22
Lost to Tigers (87–66) 5–4, Tiger Stadium (4–3), 94–58
W: Doug Bair (7–4); L: Sammy Stewart (9–4)
First

Friday, September 23
Defeated Brewers (81–73) 4–2, County Stadium (3–1), 95–58
W: Scott McGregor (18–6); L: Bob Gibson (2–4); S: Sammy Stewart (7)
First

Saturday, September 24
Lost to Brewers (82–73) 5–2, County Stadium (3–2), 95–59
W: Jaime Cocanower (1–0); L: Dennis Martinez (7–16); S: Pete Ladd (23)
First

Sunday, September 25
Defeated Brewers (82–74) 5–1, County Stadium (4–2), 96–59
W: Storm Davis (13–6); L: Chuck Porter (6–9); S: Tippy Martinez (19)
First

Baltimore clinches the AL East title as Storm Davis and Tippy Martinez combine on a six-hitter.

Tuesday, September 27

Lost to Tigers (90–67) 9–2, Memorial Stadium (48–27), 96–60
W: Jack Morris (20–12); L: Scott McGregor (18–7)
First

Wednesday, September 28

Lost to Tigers (91–67) 9–5, Memorial Stadium (48–28), 96–61, Lost 2
W: Dan Petry (19–10); L: Mike Boddicker (15–8)
First

Thursday, September 29

Lost to Tigers (92–67) 9–4, Memorial Stadium (48–29), 96–62, Lost 3
W: Milt Wilcox (11–10); L: Mike Flanagan (12–4)
First

Friday, September 30

Lost to Yankees (90–69) 6–4, Memorial Stadium (48–30), 96–63, Lost 4
W: John Montefusco (14–4); L: Storm Davis (13–7); S: George Frazier (8)
First

Defeated Yankees (90–70) 3–2, Memorial Stadium (49–30), 97–63
W: Jim Palmer (5–4); L: Jay Howell (1–5); S: Tippy Martinez (20)
First

Saturday, October 1

Lost to Yankees (91–70) 5–4, Memorial Stadium (49–31), 97–64
W: Rich Gossage (13–5); L: Bill Swaggerty (1–1)
First

Sunday, October 2

Defeated Yankees (91–71) 2–0, Memorial Stadium (50–31), 98–64
W: Mike Boddicker (16–8); L: Shane Rawley (14–14); S: Tippy Martinez (21)
First

Appendix III
1983 Regular-Season Team Statistics

Pos	Player	Ag	G	AB	R	H	2B	3B	HR	RBI	BB	SO	BA	OBP	SLG	SB	CS
C	Rick Dempsey	33	128	347	33	80	16	2	4	32	40	54	.231	.311	.323	1	1
1B	Eddie Murray	27	156	582	115	178	30	3	33	111	86	90	.306	.393	.538	5	1
2B	Rich Dauer	30	140	459	49	108	19	0	5	41	47	29	.235	.306	.309	1	1
3B	Todd Cruz	27	81	221	16	46	9	1	3	27	15	52	.208	.259	.299	3	4
SS	Cal Ripken Jr.	22	162	663	121	211	47	2	27	102	58	97	.318	.371	.517	0	4
OF	John Shelby	25	126	325	52	84	15	2	5	27	18	64	.258	.297	.363	15	2
OF	John Lowenstein	36	122	310	52	87	13	2	15	60	49	55	.281	.374	.481	2	1
OF	Al Bumbry	36	124	378	63	104	14	4	3	31	31	33	.275	.328	.357	12	5
DH	Ken Singleton	36	151	507	52	140	21	3	18	84	99	83	.276	.393	.436	0	2
	Dan Ford	31	103	407	63	114	30	4	9	55	29	55	.280	.328	.440	9	2
	Gary Roenicke	28	115	323	45	84	13	0	19	64	30	35	.260	.326	.477	2	2
	Leo Hernandez	23	64	203	21	50	6	1	6	26	12	19	.246	.287	.374	1	0
	Jim Dwyer	33	100	196	37	56	17	1	8	38	31	29	.286	.382	.505	1	1
	Joe Nolan	32	73	184	25	51	11	1	5	24	16	31	.277	.342	.429	0	0
	Lenn Sakata	29	66	134	23	34	7	0	3	12	16	17	.254	.338	.373	8	4
	Benny Ayala	32	47	104	12	23	7	0	4	13	9	18	.221	.278	.404	0	0
	Aurelio Rodriguez	35	45	67	0	8	0	0	0	2	0	13	.119	.130	.119	0	0
	Glenn Gulliver	28	23	47	5	10	3	0	0	2	9	5	.213	.333	.277	0	1
	Tito Landrum	28	26	42	8	13	2	0	1	4	1	11	.310	.318	.429	0	2
	Mike Young	23	25	36	5	6	2	1	0	2	2	8	.167	.231	.278	1	0
	John Stefero	23	9	11	2	5	1	0	0	4	3	2	.455	.571	.545	0	0
	Bobby Bonner	26	6	0	0	0	0	0	0	0	0	0	.000	.000	.000	0	0
	Dave Huppert	26	2	0	0	0	0	0	0	0	0	0	.000	.000	.000	0	0
TOTAL		29.7	162	5,546	799	1,492	283	27	168	761	601	800	.269	.340	.421	61	33

Batting Table Key

Pos = position; **Ag** = age; **G** = games; **AB** = at-bats; **R** = runs; **H** = hits; **2B** = doubles; **3B** = triples; **HR** = home runs; **RBI** = runs batted in; **BB** = walks; **SO** = strikeouts; **BA** = batting average; **OBP** = on-base percentage; **SLG** = slugging average; **SB** = stolen bases; **CS** = caught stealing

1983 Regular-Season Team Pitching Statistics

Pitcher	Ag	G	ERA	W	L	SV	GS	CG	SH	IP	H	ER	BB	HR	SO
Scott McGregor	29	36	3.18	18	7	0	36	12	2	260.0	271	92	45	24	86
Storm Davis	21	34	3.59	13	7	0	29	6	1	200.3	180	80	64	14	125
Mike Boddicker	25	27	2.77	16	8	0	26	10	5	179.0	141	55	52	13	120
Dennis Martinez	28	32	5.53	7	16	0	25	4	0	153.0	209	94	45	21	71
Mike Flanagan	31	20	3.30	12	4	0	20	3	1	125.3	135	46	31	10	50
Jim Palmer	37	14	4.23	5	4	0	11	0	0	76.7	86	36	19	11	34
Allan Ramirez	26	11	3.47	4	4	0	10	1	0	57.0	46	22	30	6	20
Tippy Martinez	33	65	2.35	9	3	21	0	0	0	103.3	76	27	37	10	81
Sammy Stewart	28	58	3.62	9	4	7	1	0	0	144.3	138	58	67	7	95
Tim Stoddard	30	47	6.09	4	3	9	0	0	0	57.7	65	39	29	10	50
Dan Morogiello	28	22	2.39	0	1	1	0	0	0	37.7	39	10	10	1	15
Don Welchel	26	11	5.40	0	2	0	0	0	0	26.7	33	16	10	1	16
Bill Swaggerty	26	7	2.91	1	1	0	2	0	0	21.7	23	7	6	1	7
Paul Mirabella	29	3	5.59	0	0	0	2	0	0	9.7	9	6	7	1	4
TOTAL	28.1	162	3.63	98	64	38	162	36	15	1452.0	1,451	585	452	130	774

Pitching Table Key

Ag = age; G = games; ERA = earned run average; W = wins; L = losses; SV = saves; GS = games started; CG = complete games; SH = shutouts; IP = innings pitched; H = hits; ER = earned runs; BB = walks; HR = home runs; SO = strikeouts

Appendix IV
1983 American League
Championship Series Statistics

Baltimore Orioles (E) 3 vs. Chicago White Sox (W) 1

GAME 1 at Baltimore, October 5
Attendance: 51,289

		Runs	Hits	Errors
CHI	001 001 000	2	7	0
BAL	000 000 001	1	5	1

Pitchers
CHI: Hoyt (W)
BAL: McGregor (L), Stewart (seventh inning), T. Martinez (eighth inning)

GAME 2 at Baltimore, October 6
Attendance: 52,347

		Runs	Hits	Errors
CHI	000 000 000	0	5	2
BAL	010 102 00X	4	6	0

Pitchers
CHI: Bannister (L), Barojas (seventh inning), Lamp (eighth inning)
BAL: Boddicker (W)
Home Runs
BAL: Roenicke

GAME 3 at Chicago, October 7
Attendance: 46,635

		Runs	Hits	Errors
BAL	310 020 014	11	8	1
CHI	010 000 000	1	6	1

Pitchers
BAL: Flanagan (W), Stewart (S, sixth inning)
CHI: Dotson (L), Tidrow (sixth inning), Koosman (ninth inning), Lamp (ninth inning)
Home Runs
BAL: Murray

GAME 4 at Chicago, October 8
Attendance: 45,477

		Runs	Hits	Errors
BAL	000 000 000 3	3	9	0
CHI	000 000 000 0	0	10	0

Pitchers
BAL: Davis, T. Martinez (W, seventh inning)
CHI: Burns (L), Barojas (tenth inning), Agosto (tenth inning), Lamp (tenth inning)
Home Runs
BAL: Landrum

ALCS Statistics

Batting Table Key

POS = position	H = hits	BB = walks
BA = batting average	2B = doubles	SO = strikeouts
G = games	3B = triples	SB = stolen bases
AB = at-bats	HR = home runs	
R = runs	RBI = runs batted in	

Baltimore

Player/POS	BA	G	AB	R	H	2B	3B	HR	RBI	BB	SO	SB
Gary Roenicke/of	.750	3	4	4	3	1	0	1	4	5	0	0
Cal Ripken Jr./ss	.400	4	15	5	6	2	0	0	1	2	3	0
Eddie Murray/1b	.267	4	15	5	4	0	0	1	3	3	3	1
Jim Dwyer/of	.250	2	4	1	1	1	0	0	0	1	0	0
Ken Singleton/dh	.250	4	12	0	3	2	0	0	1	2	2	0
John Shelby/of	.222	3	9	1	2	0	0	0	0	1	3	1
Dan Ford/of	.200	2	5	0	1	1	0	0	0	0	1	0
Tito Landrum/of	.200	4	1	2	2	0	0	1	1	0	2	0
John Lowenstein/of	.167	2	6	0	1	1	0	0	2	1	2	0
Rick Dempsey/c	.167	4	12	1	2	0	0	0	0	1	1	0
Todd Cruz/3b	.133	4	15	0	2	0	0	0	1	0	5	0
Al Bumbry/of	.125	3	8	0	1	1	0	0	1	0	2	0
Rich Dauer/2b	.000	4	1	0	0	0	0	0	1	0	0	0
Benny Ayala/ph	.000	1	0	0	0	0	0	0	1	0	0	0
Joe Nolan/ph	.000	1	0	0	0	0	0	0	1	0	0	0
Jim Palmer/pr	—	0	0	0	0	0	0	0	0	0	0	0
TOTAL	.217	4	129	19	28	9	0	3	17	16	24	2

Chicago

Player/POS	BA	G	AB	R	H	2B	3B	HR	RBI	BB	SO	SB
Rudy Law/of	.389	4	18	1	7	1	0	0	0	0	1	2
Julio Cruz/2b	.333	4	12	0	4	0	0	0	0	3	4	2
Greg Walker/1b	.333	2	3	0	1	0	0	0	0	1	2	0
Ron Kittle/of	.286	3	7	1	2	1	0	0	0	1	2	0
Jerry Dybzinski/ss	.250	2	4	0	1	0	0	0	0	0	0	0
Tom Paciorek/1b, of	.250	4	1	1	4	0	0	0	1	1	2	0
Vance Law/3b	.182	4	11	0	2	0	0	0	1	1	3	0
Carlton Fisk/c	.176	4	17	0	3	1	0	0	0	1	3	0
Greg Luzinski/dh	.133	4	15	0	2	1	0	0	0	1	5	0
Harold Baines/of	.125	4	16	0	2	0	0	0	0	1	3	0
Mike Squires/1b	.000	4	4	0	0	0	0	0	0	0	0	0
Scott Fletcher/ss	.000	3	7	0	0	0	0	0	0	1	0	0
Jerry Hairston/of	.000	2	3	0	0	0	0	0	0	1	1	0
Auerilio Rodriguez/3b	—	2	0	0	0	0	0	0	0	0	0	0
TOTAL	.211	4	133	3	28	4	0	0	2	12	26	4

		Pitching Table Key		
W = wins	CG = complete games	ER = earned runs
L = losses	SH = shutouts	BB = walks
ERA = earned run average	SV = saves	SO = strikeouts
G = games	IP = innings pitched	
GS = games started	H = hits	

Baltimore

Pitcher	W	L	ERA	G	GS	CG	SH	SV	IP	H	ER	BB	SO
Mike Boddicker	1	0	0.00	1	1	1	1	0	9.0	5	0	3	14
Storm Davis	0	0	0.00	1	1	0	0	0	6.0	5	0	2	2
Tippy Martinez	1	0	0.00	2	0	0	0	0	6.0	5	0	3	5
Sammy Stewart	0	0	0.00	2	0	0	0	1	4.1	2	0	1	2
Scott McGregor	0	1	1.35	1	1	0	0	0	6.2	6	1	3	2
Mike Flanagan	1	0	1.80	1	1	0	0	0	5.0	5	1	0	1
TOTAL	3	1	0.49	4	4	1	1	1	37.0	28	2	12	26

Chicago

Pitcher	W	L	ERA	G	GS	CG	SH	SV	IP	H	ER	BB	SO
Dennis Lamp	0	0	0.00	3	0	0	0	0	2.0	0	0	2	1
Juan Agosto	0	0	0.00	1	0	0	0	0	0.1	0	0	0	0
Britt Burns	0	1	0.96	1	1	0	0	0	9.1	6	1	5	8
La Marr Hoyt	1	0	1.00	1	1	1	0	0	9.0	5	1	0	4
Dick Tidrow	0	0	3.00	1	0	0	0	0	3.0	1	1	3	3
Floyd Bannister	0	1	4.50	1	1	0	0	0	6.0	5	3	1	5
Richard Dotson	0	1	10.80	1	1	0	0	0	5.0	6	6	3	3
Salome Barojas	0	0	18.00	2	0	0	0	0	1.0	4	2	0	0
Jerry Koosman	0	0	54.00	1	0	0	0	0	0.1	1	2	2	0
TOTAL	1	3	4.00	4	4	1	0	0	36.0	28	16	16	24

Appendix V
1983 World Series
Statistics

Baltimore Orioles (AL) 4 vs. Philadelphia Phillies (NL) 1

Game 1 at Baltimore, October 11
Attendance: 52,204

		Runs	Hits	Errors
PHI	000 001 010	2	5	0
BAL	100 000 000	1	5	1

Pitchers
PHI: Denny (W), Holland (S, eighth inning)
BAL: McGregor (L), Stewart (ninth inning), T. Martinez (ninth inning)
Home Runs
PHI: Morgan, Maddox
BAL: Dwyer

Game 2 at Baltimore, October 12
Attendance: 52,132

		Runs	Hits	Errors
PHI	000 100 000	1	3	0
BAL	000 030 10X	4	9	1

Pitchers
PHI: Hudson (L), Hernandez (fifth inning), Andersen (sixth inning), Reed (eighth inning)
BAL: Boddicker (W)
Home Runs
BAL: Lowenstein

Game 3 at Philadelphia, October 14
Attendance: 65,792

		Runs	Hits	Errors
BAL	000 001 200	3	6	1
PHI	011 000 000	2	8	2

Pitchers
BAL: Flanagan, Palmer (W, fifth inning), Stewart (seventh inning), T. Martinez (S, ninth inning)
PHI: Carlton (L), Holland (seventh inning)
Home Runs
BAL: Ford
PHI: Matthews, Morgan

Game 4 at Philadelphia, October 15
Attendance: 66,947

		Runs	Hits	Errors
BAL	000 202 100	5	10	1
PHI	000 120 001	4	10	0

Pitchers
BAL: Davis (W), Stewart (sixth inning), T. Martinez (S, eighth inning)
PHI: Denny (L), Hernandez (sixth inning), Reed (sixth inning), Andersen (eighth inning)

Game 5 at Philadelphia, October 16
Attendance: 67,064

		Runs	Hits	Errors
BAL	011 210 000	5	5	0
PHI	000 000 000	0	5	1

Pitchers
BAL: McGregor (W)
PHI: Hudson (L), Bystrom (fifth inning), Hernandez (sixth inning), Reed (ninth inning)
Home Runs
BAL: Murray (2), Dempsey

Series MVP: Rick Dempsey

World Series Statistics

Batting Table Key		
POS = position	H = hits	BB = walks
BA = batting average	2B = doubles	SO = strikeouts
G = games	3B = triples	SB = stolen bases
AB = at-bats	HR = home runs	
R = runs	RBI = runs batted in	

Baltimore

Player/POS	BA	G	AB	R	H	2B	3B	HR	RBI	BB	SO	SB
Benny Ayala/ph	1.000	1	1	1	1	0	0	0	1	0	0	0
Mike Boddicker/p	.000	1	3	0	0	0	0	0	1	0	1	0
Al Bumbry/of	.091	4	11	0	1	1	0	0	1	0	1	0
Todd Cruz/3b	.125	5	16	1	2	0	0	0	0	1	3	0
Rich Dauer/2b, 3b	.211	5	19	2	4	1	0	0	3	0	3	0
Storm Davis/p	.000	1	2	0	0	0	0	0	0	0	2	0
Rick Dempsey/c	.385	5	13	3	5	4	0	1	2	2	2	0
Jim Dwyer/ph, of	.375	2	8	3	3	1	0	1	1	0	0	0
Mike Flanagan/p	.000	1	1	0	0	0	0	0	0	0	1	0
Dan Ford/ph, of	.167	5	12	1	2	0	0	1	1	1	5	0
Tito Landrum/of	.000	3	0	0	0	0	0	0	0	0	0	1
John Lowenstein/of	.385	4	13	2	5	1	0	1	1	0	3	0
Tippy Martinez/p	.000	3	0	0	0	0	0	0	0	0	0	0
Scott McGregor/p	.000	2	5	0	0	0	0	0	0	0	0	0
Eddie Murray/1b	.250	5	20	2	5	0	0	2	3	1	4	0
Joe Nolan/ph, c	.000	2	2	0	0	0	0	0	0	1	0	0
Jim Palmer/p	.000	1	0	0	0	0	0	0	0	0	0	0
Cal Ripken Jr./ss	.167	5	18	2	3	0	0	0	1	3	4	0
Gary Roenicke/ph, of	.000	3	7	0	0	0	0	0	0	0	2	0
Lenn Sakata/pr, 2b	.000	1	1	0	0	0	0	0	0	0	0	0
John Shelby/ph, of	.444	5	9	1	4	0	0	0	1	0	4	0
Ken Singleton/ph	.000	2	1	0	0	0	0	0	1	1	1	0
Sammy Stewart/p	.000	3	2	0	0	0	0	0	0	0	1	0
TOTAL	.213	5	164	18	35	8	0	6	17	10	37	1

Philadelphia

Player/POS	BA	G	AB	R	H	2B	3B	HR	RBI	BB	SO	SB
Larry Andersen/p	.000	2	0	0	0	0	0	0	0	0	0	0
Marty Bystrom/p	.000	1	0	0	0	0	0	0	0	0	0	0
Steve Carlton/p	.000	1	3	0	0	0	0	0	0	0	1	0
Ivan DeJesus/ss	.125	5	16	0	2	0	0	0	0	1	2	0
John Denny/p	.200	2	5	1	1	0	0	0	1	0	1	0
Bob Dernier/pr	.000	1	0	1	0	0	0	0	0	0	0	0
Bo Diaz/c	.333	5	15	1	5	1	0	0	0	1	2	0
Greg Gross/of	.000	2	6	0	0	0	0	0	0	0	0	0
Von Hayes/ph, of	.000	4	3	0	0	0	0	0	0	0	1	0
Willie Hernandez/p	.000	3	0	0	0	0	0	0	0	0	0	0
Al Holland/p	.000	2	0	0	0	0	0	0	0	0	0	0
Charles Hudson/p	.000	2	2	0	0	0	0	0	0	0	1	0
Joe Lefebvre/ph, of	.200	3	5	0	1	1	0	0	2	0	1	0
Sixto Lezcano/ph, of	.125	4	8	0	1	0	0	0	0	0	2	0
Garry Maddox/ph, of	.250	4	12	1	3	1	0	1	1	0	2	0
Gary Matthews/of	.250	5	16	1	4	0	0	1	1	2	2	0
Joe Morgan/2b	.263	5	19	3	5	0	1	2	2	2	3	1
Tony Perez/ph, 1b	.200	4	10	0	2	0	0	0	0	0	2	0
Ron Reed/p	.000	3	0	0	0	0	0	0	0	0	0	0
Pete Rose/ph, 1b, of	.313	5	16	1	5	1	0	0	1	1	3	0
Juan Samuel/pr, ph	.000	3	1	0	0	0	0	0	0	0	0	0
Mike Schmidt/3b	.050	5	20	0	1	0	0	0	0	0	6	0
Ozzie Virgil/ph, c	.500	3	2	0	1	0	0	0	1	0	0	0
TOTAL	.195	5	159	9	31	4	1	4	9	7	29	1

Pitching Table Key		
W = wins	CG = complete games	ER = earned runs
L = losses	SH = shutouts	BB = walks
ERA = earned run average	SV = saves	SO = strikeouts
G = games	IP = innings pitched	
GS = games started	H = hits	

Baltimore

Pitcher	W	L	ERA	G	GS	CG	SH	SV	IP	H	ER	BB	SO
Scott McGregor	1	1	1.06	2	2	1	1	0	17.0	9	2	2	12
Mike Boddicker	1	0	0.00	1	1	1	0	0	9.0	3	0	0	6
Storm Davis	1	0	5.40	1	1	0	0	0	5.0	6	3	1	3
Sammy Stewart	0	0	0.00	3	0	0	0	0	5.0	2	0	2	6
Mike Flanagan	0	0	4.50	1	1	0	0	0	4.0	6	2	1	1
Tippy Martinez	0	0	3.00	3	0	0	0	2	3.0	3	1	0	0
Jim Palmer	1	0	0.00	1	0	0	0	0	2.0	2	0	1	1
TOTALS	4	1	1.60	5	5	2	1	2	45	31	8	7	29

Philadelphia

Pitcher	W	L	ERA	G	GS	CG	SH	SV	IP	H	ER	BB	SO
John Denny	1	1	3.46	2	2	0	0	0	13.0	12	5	3	9
Charles Hudson	0	2	8.64	2	2	0	0	0	8.3	9	8	1	6
Steve Carlton	0	1	2.70	1	1	0	0	0	6.7	5	2	3	7
Larry Andersen	0	0	2.25	2	0	0	0	0	4.0	4	1	0	1
Willie Hernandez	0	0	0.00	3	0	0	0	0	4.0	0	0	1	4
Al Holland	0	0	0.00	2	0	0	0	1	3.7	1	0	0	5
Ron Reed	0	0	2.70	3	0	0	0	0	3.3	4	1	2	4
Marty Bystrom	0	0	0.00	1	0	0	0	0	1.0	0	0	0	1
TOTALS	1	4	3.48	5	5	0	0	1	44	35	17	10	37

Appendix VI
Where Are They Now?

Players

Benny Ayala lives in Toa Baja, Puerto Rico.

Mike Boddicker is a volunteer assistant baseball coach for St. Thomas Aquinas High School in Overland Park, Kansas, and throws batting practice for the Kansas City Royals.

Al Bumbry is a roving outfield instructor for the Cleveland Indians.

Todd Cruz, a former health club manager, is now on disability and gives talks to schools. He lives in Colton, California.

Storm Davis is a power lifter in Jacksonville, Florida.

Rich Dauer is the Milwaukee Brewers bench coach.

Rick Dempsey is the Orioles' first-base coach.

Jim Dwyer is a minor league hitting coach for the Minnesota Twins.

Mike Flanagan is vice president of baseball operations for the Orioles.

Dan Ford is a casino dealer on a Mississippi River boat.

Glenn Gulliver is a high school baseball coach in Allen Park, Michigan.

Leo Hernandez lives in Venezuela.

Tito Landrum is a physical therapist in New York.

John Lowenstein is a rancher in Montana and Nevada.

Dennis Martinez lives in Miami, Florida.

Tippy Martinez is a postgame analyst for Comcast SportsNet Orioles games.

Scott McGregor is a pitching coach for the Orioles' Class A club, the Frederick Keys.

Dan Morogiello lives in Whitehouse Station, New Jersey, and still plays semipro baseball.

Eddie Murray is a hitting coach for the Cleveland Indians.

Joe Nolan lives in St. Louis, Missouri.

Jim Palmer is a broadcaster for Orioles television.

Allan Ramirez is a medical equipment salesman in Victoria, Texas.

Cal Ripken Jr. is president of Ripken Baseball and owner of the minor league Aberdeen Ironbirds.

Aurelio Rodriguez died after being hit by a car in September 2000.

Gary Roenicke is a scout for the Boston Red Sox.

Lenn Sakata is a minor league roving infield instructor for the San Francisco Giants.

John Shelby is the first-base coach for the Los Angeles Dodgers.

Ken Singleton is a broadcaster for the New York Yankees on the YES Network.

Sammy Stewart's present whereabouts are unknown.

John Stefero is an automobile salesman in Odenton, Maryland.

Tim Stoddard is an assistant baseball coach at Northwestern University.

Bill Swaggerty is vice president of business development at Interfinish Flooring.

Manager and Coaches

Joe Altobelli, who served as Orioles manager from 1983 to 1985, is currently a broadcaster for the Triple-A Rochester Red Wings.

Elrod Hendricks is the bullpen coach for the Orioles.

Ray Miller, former pitching coach and Orioles manager (1998–1999), is now retired and lives in New Athens, Ohio.

Cal Ripken Sr. died in 1999.

Ralph Rowe, batting coach, died in 1997.

Jimmy Williams is retired and living in Joppa, Maryland.

Index